DUNKIRK
1940
'WHEREABOUTS UNKNOWN'

DUNKIRK 1940
1940
'WHEREABOUTS UNKNOWN'

HOW UNTRAINED TROOPS OF THE LABOUR DIVISIONS WERE SACRIFICED TO SAVE AN ARMY

TIM LYNCH

SPELLMOUNT

In memory of 4604110 Private Philip Smith,
9th Battalion West Yorkshire Regiment, 1903–1982

And the forgotten men of the battle for France.

First published 2010

Spellmount
The History Press
The Mill, Brimscombe Port
Stroud, Gloucestershire, GL5 2QG
www.thehistorypress.co.uk

British Library Cataloguing in Publication Data.
A catalogue record for this book is available from the British Library.

ISBN 978 0 7524 5490 0

Typesetting and origination by The History Press
Printed in India, Aegean Offset
Manufacturing managed by Jellyfish Print Solutions Ltd

Contents

Acknowledgements

This book began as an attempt to find out about the experiences of my grandfather in the defence of Arras in 1940. He had not spoken of it when I was a child and died a few months before I returned from the Falklands, having perhaps learned the questions I should have asked. The records of the 9th seem to have been lost in the battle and the Battalion disbanded soon after its return to England. No-one seems to have thought it necessary to record its part in the war and so far I have found only a few tantalising references, a letter on an internet auction site and a scattering of misfiled lists in other war diaries. The search, however, led me to reading of the 2/5th Battalion of the Regiment and from there to the history of 137 Brigade whose unsung experiences encapsulate all that was good and bad about the army sent to France in 1939. This book is dedicated to all those who served the lines of communication. I would like to thank Shaun Barrington of Spellmount at The History Press for recognising that this was a story worth telling.

In researching the book, I have had the pleasure of getting to know a wide variety of people whose passion for their subject and willingness to share what they know has added a depth to the story I could never have managed alone. Hugh Sebag-Montefiore was kind and courteous enough to make efforts on my behalf to track down information about the 9th. Martin Marix Evans shared his new-found details about the impact of the geography and geology of the Dunkirk area on the German attack plans.

Adrian Noble, whose father served with the Tyneside Scottish, sent me his files on the battle at Ficheux and Jeremy Moor his father's own diary of the events around Robecq. These were subsequently to form the basis of the official account given by Major Parks in his 1941 article but included insights that were later dropped. Both added the vital element of remembering that this is not ancient history.

I owe a very great debt of gratitude to Kim James, whose own excellent book *The Greater Share of Honour* (Troubador Books, 2007) is a moving account of what these events meant to real people. Kim's friendship is something to treasure and he has been generosity personified in sharing the fruits of his years of research, including a number of war diaries and personal accounts. It was he who produced Rex Flower's unpublished story that forms an important part of this book. It was also through Kim that it was possible to access the papers of Archibald Bentley Beauman, courtesy of his daughter, Lavender Scaramanga. Beauman deserves far greater recognition than he ever received.

Other accounts were gathered from the collections of the Imperial War Museum and the BBC WW2 People's War, an online archive of wartime memories contributed by members of the public and gathered by the BBC. The archive can be found at bbc.co.uk/ww2peopleswar.

Finally, as ever, my thanks go to my wife, Jacqueline and daughter Bethany for letting me get on with writing. My son, Joshua, was supportive in the way only a five-year-old can be. Had he been in France in 1940, his help for Beauman et al would have been worth another division – to the Germans. All three help keep me sane by driving me mad. Thanks.

Tim Lynch

Chapter One

'A specified dimension within a specified time'

On 11 October 1939 Minister for War Leslie Hore-Belisha announced to the Commons that he was

> … able to inform the House that we have fulfilled – and more than fulfilled – our undertaking recently given to France to dispatch to that country in the event of war a British Expeditionary Force of a specified dimension within a specified time … Within six weeks of the outbreak of war in 1914, we had transported to France 148,000 men. Within five weeks of the outbreak of this war we had transported to France 158,000 men. During this period we have also created our base and lines of communication organisation so as to assure the regular flow of supplies and munitions of every kind and to receive further contingents as and when we may decide to send them.

Further, he said, 25,000 vehicles of some 50 different types, 'some of them of enormous dimensions and weighing 15 tons apiece or more', had been delivered via harbours with specialist equipment.[1]

This, he said, was not the 'light army' that had gone to France 25 years before:

> Nearly sixty per cent of the fighting troops in 1914 were infantrymen, relying on their rifles and bayonets and two machine-guns per battalion. Now only twenty per cent of the fighting troops are infantrymen, with fifty Bren guns and twenty-two anti-tank rifles, and other weapons as well with each battalion. It will be seen from this one example how much more effectively armed with fire-power is the present Expeditionary Force.

'He might have added', wrote one observer, 'that even in 1914 the Kaiser's generals were astounded at the firepower of the British line; they could not believe that the men were armed only with rifles and not machine-guns, so rapid and accurate was their fire.'[2]

'Knowing the precise situation regarding the British Field Army in France in general, and in particular in my own division', wrote Bernard Montgomery, then a Major-General in command of 3rd Division,

> I was amazed to read in a newspaper one day in France in October 1939, the speech of the Secretary of State for War in Parliament when he was announcing the arrival of the

BEF in France. He gave Parliament and the British people to understand that the Army we had just sent to France was equipped 'in the finest possible manner which could not be excelled. Our Army is as well if not better equipped than any similar Army.'[3]

In fact, Montgomery claimed, the Army was 'totally unfit to fight a first class war on the continent of Europe … Indeed, the Regular Army was unfit to take part in a realistic exercise.'[4]

Twenty-five years on, there was much about the men arriving in France in 1939 that was familiar to the veterans of their fathers' war. Despite the introduction of new battledress and webbing equipment in 1937, many men still wore the same uniforms and equipment and carried the same basic weapons as the previous generation. Crucially, though, the men arriving in 1939 differed most from those of 1914 in their ability to make use of the firepower Hore-Belisha so admired. His emphasis on the greater number of machine guns, for example, glossed over the fact that there were now only a third the number of men available to fire them. According to his statement, 60 per cent of the 1914 BEF – 88,000 men – had been infantry soldiers able to man positions along the front. Now, even heavily armed, only 20 per cent – 31,600 – were available to do the same job.

In 1914, every soldier of the small but highly professional army prided himself in his ability to use the Short Magazine Lee-Enfield rifle to maximum effect. Every year, each soldier completed a weapons training test in which he fired 250 rounds at ranges of 100–600 yards, followed by a 'mad minute' in which he fired 15 rounds at a target 300 yards away. Part III of the test involved firing 50 rounds at various ranges. He scored four points for each 'bull' (a 24-inch wide target), three for an inner and two for an outer. To qualify as a marksman with an extra sixpence a day pay, a soldier had to score a minimum of 130 points out of a maximum 200. To be assessed as a 'first class shot', he needed 105 points and 70 to become a second class shot. Any commanding officer of an infantry unit with fewer that 50 per cent of his men qualified as marksmen after the test would be required to face a very embarrassing interview with his brigadier. As a result, the initial German attacks of the First World War faltered in the face of heavy rifle fire and any enemy showing himself within 600 yards of a British soldier would be very lucky to live long enough to learn from the experience.[5]

In marked contrast, in 1939 many men would arrive with their unused weapons still packed in greased crates having never had the opportunity to fire them. Others arrived having fired their weapons only once to complete their basic training.

Leslie Hore-Belisha, Secretary of State for War, May 1937–January 1940.

Inspecting a Regular Army machine gun battalion under his command in November, II Corps Commander Lieutenant General Alan Brooke noted, 'It would be sheer massacre to commit it to battle in its present state.'[6]

Twenty years earlier, in 1918, Britain had the largest navy in the world, a newly created Royal Air Force and fielded the biggest, most experienced and well equipped army it had ever known. That year had seen it defeat the bulk of its main enemy in a continental war for the first time in its history, yet the victories and the lessons they brought were soon forgotten and in the popular imagination the First World War became the story of mud, blood and stalemate it remains today. At the highest level, Lloyd George's hatred of the Western Front, and of Haig in particular, meant he tried to ignore the successes that had finally come from it. Disenchantment among veterans and the emergence of the 'lions led by donkeys' attitude towards the conduct of the war focused on the failures, not the victories. 'By robbing Haig and his army of their laurels', wrote historian John Terraine, 'the lessons they had so painfully learned were wasted, and this augured ill for the conduct of the next war. It also made it more certain that there would be a next war.'[7] Having defeated the German Army in the field, logistical problems had prevented the Allies from entering Germany and the only troops to parade through the streets of Berlin were Germans, proudly wearing oak leaves in their helmets and already proclaiming that they had not been defeated in battle, instead they had been betrayed by 'communists and Jews' at home. It was a legend the Nazis would trade heavily on.

For the British and French, exhausted economically, socially and psychologically by the enormous costs of the past four years, the problem was what to do with their huge forces now that the war was over. In March 1919, Parliament debated the annual army estimate and agreed that 'a number of Land Forces, not exceeding 2,500,000, all ranks, be maintained for the Service of the United Kingdom of Great Britain and Ireland at Home and Abroad, excluding His Majesty's Indian Possessions, during the year ending on the 31st day of March, 1920' and that 'a sum not exceeding £125,000,000 be granted to His Majesty on account for or towards defraying the charges for Army Services.'[8] Soon after, it agreed a budget of 'a further sum, not exceeding £50,000,000, be granted to His Majesty on account for defraying the Charges for Army Services, which will come in course of payment during the year ending on the 31st day of March, 1920.'[9] At the same time, the navy would be provided with £120,000,000[10] and the Air Force another £45,000,000.[11]

Heavy taxation to pay for the war had combined with a decline in overseas trade and particularly in Britain's traditional exports of textiles and coal. In the chaotic reorganisation of the economy after the war, rather than adapt to the new emerging industries, the narrow view prevailed that economic problems must stem from poor management of public money. In 1921 the Anti-Waste League was formed by Lord Rothermere to campaign against what they considered wasteful government expenditure and in August Sir Auckland Geddes was appointed to chair a committee to consider sweeping cuts to public expenditure with a brief to

> … make recommendations to the Chancellor of the Exchequer for effecting forthwith all possible reductions in the National Expenditure on Supply Services, having regard especially to the present and prospective position of the Revenue. Insofar as questions of policy are involved in the expenditure under discussion, these will remain for the exclusive consideration of the Cabinet; but it will be open to the Committee to review the expenditure and to indicate the economies which might be effected if particular policies were either adopted, abandoned or modified.[12]

'The tendency to waste must be reckoned as an element of original sin' wrote Henry Higgs in his report on the committee in 1922, 'and it is better to be dead than a "waster" or wastrel'.[13] Social spending on education, health and housing were all targeted under what would become known as the 'Geddes Axe' and budgets were slashed mercilessly. With peace in Europe seemingly assured, the armed forces were obvious candidates for cutbacks and a defence spending fell from £766 million in 1919–20 to £189 million in 1921–22.[14]

By that time the Government had adopted a policy known as the 'Ten Year Rule' which ordered that from 15 August 1919 'it should be assumed for framing revised estimates that the British Empire will not be engaged in any great war during the next ten years, and that no Expeditionary Force is required for that purpose.'[15] Now, the Geddes Axe fell on the Army with a vengeance. After the creation of the Irish Free State, 5 Irish infantry regiments were disbanded in their entirety followed by another 22 infantry battalions of various regiments whilst the cavalry were cut from 28 to 20 regiments and 7 battalions were withdrawn from overseas garrisons. Meanwhile, the Territorial Army establishment was cut from 216,041 in 1922–3 to 184,161 by 1925–6.[16]

The cuts were supported by the agreements reached at the Washington Naval Conference of 1921–2 – the first international disarmament meeting to be held under the auspices of the League of Nations – which decided there should be parity between the British and American navies but set a lower quota of battleships for the Japanese, French and Italian navies along with a ten-year moratorium on the building of warships. It also set down the maximum size of battleships, cruisers and aircraft carriers and limited the size of the gun armament on existing ships. For Britain, dependent on maintaining its naval power in order to protect its overseas trade, the decision was a potentially dangerous one but based on the belief that further conferences would address air and land forces it was deemed an acceptable risk. In 1927, however, a further conference in Geneva failed on the problem of reaching agreement on the number and size of cruisers needed by Britain for trade defence.

Despite this, in 1928 Winston Churchill, as Chancellor of the Exchequer, fought off doubters and succeeded in making the Ten Year Rule permanent. Whereas previously it had been reviewed on an annual basis, now each year the ten-year clock would automatically be reset back to year one and the armed forces would never get any closer than a decade away from a state of readiness for war. Initially, as well as diverting defence spending into the peacetime economy, the concept had been designed to allow equipment programmes to be smoothed out over the medium-term, with an aim of having the armed forces ready in ten years. Now, with the rule reset year by year, the forces stagnated because the government had decreed there was no need to spend money on modernising them for at least another decade. The Treasury was satisfied but the armed forces were deeply worried.

In 1930 the London Naval Conference extended the terms of the Washington Conference to last until 1936 and Britain agreed to reduce its fleet of cruisers to 50 – much against the wishes of the Admiralty. The cutbacks had already had a serious impact on the economy with the shipbuilding, steel and engineering industries and specialist manufacturers of guns, ammunition and naval equipment all being badly hit.

In April 1931 the First Sea Lord, Sir Frederick Field, claimed in a report to the Committee of Imperial Defence that the Royal Navy had declined not only in relative strength compared to other Great Powers but that 'owing to the operation of the "ten-year-decision" and the claimant need for economy, our absolute strength also has … been so diminished as to render the fleet incapable, in the event of war, of efficiently affording protection to our trade.'[17] Field also claimed that the Royal Navy was below the standard required for keeping open Britain's sea communications during wartime; that if the Navy moved to the East to protect the Empire there would not be enough ships to protect the British Isles and its trade from attack and even that no port in the entire British Empire was 'adequately defended.'

It has been said that the road to Dunkirk began in Manchuria. A few months after Field's report, Lieutenant-Colonel Ishiwara Kanji, commander of the Japanese garrison at Kwantung in Southern Manchuria was instrumental in manufacturing the 'Mukden Incident' of 18 September by sabotaging the South Manchurian Railway. Having provoked a confrontation with the Chinese, the Kwantung force used the incident to provide a pretext for its invasion. In London, Prime Minister Ramsay MacDonald quickly recognised the potential threat to Britain's Far East empire and tried to have the Ten Year Rule abolished because he thought the international situation meant it was no longer justified. This was bitterly opposed by the Foreign Secretary Arthur Henderson who succeeded in keeping the rule in place for the time being.[18]

By then, the annual Navy estimate – £120 million in 1919–20 – had fallen to an agreement that 'a sum, not exceeding £32,529,300, be granted to His Majesty, to defray the Charge which will come in course of payment during the year ending on the 31st day of March, 1933, for Expenditure in respect of the Navy Services.'[19] Air Force spending had dropped to £17,400,000,

> … down by no less a figure than £700,000 [from the previous year], a particularly heavy decline on the comparatively small total expenditure of an expanding and developing Service … As the House will realise, to effect so large an economy with a minimum of injury to the Service has been a difficult task, and one to which the Air Council have devoted long and anxious thought. That has only been achieved by a variety of expedients, many of them admittedly makeshift measures which it will not be possible to repeat another year.[20]

In a climate of fierce inter-service rivalry, the army had come off worst. Planning for the future envisaged no more than a minor role – if any – for land forces in Europe and they were primarily seen as having reverted to their nineteenth-century function as an imperial police force. To that end, its establishment fell from 2,500,000 in 1919–20 to an order that 'a number of Land Forces, not exceeding 148,700, all ranks, be maintained for the Service of the United Kingdom at Home and abroad, excluding His Majesty's Indian Possessions (other than Aden), during the year ending on the 31st day of March, 1933.' The entire Army was now no larger than the Expeditionary Force sent to France in the first months of war in 1914. The Commons vote agreed that 'a sum, not exceeding £9,039,000, be granted to His Majesty, to defray the Expense of the Pay, etc., of His Majesty's Army at Home and abroad, excluding His Majesty's Indian Possessions (other than Aden), which will come in course of payment during the year ending on the 31st day of March, 1933.'[21]

Faced with the growing threat to the Far East, the Committee for Imperial Defence (CID) recommended an end to the Ten Year Rule and the Cabinet finally revoked it on 23 March 1932 but with the proviso that, 'this must not be taken to justify an expanding expenditure by the Defence Services without regard to the very serious financial and economic situation' which the country was in.[22] Without committing itself to increasing defence expenditure and instead pinning its hopes on the wide ranging British-led General Disarmament Conference which had opened in Geneva the previous month and which would run until 1934, the government hoped that they might be spared the need to rearm.

On 10 November 1932, Sir Stanley Baldwin, acting as Lord President of the Council and leader of the Conservative Party, addressed the Commons to attack Clement Attlee's proposal 'that the British Government should give clear and unequivocal support to an immediate, universal, and substantial reduction of armaments on the basis of equality of status for all nations, and should maintain the principles of the Covenant of the League of Nations by supporting the findings of the Lytton Commission on the Sino-Japanese dispute.' Even before the Lytton Report had been completed, the Japanese had unilaterally withdrawn from the League of Nations with the increasingly militaristic Japanese Government proclaiming Manchuria a puppet state and thereby showing the League of Nations to be toothless. With what appeared to be a growing threat in the Far East, the risk of another war seemed to be growing. In Britain, the Zeppelin and Gotha raids during the First World War had had a profound effect on thinking about the use of strategic air power and Baldwin's speech would deeply affect the development of British military policy over the coming years. To a hushed house, he said

> I think it is well also for the man in the street to realise that there is no power on earth that can protect him from being bombed, whatever people may tell him. The bomber will always get through, and it is very easy to understand that if you realize the area of space. Take any large town you like on this island or on the Continent within reach of an aerodrome. For the defence of that town and its suburbs you have to split up the air into sectors for defence. Calculate that the bombing aeroplanes will be at least 20,000ft. high in the air, and perhaps higher, and it is a matter of mathematical calculation that you will have sectors of from ten to hundreds of cubic miles.
>
> Imagine 100 cubic miles covered with cloud and fog, and you can calculate how many aeroplanes you would have to throw into that to have much chance of catching odd aeroplanes as they fly through it. It cannot be done, and there is no expert in Europe who will say that it can. The only defence is in offence, which means that you have got to kill more women and children more quickly than the enemy if you want to save yourselves. I mention that so that people may realize what is waiting for them when the next war comes.[23]

As the government adjusted to the situation in the Far East and the growing fear of air attack, Hitler's seizure of power in Germany in January 1933 gave the Chiefs of Staff still more reason to press for a strong defence policy. On 14 October, they produced their annual review prepared, as usual, with assistance from the Foreign Office. In it they warned that Germany would surely rearm to the point where, in a few years, it could start a war in Europe. Two days later, almost as if in response, Germany withdrew from both the League of Nations and the ongoing Geneva Disarmament Conference. Hitler's unilateral blow to ventures in which Britain had invested heavily forced the CID and Cabinet to agree in November 1933, some 20 months after having abandoned the Ten Year Rule, to establish the Defence Requirements Committee (DRC) to examine the country's defences with the aim not of preparing for war, but rather to 'prepare a programme for meeting our worst deficiencies' and basing its recommendations for the time being on prioritising 'the defence of our possessions and interests in the Far East; European commitments; the defence of India.' Furthermore, 'no expenditure should for the present be incurred on measures of defence required to provide exclusively against attack by the United States, France or Italy.'[24] Simply put, the British needed to consider the strategic threats posed by Germany and Japan but could not afford to contemplate any other hypothetical dangers.

The DRC report of 28 February 1934 signalled the start of a fundamental change in British policy. Having previously ruled out the likelihood of war for a decade to come it now was forced to assume that one was probable in just five years. In October 1933, the CID had prepared a memorandum on the danger from Germany and the DRC report now reinforced their view. Although the committee did not consider Japan's activities in Manchuria an immediate danger to British imperial interests, it did propose strengthening its Far Eastern defences in case of emergency and attempting to regain Japan's respect and friendship by reducing Britain's 'subservience to the United States' in order to minimise the risk that 'Japan might yield to the sudden temptation of a favourable opportunity arising from complications elsewhere.' The 'elsewhere' meant Europe where Germany was identified as 'the ultimate potential enemy against whom our "long-range" defence policy must be directed.' Not yet seen as 'a serious menace' to Britain, it was felt Germany would become one 'within a few years'.[25]

The report was not recommending a full rearmament programme, but rather attempting to rectify the damage to the forces' normal development programmes caused by the Ten Year Rule. Even this, they suggested, would not be politically popular with a public 'morally disarmed' in the wake of the First World War. Throughout the 1920s the economic slump had undermined the government's 'land fit for heroes' promise to its troops. From pride in their accomplishment, the prevailing attitude had begun to drift towards a sense of betrayal of veterans by generals and politicians alike. In a worldwide economic slump, the diversion of large amounts of funding towards the military would be difficult to put into action. With limited resources, the problem became one of deciding how best to prioritise the money available. It was clear that even if Britain could afford to keep pace with the shipbuilding quotas agreed at the Naval Conferences in Washington in 1922 and London in 1930, the loss of logistical facilities since 1919 would mean that in the event of deployment to the Far East it would not arrive in the Pacific in any state to fight.

The underlying belief that air power alone could be a war-winning strategy was brought into sharp focus by the DRC report's observation that a German occupation of the Low Countries would bring their bombers within range of British cities and they would be in a position to deal a potential knockout blow before Britain could mobilise forces against them. Consequently, they said, an essential requirement was to develop the capacity to mobilise a 'Regular Expeditionary Force' of four infantry divisions, one cavalry division, two air defence brigades and a tank brigade within a month of the outbreak of war and supported by up to twelve divisions of the Territorial Army – 'a matter which will require consideration when the urgent needs of the Regular Army have been met.'

Alongside this, the Royal Air Force should be expanded to the 52 squadrons first approved back in 1923. Although not seen as one of the 'worst deficiencies', it was suggested that at least another 25 squadrons would be necessary for home defence and other tasks, especially if Germany should rapidly expand its air forces. The DRC estimated the cost of the whole program (apart from naval construction) at about £82 million over eight or nine years; of the £71 million for the first five years, £40 million would go to the Army, £21 million to the Royal Navy, and £10 million to the Royal Air Force.

If war came in the Far East, it was assumed the Navy would have the lead role. In the event of war in Europe, it was expected that Britain would be allied to France and that the roles of the forces 'would not differ very much in kind from those that they filled in the last war'. The Navy, they presumed, would protect the mainland British coast and all maritime communications whilst the Army would provide the land defence of ports, naval bases and the shoreline as well as providing anti-aircraft defence and, if required, an expeditionary

British troops in the Saarland, 1934. Sent in to police the area during the plebiscite, the French decision to deploy African soldiers in the German territory was seen by many in Britain as vindictive and insulting, leading to widespread sympathy for the Germans.

force to be sent to Europe. To that end, in 1935 responsibility for the anti-aircraft defence of the UK was given entirely to the Territorial Army and between the formation of the TA Anti-Aircraft Division in January 1936 and April 1939, its strength grew from just 2,000 men to 96,000 – on paper at least.[26] The Royal Air Force, meanwhile, would be responsible for defence against air attack and liaison with the Royal Navy and Army as well as for the provision of an air force to accompany the expeditionary force. Although they acknowledged that a European war might either lead to or coincide with a threat in the Far East and India, the DRC did not give much thought to the possibility of fighting a two-front war. Instead, it assumed that preparing the Royal Navy for a war in the Far East would enable it to accomplish its mission in any European war, and that by strengthening the Army and Royal Air Force for use in Europe would equally serve if they were deployed to India.

In late 1937, a relieved DRC under Sir Thomas Inskip had reported that 'France no longer looks to us in the event of war to supply expeditionary forces on the scale hitherto proposed, in addition to our all-important co-operation on the sea and in the air.' In fact, it claimed, 'co-operation in the defence of the territory of any allies we may have in war' was the lowest of all army priorities and far behind those of anti-aircraft duties and of garrisoning the empire, although they recognised that the government would be heavily criticised should a major European war mean that France was threatened and Britain forced to 'improvise an army to assist her'.[27] Despite the still very evident risks, on the basis that there would now be no need to significantly increase the size of the army to fulfil its expected role in any future conflict, the DRC initially recommended an increase in the defence budget of no more than £50 million by 1939.[28] Germany's invasion of Czechoslovakia in 1938 changed things. Suddenly, the threat of war increased enormously.

Even by early 1938, though, it had already become clear to British planners that the defence of France mattered a great deal to Britain even if neutral Belgium fell. As Cabinet Secretary Lord Hankey put it in a letter to Prime Minister Chamberlain on 28 April 1938, 'It would be a nuisance to have the Germans in Belgium again, but better in Belgian ports than in French ports.' Britain, he argued, should therefore concentrate on France alone. Ideally, Hankey suggested, Britain should encourage France to extend its Maginot Line defences from Longuyon on the Luxemburg border – where the fortifications currently ended – to the Channel coast. It would not be possible to build the heavy forts of the Maginot Line in the lowland areas along the Franco-Belgian border, but other types of defences were considered possible. Since the size and effectiveness of the French defence line would have a direct impact on the need to prepare and deploy a British Expeditionary Force, the stronger the line, the less Britain would need to contribute. The groundwork for the later claims and counterclaims of the respective failures of each nation was laid in the political wrangling over cost. 'All our co-operation with France,' Hankey wrote,

> whether by air or sea and eventually by land, will be very much less effective if the Germans get the [French] channel ports. It is therefore a strong *French* interest to cover them by an extension of the Maginot Line [to the coast] … Incidentally it is a strong British interest, but it would be advisable *not* to say so or else the French might ask us to pay![29]

The political cost of France's militarising its border with neutral Belgium was too high to bear. Just as the British worried about bombing, the French needed to keep the Germans as far away as possible from their industrial heartlands of northern France and hoped to fight their war on Belgian soil. To build defences along the Belgian border would be a clear signal that they would abandon their potential allies to the north at a time

Neville Chamberlain, who was widely condemned for his policy of appeasement. Chamberlain was constrained as much by an awareness that Britain could offer no resistance to Hitler as by his pacifist beliefs.

when there was still an expectation that the Belgian's own forts along the Albert Canal – including the apparently impregnable state-of-the-art defences of Eben Emael – would serve to delay any attacking army long enough for a combined Allied army to rush to their support. It was widely believed by the French High Command that the coming war could be fought primarily around the Gembloux Gap in eastern Belgium and the Maginot Line was intended not to be France's first line of defence but as a deterrent to a costly frontal assault that would channel any German attack through the Low Countries for this very reason.

In the wake of Munich and the invasion of Czechoslovakia, British concerns for French security – or more accurately for the ability of the French to keep German bombers out of range of the UK – further increased. Britain was now prepared to discuss the alliance France had tried for nearly 20 years to achieve. In February 1939, the Chiefs of Staff reported that 'It is difficult ... to say how the security of the United Kingdom could be maintained if France were forced to capitulate.'[30] Despite this, some measure of the importance Britain still placed on assisting the French can be seen in the fact that in February 1939, when planning began under the direction of Brigadier L.A. Hawes for the deployment of the BEF to France, Hawes was unable to find a single up-to-date map of France held by the War Office or the Foreign Office. His team worked from maps produced from a survey completed before the Franco-Prussian war 70 years earlier.[31]

Having controversially succeeded the popular Alfred Duff Cooper as Secretary of State for War in 1937, Leslie Hore-Belisha had made a number of attempts to modernise the British armed forces and to boost recruitment by introducing improved pay, pension and promotion prospects. He also sought to make the army a more attractive career choice for ordinary soldiers with better barrack conditions including, for example, installing showers and recreation facilities and giving married soldiers the right to live with their families on or near their bases. The reduction in the size of the army over the previous two decades had left a glut of senior officers who were by now largely redundant and simply biding their time until retirement in unnecessary posts with little or nothing to do. The new 'youth at the helm' policy pushed these men into what they, of course, considered premature retirement to make room for up and coming junior officers. Almost overnight,

British infantryman and equipment, 1939.

An anti-aircraft Bren gun team. Hore-Belisha spoke of how much better armed the modern BEF was compared to its 1914 predecessor, with 50 of these light machine guns per battalion. In reality, many battalions held just a handful.

men who had waited years to reach the next rung of the promotion ladder found themselves granted the ranks a stagnated army had not been able to afford to give them.

Hore-Belisha's policies were attacked by both the army and Parliament but frequently not because of any inherent fault in the logic behind them. Many of the men in senior army posts in the late thirties had never led formations of troops in combat and had instead been promoted on the strength of administrative or political skills and for them, the purge hit close to home. Men like Generals John Dill and John Gort – whose suitability for high rank in a wartime army was the subject of much private debate as war loomed – were alienated to the point that it was said Gort could not bear to be in the same room with the minister.

Chief among Hore-Belisha's critics was Archibald Ramsay of the Conservative Party. Elected to the House of Commons in 1931, Ramsay had developed extreme right-wing political views and had become convinced that the Russian Revolution was the start of an international Communist plot to take over the world. In 1935, two German agents established an anti-Semitic group in the UK known as the White Knights of Britain or the Hooded Men – later to become the Nordic League. The Nordic League was primarily an upper-middle class association far removed from the working class British Union of Fascists but sharing the same ideas. Having introduced his Private Members' 'Aliens Restriction (Blasphemy) Bill' in June 1938, Ramsay now turned his attention to Hore-Belisha and began a campaign to have him sacked as Secretary of War. In one speech on 27 April he warned that Hore-Belisha 'will lead us to war with our blood-brothers of the Nordic race in order to make way for a Bolshevised Europe.'[32] His efforts to, in his words, 'clear the Conservative Party of Jewish influence' would continue into 1940 but even after his eventual arrest and imprisonment he was influential enough to be able to submit questions to Parliament about Jews serving in the British Army and to have MPs prepared to demand his release.

Facing such opposition, Hore-Belisha continued to press ahead with plans to develop the armed forces. One of the effects of the First World War had been to create a decline in the birth rate between 1915 and 1919 that now showed itself as a shortage of men aged 21–26 – the prime age for fighting troops – and normal recruitment could not meet this gap. Conscription legislation put in place to supply manpower for the First World War had lapsed in 1920 and there had been no need to reconsider it but now,

Prime Minister Chamberlain returns from Munich.

for the first time in its history, Britain was forced to put plans in place for the introduction of peacetime conscription. The initial plans put forward in 1938 were blocked by Chamberlain, who refused to allow any increase in defence spending beyond that already agreed and who still believed that appeasement could work, but the rapidly deteriorating international situation after Czechoslovakia changed things.

With the increasing German threat after Munich, Britain's plans had to be quickly reconsidered. The initial plan, based on that outlined by the DRC back in the early 1930s, envisaged sending only two advance divisions before a declaration of war followed by up to ten more to be sent in two batches, one 60 days after the outbreak and the next about six months into the war.

Perhaps not surprisingly given its frontline position in any war, France was clearly unhappy about Britain's proposed level of commitment to European defence. British Ambassador Sir Eric Phipps had reported to London in September 1938 that 'all that is best in France is against war, almost at any price' and that they were being opposed only by a 'small, but noisy and corrupt, war group'.[33] He went on to say that the small size of the projected British Expeditionary Force had convinced some French observers that 'France can only rely on Great Britain to fight to the last Frenchman.'[34] As French General Henri-Fernand Dentz put it, 'France does not intend to allow England to fight her battles with French soldiers.'[35] Reinforcing this belief, French statistics apparently showed that the British government was only preparing to mobilise at no more than one-fifth of the rate France planned to, a claim angrily rejected by the British in bilateral discussions. General Edmund Ironside, who would be appointed Chief of the Imperial General Staff in September, noted that

> When Reynaud was recently in England he had complained that whereas one man in eight was mobilized in France, only one in forty was mobilized in England; but, on going into his figures, it was found that Reynaud had included police, railway and dock workers, etc., in the French mobilisation who were not included in the British figures. When these were eliminated, the proportions were much about the same.[36]

Phipps's damning assessment of France's lack of willingness or even its ability to go to war with Germany in 1938 had already created major doubts in London about the value of France as an ally but for their part, the French regarded Britain's strategy for another long, defensive war of attrition to be a real danger to them. France could not afford such a luxury if it was to emerge from the coming war with its economy in any fit state to rebuild itself. As a result, it became clear that France wanted help in the short term rather than the promised long-haul approach the British were offering and Charles Corbin, the highly experienced ambassador in London, recommended to Daladier in January 1939 that he should remind the British as often as possible about 'the inequality of sacrifice to which our two populations would have to consent in time of war'.[37]

With the situation across Europe rapidly deteriorating France's resolve seemed to be faltering. Guided by Phipps' comments, Britain now sought to reassure France of its full support in order to prevent it seeking any sort of accommodation with Hitler and so, on 8 March 1939, during the Parliamentary debate on the Army Estimates for the following financial year, Hore-Belisha announced:

> It will now be convenient to appraise the dimensions of the field force [to be sent to France in the event of war]. The whole, or any part of it, will be used, of course, as and

how the future may require, but this is the size of the instrument our plans are shaping: Regular, four infantry divisions and two armoured divisions; Territorial, nine infantry divisions, three motorised divisions and an armoured division. In addition, there are two Territorial cavalry brigades, and a number of unbrigaded units, Regular and Territorial – making more than nineteen divisions in all. Mr Haldane projected a field force of six Regular divisions and one cavalry division only. He had not equipped the Territorial force for a European war. Our Territorial Army will be so equipped.[38]

The French were delighted by the implied promise of nineteen divisions whilst the German military attaché 'listening in the diplomats' gallery, was observed to be completely stunned, which is not surprising'.[39] Although plans had already been discussed the previous week with the CID for an eventual commitment of 32 divisions or even as many as 55, Hore-Belisha's apparent offer of 19 divisions in the short term was seen by senior commanders as little more than a political gambit.[40] General Henry Pownall, who would become Chief of Staff to Lord Gort when war broke out, noted in his diary in April that it may be 'Better late than never, but late it is, for it will take at least eighteen months more … before this paper army is an army in the flesh.'[41] General Ironside argued that it would take another year for Britain to provide even fifteen combat-ready divisions.

On 27 April 1939, Hore-Belisha secured the agreement of the Cabinet to allow restricted conscription on a temporary basis and on 26 May Royal Assent was given to a Military Training Act that would apply to males aged 20 and 21 years old.[42] They were to be called up for six months full-time military training before being transferred to the Army Reserve and released from service. The Act was intended to be temporary for a period of three years unless an Order in Council declared it was no longer necessary before the Act expired.

By 1918, there had been four British armies made up, in Richard Holmes' phrase, of the 'old, new, borrowed and blue'. The remnants of the old, pre-war professional army were still figures of influence but had been joined in 1915 by the 'borrowed' men of the Territorial Army, whose terms of service did not require them to serve overseas unless they chose to do so. In 1916 came the 'new' army of men who had answered Kitchener's call and, after the horrors of the Somme, came the first of the 'blue' – conscripts enlisted involuntarily by new legislation to fill the gaps in the ranks of the old, new and Territorial Armies. This time, it was decided, there would be an integrated army from the outset. By using the time available to create and train a reserve force, Britain would, like its European neighbours, have a ready made pool of trained soldiers if and when it needed them.

As staff talks between British and French commanders progressed in four phases between late March and late August 1939 markedly divergent views on the deployment of the BEF in France quickly emerged. The British concentrated on planning for the medium and long term so as to allow time to create, train and deploy the later echelons of the big 'Belisha army' as a complete fighting force. Gamelin, in contrast, had a much more short-term agenda. He prioritised first and foremost the move to France of the limited forces actually available in 1939: five regular divisions and the first four divisions of Territorials. For his part Lord Gort – at that time Chief of the Imperial General Staff – shared the view that Britain should quickly deploy whatever it had available. Opposing them, and by now accused by his critics of assuming the role of a latter day Kitchener, Hore-Belisha was said to be less concerned with the best interests of the strategic military situation than with calculating the political good for his own ministerial career of being seen as the father of the revitalised British Army.

Churchill, like the French High Command, cared mainly about numbers. For him, the prospect of being able – albeit not until at least 1941 – to put a large army into the field alongside the French salved at least some of the humiliation of the failure of appeasement. In Paris for the Bastille Day parade of 14 July 1939, Pownall reported hearing Churchill mutter 'Thank God we've got conscription or we wouldn't be able to look these people in the face.'[43] Later, he would write, 'Britain's introduction of conscription … did not give us an army … It was, however, a symbolic gesture of the utmost consequence to France and Poland.'[44]

By August, amicable agreements were reached about the size and speed of the deployment of the BEF, with Pownall announcing that the first two divisions were now expected to arrive 19 days after mobilisation and the whole Regular Army contingent in 34 days.[45] Compared to France's 117 available divisions of varying quality or even to the 10 Dutch divisions or the 22 divisions 'little Belgium' was able to field (despite its declared neutrality), the BEF was little more than a gesture but it was recognised as representing the best that Britain had available at the time.[46] This tiny contribution forced BEF commanders to defer to the French High Command on matters of policy and in particular to their commander-in-chief General Maurice Gamelin, who freely admitted that he was relying on any future war being confined initially to the east before spreading westwards, in order to buy time for mobilisation.

When war came on 3 September, as agreed, the BEF began to mobilise and advance elements arrived in France to organise the lines of communication and set up base areas. In 1914, the original BEF had been in action against the advancing Germans just sixteen days after war was declared. This time, with Germany occupied in subduing the Poles, it would take nineteen days before the first combat troops even reached French shores. By the time the first British infantrymen reached their assigned positions in northern France, the first – and only – French offensive of the war had already ended.

The Franco-Polish military convention held that when war came the French Army would immediately begin preparations for a major offensive and on the fifteenth day after mobilisation began they were to launch a full-scale assault on Germany itself. Pre-emptive mobilisation was declared in France on 26 August and full mobilisation began on 1 September. Four days after war was declared, a French offensive pushed into the Rhine valley. With the Wehrmacht fully engaged in Poland, Germany had just 22 divisions along the French border and no armoured forces of any kind, but instead of pushing home their huge numerical advantage, the French advanced along a 32-kilometre line in the Saarbrücken area against weak German opposition and penetrated about eight kilometres into Germany. They captured approximately 20 abandoned villages before stalling after the Anglo-French Supreme War Council gathered for the first time at Abbeville on 12 September and agreed that all offensive actions were to be halted immediately.

The Phoney War had begun.

Notes

1 Hammerton, Sir John. *The Second Great War* Vol 1 London: Waverley *c*.1941 p208–211
2 Ibid 212
3 Montgomery, B.L. *The Memoirs of Field Marshal the Viscount Montgomery of Alamein*, KG London: Companion Books 1958 p44
4 Ibid p43
5 HMSO *The NCOs Musketry Small Book* London: 1915 pp3, 103 quoted in Holmes, R. *Tommy* London: HarperCollins, 2004 p345
6 Bryant, A. *The Turn of the Tide 1939–43* London: Collins 1957 p67

7 Terraine, J. *To Win a War: 1918 The Year of Victory* London: Macmillan 1978 p14

8 Hansard House of Commons Debate 03 March 1919 vol 113 cc69–184

9 HC Deb 07 July 1919 vol 117 cc1567–70

10 HC Deb 11 December 1919 vol 122 cc1743–58

11 HC Deb 15 December 1919 vol 123 cc87–147

12 Henry Higgs, 'The Geddes Reports and the Budget', *The Economic Journal*, Vol. 32, No. 126. (Jun., 1922), p253

13 Ibid 'Introduction'

14 Barnett, C., *The Collapse of British Power* London: Eyre Methuen, 1972 p297

15 National Army Museum. *Against All Odds* London: National Army Museum 1990 p6

16 Ibid

17 Barnett, op cit. p. 301

18 Paul Kennedy, *The Realities behind Diplomacy* (Fontana, 1981) p231

19 HC Deb 06 July 1932 vol 268 cc515–9

20 HC Deb 10 March 1932 vol 262 cc2007–73

21 HC Deb 15 March 1932 vol 263 cc241–2

22 Kennedy, P. *The Rise and Fall of British Naval Mastery* (London: Penguin, 2004), p285

23 Reported in *The Times*, 11 November 1932, p7

24 DRC report (DRC 14), 28 February 1934, CAB 4/23 in *Dilemmas of Appeasement: British Deterrence and Defense, 1934–1937* Gaines Post Jr Ithaca, NY: Cornell University Press. 1993 p32

25 Ibid. p33

26 Hammerton, op cit p135

27 Inskip. Defence Expenditure in Future Years, Interim Report By The Minister For Co-Ordination of Defence, C.P. 316(37), Cab. 24/273 quoted in Sebastian Cox 'British Military Planning and the Origins of the Second World War' in B.J.C. Coercer & Roch Legault. *Military Planning and the Origins of the Second World War in Europe* Westport CT: Praeger, 2001 p117

28 McKersher, B.J.C. 'The Limitations of the Politician-Strategist: Winston Churchill and the German Threat 1933–1939' in Michael I. Handel, John H. Maurer (eds) *Churchill and Strategic Dilemmas Before the World Wars: Essays in Honor of Michael I. Handel* London: Routledge, 2003 p105

29 Hankey to Prime Minister, 28 April 1938, in CAB 21, 554 14/4/13, PRO. Emphases and exclamation original.

30 Howard, M. 1972 *The Continental commitment: The dilemma of British defense policy in the era of two world wars* London: Temple Smith p127

31 Hawes, L.A. 'The Story of the "W Plan": The Move of Our Forces to France in 1939.' *Army Quarterly* 101 (1970–71): 445–56

32 http://www.spartacus.schoolnet.co.uk/PRramsayA2.htm

33 Adamthwaite, A. *France and the coming of the Second World War, 1936–39* London: Frank Cass 1977, p177

34 Phipps to Halifax, 16 November 1938, FO 371 21600 C 14025/55/17, PRO

35 Adamthwaite 1977, p246

36 Gates, E.M. *The end of the affair: The collapse of the Anglo-French alliance, 1939–40* London: George Allen and Unwin 1981, p29 Ironside quote from MacLeod, R & Kelly, D (Eds) *Time Unguarded: The Ironside Diaries, 1937–1940*. New York: D. McKay 1963 p162

37 *Corbin to Daladier*, 26 Jan. 1939, in Etat-Major de L'Armée: *2e Bureau – Grande- Bretagne*, Carton 7N 2816, SHAT.

38 Hansard H.C. Deb 08 March 1939 vol 344 cc2161–302

39 Blaxland, G. *Destination Dunkirk: The Story of Gort's Army London* Military Book Society 1973 p23

40 'Committee for Imperial Defense Strategical Appreciation Sub-committee Procedure for Meeting to be held on the 1st March, 1939,' section 6, FO 371 22923 C2751/281/17, PRO. For the Hore-Belisha statement, see also Adamthwaite, 1977, Op cit. p253.

41 Bond, B. (Ed) *Chief of Staff: The Diaries of Lieutenant General Sir Henry Pownal* London: Leo Cooper 1972 p178

42 Hansard H.C. Deb 26 May 1939 vol 347 c2703)

43 Recorded by Pownall (see Bond, *Chief of Staff, I*, p213, diary entry of 10 July 1939)

44 Churchill, W.S. *The Second World War: The Gathering Storm* (London, 1948), pp.318–319

45 Bond, B. *British Military Policy Between the Two World Wars* Oxford: OUP 1980 p319–20

46 Freiser, K-H. *The Blitzkrieg Legend* Anapolis, Maryland: Naval Institute Press 2005 p36

Chapter Two

Wagging the Dog

Even before the last Polish resistance in the east had been crushed, Hitler was urging his generals to turn and strike west. Like Britain and France, Germany had huge deficiencies in its forces, but Hitler was convinced that if he attacked immediately his forces had enough momentum to break through. The success in Poland had been astonishing but Army Chief of Staff General Franz Halder advised caution, noting in his diary; 'The techniques of Polish Campaign [are] no recipe for the West. No good against a well-knit army.'[1] In fact, German High Command were, like their British and French counterparts, strongly of the opinion that no offensive would be possible in the west for some time – many suggesting the Spring of 1942 as being the earliest a successful attack on the Franco-Belgian defence lines could be mounted.[2] For Hitler, to delay courted disaster since, he thought, within six to eight months the Allies would be powerful enough to withstand a German attack and the result would be a long, drawn-out affair that Germany could not afford. By 1939, the country was still short of trained men and war material and it was clear that it could not withstand a lengthy blockade that would starve it not only of food but also of the raw materials for weapons production – in the official German account of the campaign, Karl-Heinz Freiser claims that of the 30 most important materials for the armaments industry, Germany had only seven in adequate quantities. Determined to finish the war quickly, on 27 September Hitler announced to his staff that he intended to attack as soon as possible and set a provisional date of 25 November. After much persuasion, his commanders were able to negotiate a series of what would amount to 29 postponements over the coming winter in order to buy the time they needed to prepare their forces.[3]

In the absence of any immediate German moves against the borders, the Allies began to settle in for what most envisaged would be another protracted, static war in which waves of advancing Germans would be broken against a solid line of defensive fortifications. At Churchill's insistence, heavy siege guns were moved to France and placed in specially constructed bunkers. These were not weapons for a modern, mobile war – their emplacements needed a dedicated light railway track to carry ammunition supplies to the guns. Along the Franco-Belgian border, the BEF prepared an elaborate line of pillboxes and trenches and settled down to wait.

Behind the front lines, the Lines of Communication (L of C) set out by Brigadier Hawes and his staff were growing in complexity to the extent that Lord Gort has been criticised on the grounds that his 'failure to curb what amounted to over-enthusiasm on

Above: The BEF
anticipated a repeat of
the previous war and
trained extensively
in trench fighting
throughout the
'Phoney War'.

Right: Troops on
exercise in France.

The British had forgotten the late successes of the *Stosstruppen* of the Great War; the Germans had not. Blitzkrieg was imminent.

the part of the supply services in demanding the construction of larger and larger depots and equivalent services meant that the "tail" was beginning to "wag the dog".[4]

Although Hore-Belisha had spoken of 25,000 vehicles being delivered to France, pre-war cutbacks had reduced the Royal Army Service Corps, responsible for the army's transport, to just 2,000 vehicles spread across the empire and the transport shortfall had, until now, been made up by hiring vehicles from specialist local civilian contractors such as the Artillery Transport Company based in York.[5] Hastily requisitioned civilian vehicles were now being repainted and sent out to France with the result that Montgomery's divisional transport had been held up at Falmouth for days by movements officers who refused to accept that a spearhead Regular Army infantry division needed quite so many laundry vans.[6] In the cash starved economy of the 1930s, competition within the army for resources had been so fierce that no money was available to support units that would only become useful in time of war. As a result, the army's tiny logistical service was now expanding out of all expectation.

With supply lines stretching up to 500 miles from the Atlantic seaboard ports to reach the BEF along the Belgian border, and ammunition dumps around Rouen alone covering some 36 square miles, maintaining security and moving supplies forward became a major problem. Theft from ships and supply dumps was so endemic that on the recommendation of Detective Chief Inspector George Hatherill 20 Scotland Yard detectives were specially enlisted into the Corps of Military Police to form the new Special Investigations Branch under the command of Detective Superintendent Clarence Campion, formerly head of Scotland Yard's Criminal Record Office and granted an automatic commission as a Major.[7] The continuing trickle of thefts also served to highlight the vulnerability of the L of C to the added threat of fifth column spies and saboteurs. It was clear that the Ordnance and Service Corps troops working at these depots could not be expected to maintain a 24 hour a day presence and complete their tasks and that more troops were needed.

British and French troops enjoy a drink together during the 'Phoney War'.

With the expectation being that the army would only be involved in policing small scale tribal wars, little thought had been given to the need to expand logistical services beyond the hiring of cheap local labour on arrival in the theatre of operations. France, however, had no cheap local labour available for hire. Its mobilisation process had been so sweeping and thorough that arms production fell in the first few months of the war and manufacturers frantically lobbied the government and military for the release from service of the key workers needed to keep the factories running. Nevertheless, thousands of tons of food, fuel and ammunition needed to maintain the BEF sat on docksides waiting to be moved.

In response to the growing need for a labour force, the Auxiliary Military Pioneer Corps (AMPC) was hastily created on 17 October 1939 and direct enlistment into the Corps began the same day. The Corps formed around a nucleus of men recalled from the reserve but considered too old or unfit for frontline duties along with some civilian volunteers including 'enemy aliens' – many of them of German, Austrian and Italian descent – and a smattering of conscripts.[8] They were immediately put to work but it was not a happy corps. The reservists were often bitter about not being allowed back to their old regiments, the conscripts complained that if they were forced to be soldiers, they'd rather be 'proper' soldiers, the 'enemy aliens' were treated with suspicion and the civilian volunteers were frequently men who were not registered as conscientious objectors but who had no interest in the military or its aims. As a cost cutting measure, they were issued with only one set of uniform for both work and parade and consequently soon earned a reputation for scruffiness. With only a small number of elderly officers to manage large groups of men on often widely dispersed sites, discipline was also a constant problem. To add insult to the reservists' injury, 75 per cent of the rifles issued to the AMPC were then withdrawn to be given to combatant troops.[9] By the end of 1939, the AMPC had 18,600 largely unarmed men working as navvies in France.[10]

To help with guard duties, garrison battalions were also formed from the ranks of returning ex-servicemen and fed into the L of C. The 9th (Overseas Defence) Battalion of the

The formation of the AMPC was given a positive spin to hide the desperate lack of manpower among the BEF.

West Yorkshire Regiment was one such unit, sent to Arras and deployed on airfield guard duties. By any definition a veteran unit, the battalion commander, Lieutenant-Colonel Luxmore-Ball, was now on his third war and among his men was Private Gordon Smith who, at the age of 34, had been considered old by infantry standards when he won the Distinguished Conduct Medal in 1918. Now, at the age of 55, Private Smith would again be called upon to fight over country he had first seen a generation before.[11] Widely scattered at designated Vulnerable Points around supply dumps and airfields across France, veterans' battalions like the West Yorkshires and the 12th Royal Warwicks were at least made up of trained and experienced soldiers, albeit frequently unarmed, carrying only sticks as deterrents to intruders. Other units began to arrive totally unprepared for what lay ahead as the Army Council turned to the deployment of the Territorial Army.

In 1914, General Sir John French's 'contemptible little army'[12] of four infantry divisions, one of cavalry and a single independent brigade was small even by comparison with that

fielded by the 'plucky little Belgium' it had come to defend. Even added to the 62 infantry
and 10 cavalry divisions of the French, the Allies were outnumbered by Germany's 100
infantry and 22 cavalry divisions and when the Germans pushed forward into Belgium
and northern France, were soon in headlong retreat.[13] In August alone, the BEF lost 1,382
men killed; September saw the loss of another 2,717 and by the end of the year 16,915
men were dead – well over 10 per cent of the original force – with many more wounded
or missing.[14] At one point, with losses mounting at a rate far outstripping his ability to
replace them, General French was even thought to be considering the need to evacuate
the British force via the channel ports for use in defending Britain rather than have them
wasted in a defence of Paris, an option that made military sense but which convinced the
French High Command for an entire generation that British strategy would always be to
run for the ports at the first opportunity.[15] With Regular Army manpower dwindling, the
British government looked to its Territorial Force for reinforcements.

The Territorial Force had been created by the Haldane Reforms of 1907 and had come
into being the following year to restructure the various strands of Britain's part-time armies.
Since medieval times, able-bodied men aged between 16 and 60 had a common law duty
to protect their county and to do this the Shire Reeve – or Sheriff – of a county had held
the power to conscript a local force as and when necessary under the principle of *Posse
Comitatus*.[16] Fearing a spread of rebellion in the wake of the French Revolution, Britain
passed the Defence of the Realm Act in 1798 which required the constables of every
parish in the country to list the names and occupations of all able-bodied men (excluding
peers and clergymen) between the ages of 15 and 60 not already engaged in military activities who could act as a Home Guard were the French to invade, or who could be used
as a force which the High Sheriff could raise to suppress a riot or call upon for any other
emergency. These later evolved into local militias who remained actively embodied during
the Napoleonic invasion scares of the early nineteenth century. Alongside them were the
Volunteers – men who were not full time soldiers and who even had to buy their own
uniforms and equipment – keen amateurs who joined in large numbers when another
French invasion scare swept the country in the 1860s.

A third element – created even earlier in 1794 – was the Yeomanry. Recruited from the
ranks of men who, by the requirement that they own a horse, were almost entirely of the
middle and upper classes, the Yeomanry were seen as an important safeguard against rebellion amongst the lower orders and it was they who would be sent to quell demonstrations
and strikes – most notably at the infamous Peterloo Massacre of 1819. Unlike their Militia
and Volunteer counterparts, the Yeomanry fitted in well with their Regular Army counterparts and enjoyed far greater political support in both Houses of Parliament through the
influence of Yeoman officers like the young Winston Churchill and the Earl of Longford.

The Haldane Reforms set out to create a single Territorial Force (TF) by merging
these existing units into a more streamlined second line army able to work closely with
the Regulars. The Militia, being the best trained, would now become Special Reserve
battalions of the Regular Army to supply reinforcements in time of war and the others
would be formed into 14 mounted brigades, each of 3 regiments of Yeomanry, 14 infantry
divisions with 12 battalions per division and the whole supported by its own artillery,
engineers, transport and medical services to provide a self contained home army. With
the main threat still seen as the invasion of the United Kingdom's mainland, they would
be used primarily for home defence, freeing up the Regular Army to serve overseas, but
Haldane also hoped that with additional training, they might be deployed overseas as reinforcements six months after general mobilisation had been declared.

Militia registration.

However, the reforms were a compromise. The early years of the twentieth century had seen growing demands for the introduction of conscription after the Boer War had highlighted the weaknesses of the standing army and the growing need to police the empire. Groups like the National Service League saw the new force as little more than a gimmick to avoid having to make the politically awkward decision to overturn Britain's longstanding opposition to enforced military service. Equally, since TF soldiers were to be paid only for the time they spent in uniform whilst conscripts would have to be employed full time, the decision to reform the force could be seen as an attempt to save money by training a second rate army on a part time basis. The long term effect could be the same, but with a set number of training sessions per year and an annual camp being the whole requirement for the TF it would take a Territorial soldier several years to acquire the experience a militiaman could gain in six months intensive service. Politically, though, the introduction of peacetime conscription was unacceptable.

Instead, Territorial Forces would form as additional battalions of the Regular Army and on paper at least, would be given the same training and equipment to allow them to work alongside their regular colleagues. At the same time, Haldane recognised that in the economic climate of the time, the Regular Army would be likely to maintain its own strength by drawing resources away from those allocated to the amateur 'Saturday Night Soldiers' and so created County Territorial Associations to manage the buildings and equipment of their local units. As a result, training and equipment varied from area to area with many battalions using obsolete weapons whilst others, in wealthier areas, having facilities that would be the envy of regular troops.

As an incentive to join, volunteers would enlist for a period of four years and would not be liable for foreign service unless they volunteered to sign the Imperial Service Obligation, but with BEF losses mounting, the Territorial Force was seen as being the logical source of reinforcement once the primary requirements for home defence had been met. Many among the Territorials saw this as unreasonable and complained about being asked to go against the terms of their enlistment. They had joined to defend their country and were willing to do so, but they did not see how serving overseas would serve that purpose. In some cases, officers were even reported to have urged their men not to give in to government blackmail and advised against signing the Obligation papers. Feelings ran high that the government had no right to pressure the Territorials into fighting a foreign war. W.N. Nicholson, a Regular officer serving with a Highland Territorial division, recalled a conversation with one of the Territorial officers: 'The Territorial Force was a last resort, in his opinion; it was not meant to come into the war until all the Regulars had been killed; a regular was not playing the game if he let a Territorial come and fight alongside him so early in the war as this.'[17] In some units acceptance of the Imperial Service Obligation was unanimous, some even agreed before the war broke out. Others were less enthusiastic. When the request was put to a parade of the 4th Battalion of the Northamptons, the commanding officer and brigade commander both explained that no-one would be forced to volunteer to serve overseas. Of 950 men, just 200 agreed to sign the papers.[18] A battalion was deemed available for foreign service if 80 per cent of its men volunteered. By the end of 1914, the requirement had dropped to just 50 per cent yet still there were problems recruiting enough men willing to go overseas.

Even in those units willing to serve overseas, differences in recruiting created still further problems. The Territorial Force allowed recruitment at the age of seventeen but the law required that a soldier was nineteen before he was allowed to serve overseas.[19] The presence of underage troops among the TF drafts leaving for France had prompted a sharp rebuke from the War Office, who insisted that no Territorial was to be sent to join the BEF 'unless he is medically fit, fully trained and is nineteen years of age or older'.

Kitchener, himself a critic of the Territorial Force, had already launched his campaign to create a 'New Army' in order to bypass them altogether so that by 1915 there were, in effect, three British armies – the 'old' pre-war regulars, the 'New Army' men who had responded to Kitchener's call and the 'borrowed' men of the TF. By 1916, a fourth group had been added when conscription swept up all those who had not yet enlisted (including the TF men who had not volunteered for foreign service), creating yet another class of soldier.[20] Whilst promotion could be rapid with men who had joined the New Army

War Office Notes.

The War Office,
Hobart House, Grosvenor Place,
9/N.D.C./159 (A.G.2.A/D.B.).   London, S.W.1.,
                                              24th November, 1939.

Sir,
I am directed to inform you that the National Defence Companies (Territorial Army Reserve) have recently been reorganised as Home Defence battalions of regiments of infantry of the Line.

These battalions are now open for enlistment to men between the ages of 35—50, fit for home service. Men are enlisted for home service for the duration of the war and, whilst serving, will receive current Army rates of pay and allowances. Those with previous service who are recommended by their commanding officer are eligible to draw military proficiency pay at the rate of 3d. per day in respect of their first three years' service.

Those with an Army second class certificate of education are eligible for the issue of educational proficiency pay at the rate of 3d. per day.

I am to say that any publicity which you can give to the above facts, through branches of the Regimental Association, or in the Regimental journal, will be much appreciated.

I am, Sir, your obedient servant,
A. A. L. CORBETT, D.A.A.G.,
for Director of Recruiting and Organisation.

The Secretary, Old Comrades' Association (The Duke of Wellington's Regiment)
(West Riding), The Depot, Halifax.

Letter requesting the recruitment of home defence battalions.

as privates commanding battalions by the end of the war, promotion above the rank of brigadier was strictly for Regular Army officers only and there was a clear hierarchical distinction made between 'real' officers and the 'temporary gentlemen' they had been forced to endure.

The return to peacetime soldiering brought with it a parting of the ways as the various constituents of the British Army reverted to their old roles and competition began again for the ever scarcer funding available to equip and train men. Reconstituted on 7 February 1920, the Territorial Force began recruiting again on the same terms as before – a four year enlistment with a requirement to attend a set number of training sessions and an annual camp in order to qualify for a bounty payment. Renamed the Territorial Army (TA) in October of that year it almost immediately fell victim to the 'Geddes axe' with the size and scale of equipment slashed to the minimum needed to perform its task. In 1922, two Air Defence Brigades were established to provide anti-aircraft cover for London and by 1935 it had been decided that the TA should assume responsibility for all anti-aircraft cover for the UK. In January 1936, the first anti-aircraft division had been formed and by 1939 the establishment of air defence units had been set at 96,000 TA troops. A Territorial Field Force establishment of 170,000 men was also created as a second line intended to follow the Regular Army into battle within six months of mobilisation.

In the wake of the Munich Crisis, recruitment for the forces was stepped up and the TA in particular began to actively campaign across the country to bring it up to strength. Typical of those the campaign targeted was eighteen-year-old Don Clark, a former member of the Army Cadet Force at Dewsbury Grammar School who, with his friends, was impressed when a squadron of the new, tracked Bren gun carriers drove into Dewsbury market place as part of a TA recruitment drive in late 1938. 'We virile teenagers were bowled over by the sight of them, their power and speed and our minds filled with dreams that we were actually driving them! It was no contest, we would definitely join up and get a baby tank!'[21] The campaign was very successful, but there was still a need for more men than the current establishment allowed for. Then, in late March 1939, and seemingly on a whim, Hore-Belisha suddenly decreed that the TA would recruit to wartime establishment and then double its size to create a total of 26 divisions for the proposed Territorial Field Force. The *Daily Telegraph* of 30 March reported:

Immediate steps are to be taken to provide equipment and accommodation for the 210,000 additional members of the Territorial Army involved in the decision, announced by Mr. Chamberlain in the House of Commons yesterday, to double the strength of the Territorial Field Army … Mr. Chamberlain made his statement in reply to Mr. Greenwood, Deputy Leader of the Opposition, who asked what were the intentions of the Government regarding the Territorial Army. The Prime Minister said: 'The House will remember that in a recent statement I announced that every aspect of our national life, including the national defence programmes, would be examined anew. In the course of this review His Majesty's Government have been impressed with the need for availing themselves still further of the spirit of voluntary service which is manifest throughout the country. (Cheers) In particular they feel that they cannot allow would-be recruits for the Territorial Army to be refused because the units in which they apply are clearly over strength. Accordingly they have been giving consideration to the position and have come to the following conclusion:

'The Territorial Field Army which is now on a peace establishment of 130,000 men, will be raised forthwith to war establishment, which will involve an addition of about 40,000 men to this figure.

'The Territorial Field Army so brought up to war establishment will be doubled and will therefore be allotted an establishment of 340,000 men.

'The House will appreciate that these important decisions will involve a number of consequential decisions to provide for the necessary increases in accommodation, in the number of competent instructors, in equipment and reserves and in the war potential necessary to maintain the increased forces. Plans for all these matters are being worked out and further information about them will from time to time be given to the House. It will be realised that a further and much augmented effort will be required to bring home to the nation the need for obtaining the numbers aimed at in the shortest possible time, and I trust that all members of the House will be willing in one form or another to give their aid to such an effort.'

He also pointed out ... that his announcement showed that double the number of divisions would in time be available for overseas service.

The report went on to claim that

By the time training is over, full war equipment will be ready. The decision to train the Territorial Army for war in a European centre means the provision of full-scale equipment similar to that of the Regular Army. That equipment is being ordered at once. A notable innovation is that the officers will be recruited as far as possible from the rank. This principle, though followed throughout the anti-aircraft units, has not formerly been put into general practice in the Territorial Army and artillery.[22]

As the *Telegraph's* special correspondent noted in the following day's edition; 'I understand that the Army Council did not reach its decision to double the strength of the Territorial Army until shortly before the Prime Minister made his statement in the House of Commons. Consequently all the Territorial Associations responsible for administration were taken by surprise.'[23] Despite the promise that 'there is already a plentiful supply of rifles. There will be one for all who

SAFEGUARD YOUR LIBERTIES!

Lance Cattermole 1938

JOIN THE TERRITORIAL ARMY

TA recruitment poster, 1938. After the Munich Crisis, recruitment to the TA was stepped up in an intensive drive.

join, however swift the rush', it was clear that the 'cost of the new Territorial Army developments alone will be more than the total cost of the whole Army three or four years ago' and that the army's infrastructure was in no state to accept a flood of new recruits. Frantic efforts began to find suitable accommodation in drill halls, church halls and private billets and for staff to help train and administer the new units by calling on retired officers, NCOs and soldiers – and even members of the British Legion – to offer their services. Special arrangements were to be made for night workers who could not attend evening training. In an echo of the spirit of Kitchener's New Army, it was even suggested that chauffeurs and male domestic workers could be formed into special units and that large employers should form their own units.

To many, the seemingly snap decision was yet further evidence of Hore-Belisha's cavalier attitude to the military. Politically, though, it was an astute move. With the announcement of the unpopular introduction of peacetime conscription only a matter of weeks away, the increase of the TA offered the chance to escape liability for full time service whilst committing to military training in a regiment or corps of one's choice. At the same time, it also pre-empted any attempt by his enemies at the War Office to undermine him by a repeat of Kitchener's creation of the New Army.

As volunteers came forward, the TA quickly grew. The 5th Battalion of the West Yorkshire Regiment, for example, grew from 27 officers and 528 other ranks in March to 47 officers and 1,032 other ranks by June, 346 over wartime establishment. Under Lieutenant-Colonel Pulleyn, these 346 were to form the nucleus of a duplicate battalion and recruitment began in May to bring this up to full strength. Training schedules and equipment though, had been prepared on the peacetime strength and linked to plans by the parent regiments. Many of those recruited had not, by September 1939, had chance to even attend the annual training camp.

Impressive though the figures for recruitment were, they hid some painful truths. As Parliament prepared to agree to allow limited conscription in a debate long into the night of 27 April, Hore-Belisha explained:

> May I ask the House to consider our military resources? The Regular Army has an establishment of 224,000 men. The right hon. Gentleman the Leader of the Opposition was good enough to say that we have instituted many reforms to make the Regular Army more attractive, and that the recruiting had thereby considerably improved. That is true. The establishment is 224,000, but the strength is 204,000. I shall at a later stage be asking the House to increase that establishment. The Territorial Field Army has an establishment of approximately 325,000 men. Its strength is 167,000 men. The Anti-Aircraft Army, if I may so describe it, has an establishment of 96,000 men and a strength of 80,000. Let us take each of these forces in turn. In the Regular Army the difference between the figures of establishment and strength shows that we are short of trained men. Those who will be at the disposal of the Regular Army under the new scheme, for which we are asking approval in principle to-night, will, in the event of war, make the shortage less inconvenient. I would point out that, although doubt has been thrown upon the value of the numbers of men we shall engage each year, a number approximating to the whole strength of the Regular Army will be trained each year.
>
> In regard to the Territorial Field Army, the new divisions will be composed in time of the best material that we have, of volunteers who have sacrificed their leisure and their holidays to fit themselves to defend our cause. We shall fill the ranks in time. We shall train the men in time. Yet time is a factor in international events which we cannot control. The

response to our appeal for recruits to double the Territorial Army is most encouraging and the Government hope that no effort will be relaxed. The number of recruits enlisted since 1st April has been no fewer than 2,000 a day, a figure which far exceeds any record previously attained. The plan announced by my right hon. Friend yesterday, under which six months' intensive training will be given to all men between the ages of 20 and 21, will fill the gap while the slower process of assembling and preparing the new Territorial formations is taking place.[24]

The plan Hore-Belisha referred to was the new Military Training Act, intended to create a reserve of fully trained troops who could be recalled to the service if necessary but who would not be as costly as maintaining a fulltime conscript army. The relatively short period of service would also cushion the blow. Twenty-year-old Rex Flowers, working in a Yorkshire Co-Op store, welcomed the idea:

> Then we got the news that there was going to be a militia, six months service, nice blue uniforms, and then back home. I was looking forward to it very much. Just think of it, Six months playing soldiers, firing guns. The nice blue uniforms would turn the girls' heads – they might have done too, we all thought it was a great idea. We got the news. First militia was to go up in June or July, I can't remember which. My friend Harry Pattison was in the First lot. How I envied him.[25]

In May, Peter Walker and John Marsland, working together at a Halifax mill, decided that 'rather than wait until the balloon went up and probably lose all chances of making up our own minds as to where and in what we served' they would join the TA. After a medical conducted in an empty shop premises in Cow Green, Halifax, they were duly signed on as members of the 2/7th Duke of Wellington's Regiment. Training would take place in a gym in Great Albion Street every Tuesday and Thursday night where, between 7 and 9pm, the recruits were taught basic weapons skills and foot drill and earned a day's pay for every eight hours they attended. Despite his lack of experience and military knowledge, Peter soon found himself promoted to Corporal even before he was issued with his first pieces of kit or fired a rifle. It would not be until August that the unit attended a live firing train-ing weekend and he was issued with some surplus First World War pattern webbing to take home. On Friday 1 September, a call from John Marsland had him leave work and report to the gym immediately with his webbing and washing kit. On the way he recalled hear-ing radio announcements telling reservists where to report. 'It filled me with excitement; tinged with apprehension and, I suppose, fear.'[26]

By the time Walker reported for duty, the establishment of a total of 645,000 troops described by Hore-Belisha in April had been increased by the inclusion of the 34,000 men of the Militia and 150,000 of the Army Reserve – bringing the army up to a nominal establishment of around 865,000 men with the possibility, it was claimed, of raising this to a million by November 1939.[27] Crucially, these forces were not to be regarded as different armies but as one whole. In the First World War TF men completing their four-year term of enlistment had been discharged and sent home from units in the front lines. This time the TA would not be a separate force with its own rules.

'During the last war, at the end of 1914', wrote one observer in 1940, 'Britain had three separate armies in existence and in preparation, all with competing interests … In less than a week from the outbreak of war in 1939 Britain had a single army, well equipped, well trained, and well led.'[28] The truth, though, was rather different.

NOTES

1 Burdock, C. & Jacobsen, H-A. Halder *War Diary 1939–42* Novato, California: Presidio Press 1988 p67

2 Frieser, K-H. *The Blitzkrieg Legend* Anapolis: Naval Institute Press 2005 p20

3 Ibid p21

4 Karslake, B. 1940: *The Last Act* London: Leo Cooper 1979 p27

5 National Army Museum *'Against All Odds' The British Army of 1939–40* London: National Army Museum. Limited Edition p23

6 Hamilton, N. *Monty: The Making of a General 1887–12* London: Hamish Hamilton 1981 p325

7 See Hatherill, G. *A detective's story: George Hatherill of Scotland Yard* New York: McGraw-Hill 1972. Hatherill later went on to investigate the serial killers John Reginald Christie and John George Haigh and the Great Train Robbery

8 www.royalpioneercorps.co.uk/rpc/history

9 Glover, M. *The Fight for the Channel Ports* London: Leo Cooper 1985 p77

10 *Against all Odds* Op cit p47

11 *Ça Ira* Journal of the West Yorkshire Regiment Vol 9. No 4 March 1940 p372

12 'It is my Royal and Imperial command that you concentrate your energies, for the immediate present, upon one single purpose, and that is that you address all your skill and all the valour of my soldiers to exterminate first the treacherous English and walk over General French's contemptible little army.' Army Order Issued by Emperor William II, 19 August 1914 Headquarters, Aix-la-Chapelle. Source Records of the Great War, Vol. II, ed. Charles F. Horne, National Alumni 1923

13 Corrigan, G. *Mud, Blood and Poppycock* London: Cassell 2003 p48

14 Corrigan p63

15 Jackson, J. *The Fall of France* Oxford: Oxford University Press 2003 p66. See also McDonald, L. *1914* London: Penguin 1989 p243

16 From the Latin meaning 'The power of the county.' The Posse Comitatus Act of June 16, 1878 passed the principle into US Federal Law and gave birth to the Sherriff's posse of western fame.

17 Nicholson, WN. *Behind the Lines: an Account of Administrative Staff Work in the British Army* Cape Publishing 1939 p19–20 quoted in Messenger, C. *Call to Arms: The British Army 1914–18* London: Cassell 2005 p70

18 Messenger Op cit p71

19 The many stories of underage troops in the trenches are true, but the key factor is that they were boys who had lied about their age to enlist. Only in the last stages of the First World War was the minimum age for overseas service reduced to eighteen and a half. It is only in the last quarter of the twentieth century that the British Army has knowingly sent soldiers still legally classified as children into combat. For example, Neil Grose, Jason Burt and Ian Scrivens of 3rd Battalion of the Parachute Regiment were all aged just seventeen when they were killed in the battle for Mount Longdon during the 1982 Falklands war.

20 The role of conscripts in the First World War remains an apparent source of embarrassment with many books devoted to the famous 'Pals' battalions but very little attention given to the larger numbers of men who chose not to enlist yet who became part of the war-winning army of 1918. As Ilana R. Bet-El points out in her study of conscripts in 1916–18, when the BBC began researching its groundbreaking 'Great War' documentary series in the 1960s it deliberately limited its requests for participants to those who served before the end of 1915 to exclude former conscripts. (Bet-El, IR. *Conscripts* Stroud: Sutton Publishing 2003 p201–204)

21 Don Clark. Personal account (Imperial War Museum Documents 99/16/1)

22 *Daily Telegraph* 30 March 1939

23 NATION ANSWERS THE CALL: RECRUITMENT BEGUN. From A Special Correspondent *Daily Telegraph* 31 March 1939

24 Hansard House of Commons Debates 27 April 1939 vol 346 cc1343–464

25 Rex Flowers. Personal account.

26 Peter Walker, Personal account. See http://www.dwr.org.uk/dwr.php?id=119&pa=121

27 Hammerton, Sir John (Ed). *The Second Great War*, Vol One, London: Waverley Book Company (Not dated *c* 1941) p134

28 Hammerton p134–5

Chapter Three

'You are no longer Saturday night soldiers'

Training for the TA took on a new impetus over the summer of 1939 but for Don Clark, by now a private in the 4th Battalion of the King's Own Yorkshire Light Infantry, the big event of their two weeks of camp on the Isle of Man was not weapons or tactical training but four days of rehearsal for a parade of the whole 49th Infantry Division to which they were attached. The parade went well and Clark recalled a tremendous sense of achievement in his ability to remain in formation for the light infantry's 140 paces per minute march past. It was, no doubt, a stirring sight but had cost almost a third of the available time for more active training – and time lost that would soon be regretted. As they prepared for the parade, men read of the deepening international crisis and it was clear to all that war was coming.

When the battalion returned from camp in August, Clark was among those ordered to remain on active duty and for the next few weeks spent his days doing various jobs around the drill hall and awaiting developments. In other areas, guards were ordered to be posted at Vulnerable Points in readiness for a possible pre-emptive sabotage attack as early as 24

Militia recruits arrive at their training depot.

Guard mounting at a railway tunnel. A posed publicity shot; few of the newly enlisted TA had full uniform at this stage.

August. On the 29th the Durham Light Infantry suffered their first casualty when Private G.R. Milburn was killed by a train as he guarded the Croxdale Viaduct in Northumberland.[1] On Sunday 3 September, men gathered around radios set up in drill halls across Britain to hear Chamberlain's speech. As the news sank in, Clark heard the Regimental Sergeant-Major's voice suddenly boom out: 'Attention you men, you are no longer Saturday night soldiers, you are in the bloody Regular Army now, or you will be when the state of war has been promulgated this afternoon, and then we'll see what you're made of.'[2]

With the declaration of war the Territorial Army effectively ceased to exist and became part of the Regular Army, its ranks now swelled by a steady stream of volunteers, militiamen, recalled reservists and in due course, conscripts. Filling the ranks was one thing, filling them with the right kind of soldier in the right kind of role was a different matter entirely. Soldiering remained, as it always had been, the least attractive of the services and men with skills and education looked first to the more glamorous Air Force and Royal Navy when volunteering – a major problem for a mechanised and increasingly technical army. Even those willing enough to serve in the army quickly became resentful when its system for handling recruits broke down under the sudden pressure. After enviously watching his friend go off for Militia training during the summer, Rex Flowers recalls:

After a while I received an official letter. I had to report to Somme barracks Sheffield. The very name filled me with awe. I had read so many books about the Great War, including the terrible battle of the Somme in 1916. At the barracks I had my medical, cough and all that, a completely new experience for me. I passed on and found wonder of wonders, that I had passed, A1. The next step was to face a board of Officers etc. My Father had said to me, 'Whatever you do son, keep out of the infantry.' Very good advice. So when the officer said 'What arm of the army do you want to serve in?' I said 'The artillery please sir.' Dad had told me how to recognise an officer and to answer with 'sir.' He replied 'No problem, We will put you down for the artillery' and that was that. I returned home well satisfied and told my Dad proudly 'I am going into the artillery', the officer had said so. I was to get to know the army a lot better before all that long. I was just an innocent well out of my depth! Time went on. It was now August 1939. I was eagerly awaiting the letter telling me when I was being called up, I was all agog, I couldn't wait. Such is the age of innocence.

At last the long awaited letter arrived, I opened it with trembling hands. I read it; I was to report on the 15th of September 1939 to Pontefract Barracks, to the K.O.Y.L.I. I rushed to my Dad; I said 'Dad, what sort of artillery is the K.O.Y.L.I.?' He said sadly, 'Son, that's the infantry. It means The Kings Own Yorkshire Light Infantry.' I burst out 'The officer said that I could go into the artillery, why is this?' He said wryly 'That's the army son, you'll learn' and I did, a lot quicker than I thought.[3]

Arriving at Strensall Barracks near York for his basic training, like many other new recruits Flowers was particularly in awe of the recalled Reservists he encountered. 'After all they were real time served soldiers, not just anybody, but more like gods.' But even these gods had to learn. Volander 'Val' Thomas had first joined the regiment at the age of eighteen in 1932 and had quickly decided he would not get along with the regimental sergeant major so, together with a friend he decided to desert the KOYLI and to go to nearby Leeds and enlist in the Cameron Highlanders instead. Two months later, the pair were arrested at the Camerons' depot and returned to the KOYLI and straight into the waiting arms of their hated RSM. Marched before their commanding officer, only Thomas' rugby skills kept him out of the glasshouse – the men arrived back just as their company was about to play an important match – but he knew it was a near thing. After that he settled down into life in the KOYLI and after three years garrison duty on Gibraltar, was effectively made redundant by the ever worsening army cutbacks and so left in November 1935 to return to civilian life. Val and his fiancée were planning for their wedding at Christmas and already had a house marked down in his home town of Wakefield when the recall notices ordering him back to the army arrived in late August. On the morning of 2 September, the couple married before Val caught the bus to the KOYLI depot at Pontefract. After just four years away, the reorganisation of the army in the 1930s had brought changes to the familiar. Gone was the time honoured command to 'form fours' on parade, replaced by the forming of three ranks instead. New drill, new weapons to learn, but still the same organisation.

For the new arrivals, the term 'organisation' was not the first they might choose to describe what they encountered. Simply working out what unit one belonged to could be a confusing hurdle. The regimental system of the British Army had evolved over two centuries into an apparently eccentric collection of battalions with local affiliations not always immediately obvious to the outsider. The basic structure of the regiment was of two or three regular battalions with associated territorial units. The 1st Battalion would be used for overseas garrison duties and would be the first into action. The 2nd Battalion would remain in the UK and would be used to reinforce the first. A 3rd (Reserve) Battalion might also exist to provide a trained pool of men in time of war. territorial battalions would then form the 4th and subsequent battalions. The new order to 'recruit to war establishment then double' meant that these territorial battalions would follow a similar pattern with, for example, the 4th battalion now expanding into two duplicate versions – 1st/4th and 2nd /4th. Again, the 1/4th would take precedence and would be used for overseas service, the 2/4th would be a second line unit used to provide reinforcements as required. Being the British Army, of course, this system was too simple to be universally accepted.

The Durham Light Infantry (DLI), for example, chose instead a completely different pattern. The regiment had recruited 37 battalions during the First World War and would raise fourteen in the Second – including the 18th Battalion which served as a 'beach brick' charged with landing the basic base installations at Salerno and Normandy. The 18th bore the DLI name but only two officers and a very few other ranks were actually from the regiment itself; most men were from logistics units. Meanwhile, the regiment also created another 18th Battalion – this one for home defence duties – seemingly without any concerns that having two 18th battalions on the regimental books might lead to the odd administrative problem. So, in 1939, the Territorial 6th, 8th and 9th battalions of the DLI were part of 151 Brigade of 50th Division whilst the 5th and 7th had already been detached to form Searchlight Regiments as part of the TA's anti-aircraft role. When the order to duplicate was issued, the regiment chose not to follow the 1/ and 2/ model but instead created the 10th, 11th and 12th as duplicates of the 6th, 8th and 9th respectively. These were formed as 70 Brigade of the 23rd (Northumbrian) Division. The 12th, having recruited largely from Scots living in Northumberland was then re-badged late in 1939 to become the 1st (and indeed only) Battalion of the Tyneside Scottish, a revival of the name adopted during the First World War by several New Army battalions of the Northumberland Fusiliers but now unaccountably under the direction of the Black Watch.

However it was applied, the duplication model continued up to divisional level with the 49th (West Riding) Infantry Division, a Territorial Division first created in 1908 and recruiting almost entirely from a small area of Yorkshire's industrial West Riding around Leeds, Bradford, Halifax and Wakefield, now being joined by a duplicate division – the 46th (North Midland and West Riding) Division – created on 2 October 1939 by reforming the North Midland Division of the First World War and incorporating elements of the West Riding units. On paper a simple and expedient exercise, duplication was not welcomed by the army. General Sherman had said of his experience of troops during the American Civil War 80 years earlier, 'I believe that five hundred new men added to an old and experienced regiment were more valuable than a thousand men in the form of a new regiment, for the former, by association with good experienced captains, lieutenants, and non-commissioned officers, soon become veterans, whereas the latter were generally unavailable for a year.' Now, the British Army was learning the same lesson. As duplication brought with it the need to move experienced men around, chaos reigned. 'In each case', wrote one unit historian, 'in place of one keen and fairly efficient unit, two untrained, ill-equipped inefficient battalions were produced.'[4]

As the 46th Infantry Division formed, Brigadier John Gawthorpe was recalled from retirement and placed in charge of its 137th Infantry Brigade in a scattered command which included the 2/5th West Yorkshire Regiment with its HQ in York and companies in Tadcaster, Knaresborough, Wetherby, Ripon, Selby, and Leeds. Alongside them were the 2/6th and 2/7th battalions of the Duke of Wellington's Regiment (DWR) covering Keighley, Bradford, Skipton, Huddersfield and Halifax. Gawthorpe, himself a former West Yorkshire Regiment officer, set up his new brigade Headquarters in Brighouse, near Huddersfield. Further afield, other retired officers were brought back to equally wide commands – Brigadier E.J. Grinling took the 2/4th King's Own Yorkshire Light Infantry from Wakefield, the 6th Lincolnshire Regiment and the 6th Yorks and Lancs as 138th Infantry Brigade whilst Brigadier R.C. Chichester-Constable assumed command of 139th Brigade with its 2/5th Leicestershire Regiment and two battalions of the Sherwood Foresters. 'These units' Gawthorpe wrote, 'had done only the barest part of recruit training and had not been to camp, as they were to have accompanied their parent units on Regular Army manoeuvres which were due to take place in Northern Command during September, 1939. War forestalled this, so they started practically from scratch.'[5]

Unable to clothe, accommodate and equip the men they already had, the TA units continued to receive more recruits to bring them up to the new establishment strength and new arrivals found themselves in for something of a culture shock. In January 1940, Arnold Straw received his call up papers and travelled to Leeds as ordered. From the city station he was marched with an assorted bunch of fellow conscripts to a nearby barracks where they were to be sorted into regiments. At eight that evening, after a ten hour wait, he and around 20 others were again marched to the railway station and put on a train, destination unknown. About two hours later they were herded off the train at Huddersfield station.

> It was bitterly cold as we marched through the darkened streets singing, with youthful enthusiasm, to our destination. This proved to be the Yorkshire Dragoons' [Territorials] Drill Hall in Fitzwilliam Street, a medium sized hall with a stage at one end and a balcony at the other … We were ushered into a small side room where there was a heap of rough hessian palliasse covers: alas there was no straw left – what irony – and no more available that night. There were two dingy army blankets each, however, so Dougie and I decided to pool our resources by using the empty palliasse covers and two blankets to lie on, and two blankets to cover us, using our civilian clothes as pillows apart from our overcoats which we used as auxiliary blankets. As we were the last party to arrive the main part of the hall was pretty well covered with 'beds', so we made ourselves as comfortable as we could on the balcony and, as there was no sign of food or drink, decided to settle down for the night. I was in no way brimming over with contentment having left home and fiancé for an unknown and precarious future – and being hungry into the bargain![6]

TA units had traditionally recruited from small geographical areas and from men who often worked together. An easy informality developed between the ranks that exasperated many of the Regular Army staff drafted in to help. Donald Edgar, serving with the 2/6th East Surreys, recalled an incident in which the captain of his unit's intelligence section came across a group of his soldiers drinking in a local hotel and immediately joined them. All went well until the captain, still wearing his full uniform, drew his sword and jumped onto a table to demonstrate how he and his men would win the war. The evening ended peacefully enough but word reached the commanding officer and the captain was quietly moved to another company.[7] Incidents like that were not unusual and now, as Straw and his comrades tried to settle down for their first night in the army, they were woken by a drunken orderly officer and two sergeants who, after asking after the new arrivals, ordered the cookhouse staff to be woken up and to produce food for them before entertaining them with an impromptu concert.

After a brief night's sleep, the recruits were processed through the paperwork and training began almost immediately, but it would not be until March that the weather improved enough to allow the new platoon to carry out any exercises outdoors. On the few occasions that the recruits were able to venture outside to do arms drill on the street behind the drill hall they could only manage a few minutes at a time before grounding their rifles and running up and down the street slapping each other on the back to restore circulation. Morning PT was conducted at the local public baths but was accompanied by much slipping, sliding and falling down on the icy cobbles rather than any disciplined march to reach it – much to the amusement of passers-by.

Training, though, was not the first priority. On Friday 25 August 1939, the 2/4th Battalion of the KOYLI was officially embodied at Dewsbury, but as the official history records, it did not exist as an organised battalion until long after that date. As platoons formed, they were immediately sent to act as guards at locations across south Yorkshire, Lincolnshire and Nottinghamshire. On that day, at 2.30 in the afternoon, a bomb produced by an IRA cell exploded inside the satchel of a tradesman's bicycle that had been left outside a shop on Broadgate, Coventry. The explosion killed five people, injured 100 more and caused extensive damage to shops in the area. The following Monday large numbers of workers went on strike in the city protesting at having to work with Irish labour. The strikers marched in procession to the Council House, where the Mayor urged them to return to work and after they had passed a vote of confidence in the Chief Constable, the crowd dispersed but memories of German support for the IRA in the First World War were still fresh.

Across the country, TA battalions were immediately deployed to guard factories, airfields, railways and other identified Vulnerable Points from German and Irish threat. Donald Edgar had been working for a company in the City of London when he received his notice of embodiment from a sympathetic policeman one evening after work. His employers made arrangements to top up his salary and gave him a farewell party a few days later. Within hours of leaving the party, he was on duty.

> Around mid-day I had been sipping champagne in a City bar in an ambience of stock-brokers, bank officials and insurance underwriters. Now here I was at midnight outside Chatham, in uniform, wearing steel helmet, carrying a rifle with five rounds of live ammunition, listening for suspicious noises which might herald the arrival of German agents or the IRA and uncomfortably aware that I was treading over thousands of tons of explosives. It was not a jolly experience![8]

With more enthusiasm than experience, men took to their duties. Among the DLI, some proved more enthusiastic than others. The official history recalls the manager of a works guarded by the local TA who arrived late one night at the gates to be told, 'If you put another foot out of the car I'll blow your _____ head off.' Another civilian inspector checking a viaduct had to crawl on hands and knees towards a sentry to produce his identity papers. Training even for this task had been limited and one new sentry stood demanding that anyone approaching should 'advance and be reconciled'.[9]

In the area covered by Gawthorpe's 137 Brigade, a Prisoner of War camp had optimistically been set up on York race course for the trickle of German sailors captured or interned at British ports and guards needed to be supplied. They were also needed to guard the BBC transmitter station on Moorside Edge and airfields around York. Worse, in the deep snows, the rail tunnels across the Pennines needed to be secured. The entrances to tunnels were relatively sheltered but the air shafts stood high on the moors and involved long and tiring treks to reach. Morale was still further sapped by a shortage of uniforms and especially greatcoats. In the freezing weather, men were paid an extra sixpence a day to use their own coats over the black army boiler suits they had been issued. The only outward signs that the new KOYLI men were even part of the army were their rifles and a red armband with the letters TA – the only known distinction made between the Territorial and Regular Army once war was declared.[10] In the West Yorkshire Regiment 'several months elapsed before there was sufficient battledress for the entire 2/5th battalion.'[11] Such was the shortage of uniforms that debate went on at high levels about whether the length of the standard issue greatcoat should be shortened to try to save enough cloth to meet the demand.[12] For battalions recruited from the woollen mills of West Yorkshire it was particularly embarrassing that they did not have a supply of the very clothing their families helped make.

The tedium of cold nights was occasionally interrupted by moments of action. In November, Private B. Pickering of the KOYLI, on guard patrol at Hemswell airfield, opened fire on an intruder and a short while later Privates Lord and Dixon challenged a running figure. Dixon fired but missed and in the excitement, Private Lord accidentally fired a round as they searched the undergrowth nearby.[13] In that case the armoury doors were found to be open but often, as Donald Edgar recalled, the 'intruders' turned out to be members of other units enjoying a little female company and the 'trigger happy TA bastards' received few thanks for their diligence. Inexperience and boredom began to take its toll and Edgar also reports the death of a young private shot in barracks when a comrade was enthusiastically explaining what he would do to any German agent attempting to get in – forgetting his rifle was still loaded.[14]

Few doubted that the guard duties were important but they were also very boring:

> No doubt it was economical in man-power to use a raw Territorial battalion for the purpose, yet it meant that the 2/4th KOYLI had a cruelly bad start to its career as a fighting unit … Duties of this type are notoriously bad for morale, for the keener a man may be on becoming a good soldier the more does he fret over the waste of time. Being scattered in platoon posts with at least a third of the men always on guard, no training could be tackled properly.[15]

Over the coming winter, the second line battalions of the TA would be employed on these guard duties and in helping the local authorities to cope with the worst winter storms in memory – but not on training for war. Men spent more time digging out snowdrifts for the council than in learning to dig trenches. For one West Yorkshire Regiment recruit, it was just too much. A Militiaman who, like the rest, had registered at the local labour exchange insisted on his right to speak to his company commander. Once in the office, he leaned confidentially across the desk and explained: 'Well, sir, I've done my best to get to like the army and fit myself to its conditions, but it's no use. I don't like it and that's flat, so I'm afraid you'll have to give me my cards back.' Others took to it more willingly but one junior recruit was asked how he liked the army. 'I like it all right, but the trouble is that everyone round here seems to be a boss but me.'[16]

The winter of guard duties and the arrival of newly trained conscripts in late 1939 and early 1940 meant the battalions grew in size but not in experience as the months went by. Slowly, as the initial rush slowed, the army began to settle down a little. Having recruited the men, it now began to take stock of what it had. Immediately, new problems arose. The introduction of conscription in September had been accompanied by the identification of key reserved occupations from which men should not be taken. One of the most vital of British industries at that time was the production of coal to power the armaments factories and an order was sent out that all miners were to be discharged with the exception of NCOs and specialists who, nevertheless, had to be offered the choice to return to their jobs at the pits. For the KOYLI, recruiting from the mining districts around Wakefield, this meant the immediate loss of over 200 often experienced soldiers. Worse was to come. The NCOs and specialists who agreed to stay on soon found that the difference between a miner's wage and that of a soldier was a significant one:

Training for trench warfare in Britain. Where would a Maginot Line cross Britain? The Thames? Any invading force, once established ashore from south or east, would cross easy terrain to London.

Some were forced to leave for the astonishing reason that they were losing the furniture from their homes. They had bought it on the hire purchase system and on army pay they were unable to keep up the full weekly payments. So the firms were removing the furniture ... Replacements for the men so lost were slow in coming and when they did they consisted of untrained recruits, so the standard of training and fitness if anything fell rather than rose.[17]

In some ways, though, the KOYLI were luckier than most. The early influx of Reservists into their TA battalions at least gave them a nucleus of trained men able to pass on informally some of the tricks of the trade. In the 2/5th West Yorkshire Regiment training was limited to a maximum of two days per week per man and instructors in such short supply that 'selected personnel were taught a portion of a lesson overnight and the whole unit was passed through this string of elementary teachers the next day. However, some individual training was achieved and relief from guard duties was promised for Spring.'[18] Such individual training was frequently heavily improvised. The 9th Battalion of the Royal Northumberland Fusiliers, designated as a machine gun battalion for 23rd Division, relied entirely on two German machine guns captured in 1918 and wheeled out of the regimental museum. Also in 23rd Division, men of the Green Howards used a wooden replica built by a local carpenter to train in the use of mortars.

In early 1940, with no sign of action in France, attention turned instead to developments elsewhere. As A.S. Bryant later wrote;

By this time the British, growing conscious of the freedom of choice given by command of the sea, were beginning, as so often in the past, to contemplate offensive adventures for which they did not possess the military power ... forgetful of the fact that, with grossly

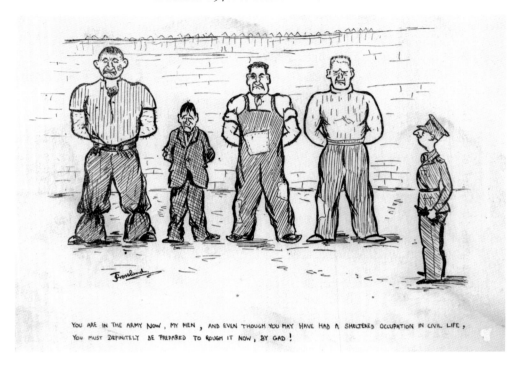

Above: Cartoon from *DWR Journal* 1940.

Right: Cartoon from West Yorkshire Journal
'*Ca Ira*' 1940.

inadequate force and armaments, they were already facing the greatest military and air power in Europe, they proceeded to plan, in concert with their French allies, an expedition as fantastic as ever a British Government had ever launched from its island-base.[19]

Over the winter plans had been developed for an Anglo-French intervention in Scandinavia. Norway had declared neutrality but both Britain and Germany had recognised its vital strategic importance since control of the country would mean control of access to the Atlantic and particularly to the approaches to Germany in the south and the Soviet Union in the north. An Allied naval presence there would add significantly to the blockade of Germany's trade. At the start of the war, Germany imported over 10 million tons of iron ore from Sweden, 90 per cent of it through the port of Luleå in the north. That port, though, freezes over in winter but the alternative route, through the Norwegian port of Narvik, does not. Therefore control of Narvik would mean both a naval base covering the north Atlantic and a blockade of the supply of iron ore crucial to Germany's war industry.

The Soviet Union and Nazi Germany had signed a mutual non-aggression pact on 23 August 1939 that included a secret clause dividing the countries of Eastern Europe between the two signatories and also stated that Finland would fall under the Soviet 'sphere of influence' in the north. After joining the German attack on Poland, the Soviets turned their attention to Finland in the autumn of 1939 and demanded that the Finns agree to move the border 25 kilometres (16 miles) back from Leningrad. It also demanded that they lease the Hanko Peninsula to the USSR for 30 years for the creation of a naval base there. In exchange, the Soviet Union offered Finland a large part of Karelia but the offer was contemptuously dismissed by the Finns as 'two pounds of dirt for one pound of gold'. In response, on 30 November, Soviet forces invaded Finland and bombed civilian boroughs of Helsinki.[20]

In December, Hitler met with Vidkun Quisling, the leader of the Norwegian *Nasjonal Samling* (National Union) party, who alleged that the Soviet Union would soon attack Norway and that British intervention was imminent. Certainly Britain had its eye firmly on Norway since on 19 September Churchill had told the Cabinet that the transportation of iron ore to Germany had to be stopped and proposed laying mines off the coast at Narvik. The invasion of Finland provided the pretext for Britain and France to make their move and present it as an attempt to defend the neutral states of Norway and Sweden whilst at the same time allowing them to garrison the port.

In February 1940, the Allies offered to help Finland by sending 100,000 British and 35,000 French troops via Narvik, moving to the Finnish front via Sweden and securing supply routes along the way. The Finns were asked to make a formal request for help to avoid German charges that the Allies had invaded and on 2 March, permission to pass through Narvik and northern Norway and through Sweden was officially requested from the respective governments so that the troops could be used to create a defence line against further attacks into Scandinavia. The plan, if successful, would significantly increase the power of the blockade of Germany and would also draw German attention away from the more vulnerable French front. Given the state of the BEF in France, the plan to send such a large force was wildly over-optimistic from the outset, but Churchill was determined to push the plan through. The already under-strength force in France found its supply of weapons and reinforcements diverted to create another Expeditionary Force – much to the anger of commanders in the field. By diverting troops from France and bringing two Territorial brigades up to full strength, a force of four brigades with attached artillery and engineers was eventually assembled.

Among those slated to join the expedition were 146th and 148th Brigades of the 49th Infantry Division and to bring them up to strength the army turned to their duplicate, second line counterparts in 46th Division. As the 1/4th KOYLI made ready, its battalion medical officer examined the men and medically downgraded about 30 per cent of them. To meet the pressing need for troops to take part in the Norwegian expedition, the War Office disallowed his assessment and ordered in a draft from the 2/4th battalion – including a new medical officer.[21] As a result, orders reached the 2/4th to 'send all private soldiers, other than immatures [those under nineteen years of age] to the 1/4th KOYLI.'[22] By careful application of the term 'specialist', the battalion managed to retain at least some of the longer standing members but at a stroke, it had lost another 212 men, leaving behind a battalion composed almost entirely of NCOs and under-age boys. An infantry battalion of the time was established for 21 officers and 752 other ranks. In a matter of weeks, the 2/4th had lost over half its men before it had even completed its first training exercise. As replacements, two new drafts – one of newly trained conscripts, the other of Reservists recently returned from France – arrived to join the KOYLI.

Having by now completed his basic training at York, Rex Flowers was among those posted to the 2/4th KOYLI at Dewsbury:

> We arrived in Wakefield on Saturday about lunchtime, we marched from the station to the drill hall – no one seemed to be about. Eventually we contacted someone but we were left hanging about for some time. Later, after a meal of sorts, we were conducted to an empty chapel and given two blankets each. We were told that there was a snack at teatime and breakfast was at eight, next morning. The old chapel was very cold, and there were no beds. A blanket on the floor was our bed, no messing about here, it was primitive! We were all a bit depressed. Said some lads 'Right we are not stopping here for the night.' One who came from my own town said 'I am going home for the night, I can catch Burrow's bus and catch it back tomorrow evening.' I questioned him on this and decided to do the same. Some of these poor chaps lived a long way off and perforce had to stay. It was bitterly cold that Winter. We distributed our blankets and kit around, so that a casual inspection would not reveal our absence, as it happened nobody inspected – no-one was bothered. We proceeded to the bus station, waited a bit. At last the bus came and transported us to that soldier's dream, home. I went to the pictures that night I recall. Next day, after enquiries, I caught the bus and got back to Wakefield without any trouble. We had not been missed!'[23]

It quickly became common practice for one man to stay at the chapel in case of checks whilst the others went home, taking friends from farther afield with them. Frequently, as the winter wore on, men living nearby were given permission to go home at weekends to save on heating costs.

Also joining C Company at Dewsbury was Val Thomas. After reporting in September, he had been part of a 100-strong KOYLI contingent of Reservists sent to France as a labour force. Together with drafts from various Lancashire regiments, they had formed 12 Labour Company working on the BEF lines of communication in Normandy and Brittany. Like many recalled soldiers, the men of 12 Labour Company were not happy in their new role and an average of 30 field punishments were being handed out every month during that freezing winter. In late January, Thomas had returned home on leave before being sent back to France. Just three weeks later, he was home again. A new War Office directive had recognised the need to stiffen the weak units at home with more experienced men and had ordered that wherever possible, ex-regulars should be sent back to their parent regiments. 78 KOYLIs began the journey back to Pontefract on 27 February. Soon, like Flowers, they would settle into a routine in which so long as they reported for duty every morning no-one questioned where they spent their nights. Thomas was within easy reach of home and took every opportunity to spend time with his new wife.[24]

Throughout the army, men were constantly on the move. In the TA, the medically unfit and 'immatures' were being weeded out of units destined for overseas service and transferred instead to home defence duties. That in itself created yet more problems. In October 1939 General Sir Frederick Pile, Commander-in-Chief of the TA Anti-Aircraft Command, had received an unplanned intake of 11,000 'immatures' from all divisions, and all of them bitter at being refused the chance to serve overseas. He reported that at a 'fairly representative battery' an intake of 25 Militiamen included one man with 'a withered arm, one was mentally deficient, one had no thumbs … one had a glass eye which fell out whenever he doubled to the guns.' Of 1,000 recruits to 31st AA Brigade, Pile estimated that as many as one in ten was either mentally or psychologically unsuitable 'even considered against an undemanding standard'.[25]

Even the 'undemanding standard' of the selection boards still left gaps in the ranks that had to be filled. James Laidler, an eighteen-year-old clerk from Durham, had tried enlisting but as an 'immature' met with little success. Then, in March 1940, he read an article in the local press about the formation of the 1st Tyneside Scottish and asking for recruits to come forward:

> I immediately volunteered and everything went well until the question of my age arose. The officer in charge, having heard what was happening, came along and said, 'Right, Sonny, today the 15th of March is your birthday.' And so began my military career. There were twenty of us that day at the recruiting office and when everything was completed we were marched over Tyne bridge in Newcastle to Gateshead where we were billeted in a school. We were a motley crowd – a rent collector, a bus conductor, clerks like myself, a sculptor and two convicts who had been released from Durham jail on condition they joined the Army.

Also among the recruits with him was 'Smithy', an awkward sixteen-year-old who had lied about his age to enlist.[26] Within six weeks, they would be in France. In nine weeks, Smithy and many of that 'motley crowd' would be dead.

Meanwhile, in France, the Regular contingent of the BEF had by now been joined by six more divisions

Private James Coutts Laidler, 1st Tyneside Scottish.

Recruit Company, 1st Tyneside Scottish. Within a few weeks, armed with rifle and bayonet, these men would face German tanks. (Courtesy Elsie Laidler)

Officers of the 1st Tyneside Scottish.

from the first line TA, but was still under-strength. Controversially, during a visit to the front, Hore-Belisha had criticised the intention to leave prepared defences on the border to advance into Belgium in a plan which even the French general Alphonse Georges had dismissed as 'happy-go-lucky'. 'If the enemy masks Belgium' Georges wrote, 'he can manoeuvre elsewhere. So do not let us pour our resources into this business. Let us stop dreaming.'[27] Despite the clear risks involved, the Dyle plan was adopted by the British and French governments and Gort expressed his willingness to comply, primarily because he considered the BEF too small to operate independently but also in no small measure because he himself lacked command experience and plans of his own. Instead, Gort had occupied his time in addressing issues such as which shoulder the men of the BEF should carry their steel helmets when not in use. Hore-Belisha's interference, if anything, made him more determined not to be directed by a man he despised and so even more eager to go along with the Dyle plan.

Hore-Belisha had also been critical of the efforts of the BEF to complete work on permanent positions, claiming that more effort should have been made to exploit civilian expertise by contracting building companies and that by doing so the French were able to construct a pillbox in just three days. He compounded this by pointing to the quality of work completed in a neighbouring French sector as an example of what he thought the BEF should be doing. Gort and his staff were furious. The winter had been the worst in memory and since concrete cannot set in sub-zero temperatures work everywhere was behind schedule. More importantly too for the BEF's pride, it turned out that in fact the French had fallen so far behind that they had asked for British help. The work Hore-Belisha had admired was, in fact, that of men from the BEF. The claim that the French could build a pillbox in three days also turned out to be a misunderstanding. It could be built in three days, but the preparatory work and delivery of the materials took three weeks for each one. The 'Pillbox Affair', as it became known, should have been a storm in a tea cup but Gort had seen his chance to get rid of Hore-Belisha, who, for his part, showed an arrogant refusal to simply apologise for his mistake. It brought matters to a head. Gort finally had the position and influence to launch a campaign to have Hore-Belisha sacked and used the 'Pillbox Affair' as the focus. Relations between the Army and Parliament were strained as Gort demanded that politicians not be allowed to criticise the Allied plan. Richard Wilkinson has argued that Hore-Belisha was the founder of the modern army, 'But was he entitled to influence the conduct of the war? Hore-Belisha thought so because he had to fight the Army's corner in Parliament and Cabinet and, if military disaster occurred, his head would roll.'[28] Nevertheless, Gort mobilised his supporters in a concerted effort to have him removed from office and in January 1940, they succeeded.

'Father-to-Son' wrote *Time* magazine on 15 January 1940,

Thus the Cabinet and the generals were well pleased when Neville Chamberlain picked as his new War Secretary last week a man of character and a great gentleman, Mr. Oliver Stanley, son of the Earl of Derby, who was Secretary of State for War in 1916–18 and again in 1922–24. If the time is coming to send Tommy Atkins to glory, death and victory, quiet Mr. Stanley … will not hold the Army back. Neither will he go-get. That is practically guaranteed by Mr. Stanley's record right up to last week as a routine President of the Board of Trade and before that as an uneventful President of the Board of Education, Minister of Labor and Minister of Transport. Incidentally, in 1934 it was Hore-Belisha who took over the Ministry of Transport from Stanley and in a few weeks was making world headlines by dotting London streets with brilliant orange 'Belisha Beacon' traffic globes set atop zebra-striped poles.

The Army objects profoundly to the zebra touch and War Secretary Oliver Stanley will certainly remember that in World War I the leading roles were legitimately played by Foch, Ludendorff, Hindenburg, Haig, Pershing – whereas today no Allied general has had a chance. Socially the new War Secretary is somewhat overshadowed by his clever and beauteous wife. Lady Maureen Stanley, daughter of the Marquess of Londonderry who used to be perhaps the chief British exponent of appeasing Germany but swung violently around after the rape of Bohemia last spring.

In Canada this week the appointment of Mr. Stanley was viewed askance, for Canadian troops have been writing home rhapsodies about the fine treatment they have been given by 'The Tommy's Friend.' In London the *Daily Express* of self-made Canadian-born Baron Beaverbrook gloomed: 'Mr. Oliver Stanley is a most unsatisfactory appointment … He belongs to the Tory hierarchy … Belisha does not belong to that class.'

In his diary entry of 26 October 1937, General 'Tiny' Ironside, later to be Gort's rival for the post of BEF commander, noted:

I had Gort round to see me in the morning. He has been some three weeks as Military Secretary and I found him already almost prepared to give it up. He had been talking with the [Adjutant-General]. He was really very upset with the new Secretary of State. As he put it, he was in the bad position of having to sell him unsound horses and Belisha was too clever to buy duds.[29]

However many were his failings in the eyes of the public and the common soldier, Stanley had one great advantage over his predecessor. He would not challenge Gort and would buy whatever he was offered.

The affair had, however, highlighted the need for more work to prepare the BEF for the coming battle. The French transport infrastructure could barely cope with the traffic it carried and new roads, railways and base depots were desperately needed. At the same time, existing facilities needed to be guarded and the demands on the troops manning front line positions were too much to bear. Individual battalions of TA troops continued to arrive into February 1940 to act as L of C troops but Gort still pressed for more. With a more compliant Secretary of State for War, he was at last able to exert the power he felt due to him.

In France, the Lines of Communication had been spreading fast and far in excess of the original estimates. Major General de Fonblanque, in overall command of the BEF supply lines, had made use of every channel port and the Auxiliary Military Pioneer Corps (AMPC), formed to act as a labour force, were stretched to the limit. The removal of experienced ex-regulars from the AMPC to reinforce the Norwegian expedition and bolster units still at home had had a significant impact on the work being carried out. It was put to the War Cabinet that the morale of the TA units still in training would suffer less by being deployed to France than by remaining on scattered guard duties in the UK and training on inadequate equipment. Finally and reluctantly, General Ironside, the Chief of the Imperial General Staff, bowed to political pressure and agreed to release three embryonic TA divisions – the 12th (Eastern), the 23rd (Northumbrian) and the 46th (North Midland) – for service in France. Not only would this provide around 18,000 men for labour duties, it would also allow British politicians to tell their French counterparts that Britain had supplied three more infantry divisions towards the prom-ised nineteen by the end of the year.

As labour troops, these men would not need their artillery and signals support and would proceed overseas with only what they needed to complete their basic training. 'Their War Office instructions were cut and dried: a straightforward coolie job until August, build-ing airfields and pillboxes, back to England for stiff training, a gradual return to France as front-line soldiers.'[30]

For the men of the TA the news was greeted with mixed feelings. 'Welcome news had arrived during March', wrote one historian. 'The greater part of the 46th Division was to proceed to France for a three months' period of intensive training interspersed with guard duties on the line of communication. This was a step in the right direction, although there seemed little immediate prospect of fighting.'[31] 'Yet it was sour reward for patriotism' noted Gregory Blaxland, 'for most had joined in response to Hore-Belisha's appeal, and although the senior battalions may have skimmed the cream in the process of doubling, there was plenty of fine material among the men who had joined to be soldiers and been given the role of labourers.'[32]

Painfully aware of their lack of equipment and training, Ironside insisted on an assur-ance from Gort that the three divisions would be allowed as much time as possible for training alongside their labouring duties and that none would be used in an operational role until they had at least been issued their full scale of equipment. The promise was duly made.

NOTES

1 Rissik, D. *The DLI at War 1939–45* Durham: Depot DLI c1952 p321
2 Don Clark. Personal account IWM Documents 99/16/1
3 Rex Flowers. Unpublished personal account Courtesy of Kim James
4 Hingston, W. History of the KOYLI Vol 5 *Never Give Up 1919–42* London: Lund Humphries 1950 p55
5 Gawthorpe, J.B. '137 Brigade: A Formation of the TA in the First Year of War 1939–40' In *Ca Ira*, the journal of the West Yorkshire Regiment Vol XII June 1948 p223
6 Arnold Straw. Personal account. BBC Wartime memories Project http://www.bbc.co.uk/ww2peo-pleswar/stories/50/a2069750.shtml
7 Edgar, D. *The Day of Reckoning* London: John Clare Books. (Not Dated) p28
8 Ibid p12
9 Rissik p321
10 Hingston p112
11 Sandes, E.W.C. *From Pyramid to Pagoda, The Story of the West Yorkshire Regiment (The Prince of Wales Own) in the War 1939–45 and Afterwards* London: FJ Parsons. 1951 p251
12 *Halifax Courier* 8 June 1940
13 2/4th KOYLI War Diary. National Archives file WO166/4375
14 Edgar, p15
15 Hingston p110
16 *Ca Ira;* West Yorkshire Regimental Journal Dec 1939 p331
17 Ibid p111
18 Gawthorpe p223
19 Bryant, A. *The Turn of the Tide* London: Collins. 1957 p74–5
20 For details see Derry, T.K. *The Campaign in Norway* London: HMSO 1952.
21 Hingston p57
22 Ibid p111
23 Rex Flowers. Personal account
24 The story of Val Thomas is told in James, K. *The Greater Share of Honour* Leicester: Troubadour Books 2007
25 Pile, Gen. Sir F. *Ack-Ack* London: Harrap 1949
    Quoted in *Against All Odds: The British Army of 1939–40* National Army Museum 1990 p59

26 Laidler, J.C. *A Slice of My Life: The War Diary, Letters and Photographs of Private James C Laidler* Private
   Published document. Wakefield Library "Smithy" is believed to refer to 2759795 James Smith, son of
   Charles and Emily May Smith of Gateshead, the only Smith listed among the battalion's casualties for
   this period. His age is recorded as 20 on his headstone at the Ficheux Cemetery.

27 Benoist-Méchin, J. *Sixty Days That Shook the West: The Fall of France, 1940* Translated by Peter Wiles and
   edited by Cyril Falls New York: G. P. Putnam. 1963 p39

28 Wilkinson, R. 'Hore-Belisha – Britain's Dreyfus?' *History Today* Vol 47 Issue 12. December 1997.

29 Kelly, D. (Ed) *Time Unguarded: The Ironside Diaries, 1937-1940* New York: D. McKay 1963 p33

30 Collier, R. *The Sands of Dunkirk* London: Fontana 1974 p78

31 Sandes, Op Cit p251

32 Blaxland, G. *Destination Dunkirk* London: Wm Kimber & Co 1973 p58

Chapter Four

Leaving Much to be Desired

The first British troops sent to France when war was declared were the advance elements of the planned Lines of Communication network sent to Cherbourg on 4 September to prepare the port for the arrival of the BEF. By the middle of the month, some 30,000 administrative troops had been deployed simply to co-ordinate the movement of the fighting forces due to begin to arrive soon after. Among the first to be deployed was Brigadier Archibald Bentley Beauman, hastily recalled after being made redundant earlier in the year under Hore-Belisha's purge of officers and who only now learned on board the destroyer taking him to France that he was to command the Cherbourg area and the main entry point for the entire army. It was a daunting task and as Beauman later recalled, it got off to a poor start. With no catering facilities aboard ship, the advance party had been allocated just one pork pie per officer to sustain them on the journey and found that no arrangements had been made to feed them on arrival. Only the efforts of the British Consul and his wife meant that bread and ham was found and at the hotel allocated to them, only full colonels and above had been given beds – anyone below that rank simply slept on the floor.

The following day, parties began to disperse to their allocated areas. The lucky ones travelled by train, others by buses provided by the French. As Beauman later wrote, all the buses provided were

> … in the last state of mechanical dissolution and were quite unable to surmount the mildest hill. Whenever a rise was met the passengers had to get out and walk, with the result that some officers took three days to get to destinations 150 miles away. Our early impressions of French organisation were not entirely favourable.[1]

The initial impression was not improved when Beauman began to seek accommodation for the 5,000-strong garrison under his command. 'We found that the minor staff officers were far less helpful than their chiefs, while the civil authorities were definitely obstructive. However after endless trouble we got shelter of sorts for all the garrison, though some of it was distinctly primitive.'[2]

Having found accommodation for his own men, Beauman now needed to prepare for the arrival of thousands of troops aboard the civilian ships commandeered as transports. These ships were to operate a shuttle service, turning around immediately and leaving their passengers on the dockside with anything up to a sixteen-hour wait for trains to

Brigadier Archibald Bentley Beauman. The third youngest brigadier of the First World War at the age of 29, Beauman fell victim to Hore-Belisha's purge and left the Army early in 1939 only to be recalled to command the Northern District of the Lines of Communication.

their destinations.[3] Drivers might arrive several days before the ships carrying their vehicles and so shelter from both the weather and possible air attack had to be provided along with catering and sanitary facilities around the *Gare Maritime*. Unlike combat operations, he later commented, the 'difficulty of Lines of Communication work is that most of it has no counterpart in peace, and as a result, commanders and staff come to it inexperienced and untried.'[4] Nevertheless, applying the skills that had made him the third youngest brigadier in the First World War, he set about the intricate task of negotiating French bureaucracy and setting up his reception centre and transport facilities.

If the British impression of the French was poor, so too was the French impression of the unskilled labour force provided by the hurriedly created Auxiliary Military Pioneer Corps – a mixed group of reservists and newly recruited civilians. The reservists resented not being allowed to rejoin their old regiments whilst the civilians were recruited without any selection and sent to France without training; Beauman:

> The civilian element recruited directly from life in particular was inclined to give trouble. These men had been put hurriedly into uniform and were sent to France without any training or knowledge of military discipline. As a result both their deportment and their behaviour left much to be desired.[5]

The poor discipline of these civilians in uniform soon manifested itself in trouble in the bars around the town. The French commanders, unable to distinguish them from the trained men, soon came to regard them as typical of the British Army and this negative judgement would affect relations throughout the coming campaign. Gradually, though, a working relationship was built up so that by April 1940, Cherbourg was a busy and slick operation handling up to 6,000 arrivals per day and moving thousands of tons of supplies and ammunition to the BEF.

From the start, the whole administrative operation was under the command of Major-General Philip de Fonblanque from his HQ at Le Mans but the huge expansion of the operation, quickly outgrowing the original plans, meant that by now the Lines of Communication covered ports from Dunkirk in the north to Marseille on the

Pioneers at work.

Mediterranean coast and spread over hundreds of miles of France. It was decided that it should be subdivided into Northern and Southern Districts, each with four sub-areas, and in March Beauman had been given command of the Northern District from a headquarters at Rouen. Despite the massive size of the task – ammunition dumps alone covered an area of some 36 square miles around the city – he found just two officers and a clerk with which to run it for the first two weeks. Responsible now for huge numbers of men, equipment and even a top secret poison gas store, it was a relief to find that two of the newly arrived digging divisions, the 12th and 23rd, would be assigned to his area as a labour force. The 46th, meanwhile, would be assigned to duties in the Southern District around Brittany.

A top secret warning order had reached the units of 137 Brigade on 9 March giving three weeks notice to move overseas for 'important national work on the lines of communication'. No details about their destination were given but one clue came when the order helpfully explained that a table of rank badges of the French Army would follow shortly.[6] The next day the same orders reached 138 Brigade and later 139 Brigade were also warned to make ready. Even as these orders reached them, the three divisions remained unsettled as the constant flow of men in and out of their units continued. A week after the order arrived, for example, 182 Reservists rejoined the KOYLI at Dewsbury from the Field Force already in France to bolster the battalion. This was offset by the end of the month with the loss of another 64 men to various other destinations. On the 19th an under-age recruit was discharged from the army and another arrived from a training course. So it went on with men coming and going so quickly that even within the tight knit communities of the regimental system, it was difficult for men to keep track of their friends or even their own future in the battalion. No-one, it seemed, knew for certain what was going on and even if anyone did; they could not say anything for fear of falling foul of draconian censorship measures. As the editor of the Duke of Wellington's regimental association journal *Iron Duke* noted in February 1940:

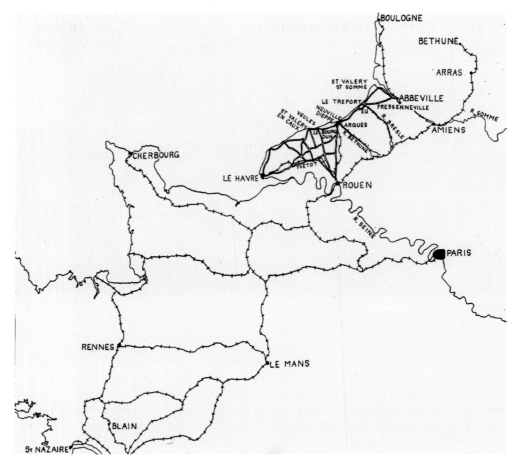

Sketch map of Northern France.

> The fog of war has descended on THE IRON DUKE with a vengeance … Here we are
> in the thick of historic and epoch-making events, yet scarcely permitted by the censor
> even to allude to their existence … The last IRON DUKE achieved a distinction unique
> in its distinguished career; it was classified as a secret document; it could only be obtained
> on signature and read at the recipient's peril. No two authorities agree as to what may or
> may not be published, and the wretched sub-editor must steer a perilous course between
> the Scylla of sheer drivel and the Charybdis of criminal indiscretion.[7]

With information at a premium, men were now told that they would be going overseas,
but not where or when as in the last days of March embarkation leave was granted to all
units. In the KOYLI, 'A' and 'B' Companies went first after a stern lecture from Colonel
Hodgkinson on 'secrecy and discipline' and by the end of the month the other companies
had followed suit. Secrecy in the military is one thing, secrecy in a small town something
else altogether. 'April came and rumours started that we were soon going to France' wrote
Rex Flowers, 'I was virtually told so at my dental appointment.' Training began in earnest
in the first week of April and was made all the harder by the effects of the last minute
typhoid and paratyphoid injections. 'I got my jab at the drill hall', he recalled,

War Office Instructions for Regimental Journals.

For the guidance of contributors of news and articles we print below the instructions which have been issued to editors by the Director of Public Relations, the War Office :—

1. No information must be published which might in any conception be of use to the enemy.

2. No description of modern doctrines as accepted in the Army, or treatises on tactical theories, must be given.

3. No description of modern weapons or equipment in possession of the Allies must appear.

4. News from units should not in any way disclose the order of battle of the Army, or any plans for its expansion.

5. Details of higher formations and publication of the names of commanders of units must not be given.

6. No units or stations must be named. There is no objection to referring to units by counties or other areas, as, for example, " Units in Gloucestershire " or " Units in Malta."

7. Names of officers should not be mentioned. There is no objection to Christian or nicknames, or to referring to officers by the first letter of their surname—*e.g.*, Capt. A. or to the command held by them—*e.g.*, in place of " Capt. Smith," write " the Commander of ' C ' Company." There is no restriction on the publication of the names of other ranks.

8. The following typify the kind of article to which no objection could be taken :— (*a*) Biographies ; (*b*) reminiscences of past campaigns ; (*c*) stories of sport and adventure ; (*d*) stories concerning the domestic affairs of a unit, so long as neither the unit nor station are identifiable.

9. Photographs of individuals and groups are admissible, provided the background is either blocked out or is of a neutral character.

Instructions for journals 1939.

… and just had time to get down to our billet down the road before I was very ill indeed. We all were. I was sick all over my blankets, which I had to clean later. Had a temperature and spent a very uncomfortable night. We soon got over it though.[8]

Speculation was rife. Most assumed they would go to France but the Norwegian campaign was still underway and the possibility of a trip to the Arctic could not be ruled out. Men began to look for clues about where and when they were going. The relative exchange rates of French francs and Norwegian krona were discussed at length and some made efforts to brush up their schoolroom French. Five weeks after the order to move had arrived, an unofficial war diarist for the 2/5th West Yorkshires noted:

14 April. York.

There is an air of expectancy in the Bn. Something is in the wind. Something big. That much has become increasingly clear in the last few weeks. Officially, we know little; in fact, we seem to have deduced a great deal from guarded hints dropped quietly from High Quarters. [The Quartermaster's] features are largely our barometer in these uncertain days. They wear a variety of expressions not unconnected, one gathers, with the mounds of strange stores which fatigue parties are daily assembling and dismantling on the Drill Hall floor … He has become much more accommodating of late, which is taken as a significant sign. He discharges equipment with a lavish hand and requests which a week ago would have elicited nothing more than the cynical smile of the disillusioned Quartermaster are now, miraculously, treated with all seriousness. Clearly some tremendous upheaval is foreshadowed.

The Commanding Officer has gone so far as to advise us to prepare against a possible move 'to camp', but we are packing and buying last-minute necessities as though our days in civilised parts were strictly numbered ...

Someone knows the answer to our queries: we sent an advance party (led by Captain C Jason Wood, OC D Coy) off into the blue a week ago. Are they, we wonder, regaling themselves in some isolated estaminet which will shortly hum to the activity of Bn HQ ... shivering somewhere amid the snows of Norway ... or what?[9]

After the departure of advance parties, detailed movement orders began to appear with more clues about departure dates. 'Immature' was now defined as any man who had not reached his nineteenth birthday by 15 April. Immediately, the 2/4th lost another 77 men, including four lance corporals with yet another 24 men now assessed as unfit. Just ten days before their actual departure, the 2/6th Battalion of the Duke of Wellington's Regiment (DWR) based in Keighley, received an intake of 124 men fresh from the training depot and 'lacking the most basic equipment such as respirators'. Thirty-seven of them had not even been medically graded.[10]

Those who could afford it, used the time to buy in extra items of equipment. In 12th Division, Donald Edgar's Adjutant gave him funds to buy as many large-scale maps of France as he could.[11] Others bought binoculars, compasses and after the order was issued that '.45 revolvers will not be taken – if the officer possesses a .38 revolver this will be taken, otherwise he will proceed unarmed',[12] some found handguns privately to make up for the shortages in every unit. Every day brought new, sometimes conflicting instructions.

On 19 April, the West Yorkshires' diarist noted that all bedding was to be handed in to stores by Monday 21st and that instructions had been issued to read the gas and electric meters and record the amount of coal available for heating 'which we take to be clear indication that the move will come Monday night at the latest'. The disappointment in his next entry is almost palpable as he notes 'yesterday's instructions are cancelled'. By the following Wednesday, however, 'Rumour and counter rumour crystallised tonight at the weekly Company Commanders' conference into hard fact at last. We leave for France on Saturday night ... That we are marked out as a working unit is clear. What that work will be is less certain.'[13]

Even as the West Yorkshires finally heard what was happening, Donald Edgar and his battalion were already on their way to France with the rest of 12th Division. As dawn broke on the 21st, Edgar, still hungover from a riotous farewell party at a local restaurant, led Headquarters Company of the 2/6th East Surreys as they marched through empty streets to the nearby railway station to begin the journey. 'The locals knew we were off to France. But no-one seemed to care.'[14] By that afternoon, the battalion was aboard the SS *Ulster Prince* and already putting to sea, a lone army chaplain standing on the quay to wave them farewell.

Others had a different send off. James Laidler of 23rd Division's 1st Tyneside Scottish recalls leaving Gateshead for France on the evening of 23 April. 'We went through the town in great style with pipes playing. Although the move was supposed to be secret, the streets were thronged with people. They gave us a terrific send off.'[15] Confined to barracks as part of the recruit company, Laidler was ready to go. Alan Forster, another member of the battalion recalled that:

The Battalion left its HQ in Gateshead for Southampton on the 23 April 1940 and embarked for Le Havre with so little notice one soldier was in the cinema with his girl

Troops of the Duke of Wellington's Regiment practise entraining.

friend when the film was interrupted with an announcement that his unit was to go to the docks. He had to change out of civvies and into his uniform whilst crossing the channel.[16]

Across the country, a select few drove in convoys of trucks as they made their way to departure ports on a journey of up to eighteen hours at the stately prescribed pace of 20mph with a density of no more than 20 vehicles to the mile, ready to join up with their battalions somewhere on the other side of the Channel. The rest of the men would follow a few days later by rail and with the attention to detail that marks the British Army, some units even used the intervening period to practise getting to the local station. Arnold Straw, still with the 2/7th DWR, recalls being marched in a column to the station where a train stood by so that they could be timed getting on board as quickly and smoothly as possible. Time and again, they were given the order to embark as the commanding officer stood by with a stopwatch. Finally, he was satisfied that his men could quickly board their train in a dignified, military fashion.

Throughout that week, the last units of the three divisions made ready to leave with another round of meter reading and coal measuring. With security still a confusing problem, commanders chose for themselves how to deal with their leaving. On the evening of the 25th, C Company of the 2/6th DWR were treated to a trip to the local cinema and a dance for friends and family at the Co-Operative Hall in Skipton. A few miles away in Huddersfield, Straw and his comrades in their sister battalion were only finally told on the 26th that they would leave the following day but that 'on no account must we divulge this information to anyone else on the grounds of security' – promptly ensuring that as the battalion marched through Huddersfield the next day with colours flying and the band playing, thousands of well wishers lined the route. At the station, the carefully rehearsed boarding procedure fell apart as relatives and girlfriends crowded the platform to say good-

Sir Cyril Deverell (front row, centre) with officers of the West Yorkshire Regiment just before embarkation.

A TA battalion prepares to move overseas. Note the 1918 pattern uniforms.

bye. With no-one there to say goodbye to, Straw gleefully bagged the most comfortable seat and settled into his compartment.

The Dukes and the West Yorkshire Regiment of 137 Brigade were the last elements of the digging divisions to set out, leaving their home towns late in the evening of the 27th for the overnight journey to Southampton. Even as they began to gather at their designated departure points in their scattered billets, the KOYLIs of 138 Brigade were already arriving at Cherbourg. Early that morning, on board the Isle of Man steam packet *Tynwald*, Rex Flowers and his mates lined the rails for their first glimpse of a foreign country as France came into view through the morning mist. Like many aboard, this was his first trip overseas and indeed his first long journey of any kind so he was disappointed to see not some bustling exotic harbour but a drab port very similar to the one he had just left. Although his first real culture shock was not far away. At 0830hrs the ship docked and the battalion disembarked to march to a waiting train of cattle trucks bearing the sign '*40 hommes, 8 chevaux*' so familiar to the men of the previous generation. Fully expecting civilian railway carriages like those used to get the battalion to Southampton, Flowers was shocked. 'I couldn't believe my eyes!' he wrote later:

> How primitive this sort of thing was, but I was to learn a lot more before it was over. It was a different world altogether. As we came up to these monstrosities I thought 'Bloody charming' … We entrained, at least someone decreed that we had less than 40 men, but it was still crowded … We sorted ourselves out reasonably and as we proceeded, some of us sat in the doorways with legs dangling. So we travelled down the Cotentin peninsula at a snail's pace. At least we had time to enjoy the pleasant rural scenery. Women came up to the train with bread. It was another first, my introduction to a yard of bread. I have loved it ever since, no one makes this kind of bread like the French. The train was so slow that men jumped off, bought some bread, then ran and caught the train easily.[17]

Arriving at a small station, the battalion detrained, formed up and set off on foot to a camp about a mile outside the village of Montreuil.

> It was a new ready-made camp, composed of wooden huts, cookhouse, dining rooms. We could not believe our luck, after Dewsbury and Wakefield, to us it was the lap of luxury. We were detailed off in platoons and companies, each to our areas and huts. After being allotted our huts, we dismissed and entered them. We had a proper bed each! Not bad! We looked around; the scenery was very nice, fields, woods and lakes. Each field was divided by a hedge on top of a bank of earth. We were in what is known as the Forêt de Tanouarn, not far from Rennes in Brittany. I liked the camp, we all did, it was brand new and we made the best of what was available. I can see the hut that I was in my mind's eye now, at the edge of the camp, near to a small stream. The weather was hot and sunny, the food was not bad, and we worked hard. I thought, I can spend the summer here. It was all too good to be true!

As Flowers continued on his journey, His Majesty's Transport *Tynwald* had returned to Southampton and stood waiting to receive the West Yorkshires. Nearby, another Isle of Man steam packet and the London and North Eastern Railways Ferry *Bruges* stood by to transport the Dukes as they arrived at the docks at 0600hrs on the 28th. Field Marshal Sir Cyril Deverell, Colonel in Chief of the West Yorkshires, arrived to wish them well and spent time talking to Brigadier Gawthorpe on the quayside. 'He was as surprised as I was' Gawthorpe wrote later, 'when another unit arrived subsequently and all the officers

SS *Tynwald*. The Isle of Man steam packet *Tynwald* was used to ferry troops across to France in the early stages of the war. Later, many of her crew refused to return to Dunkirk after coming under attack. Afterwards taken up by the Royal Navy as an anti-aircraft ship, she struck a mine off North Africa and sank on 12 November 1942.

A British unit arriving in Cherbourg.

Cartoon from the DWR Journal *Iron Duke* 1940.

"WOTS SHE MEAN, BILL, MERCY?
I HAVENT TOUCHED HER YET!
S T Swift

appeared in best Service Dress, Sam Browne belts and all, with their battle dress presumably packed as baggage. Theirs was a truly swell departure but, I say again, surprising.'[18] It was not the only surprise the Dukes had up their sleeves. Arriving at around 0700hrs, the 2/7th DWR had loaded its baggage and troops by 1000hrs and found they had the ship to themselves, allowing considerably more comfort than most other units enjoyed. Having taken their drums and instruments with them, Bandmaster W.E. Doyle gathered his men together. 'It was a decided comfort to us,' the war diary recorded.

Firstly it gave us a few selections to while away the tedium of waiting for the Trooper so leave the dockside. It was at the actual moment of leaving the dock that it surpassed itself. We drew away from England to the strains of 'Land of Hope and Glory' which seemed to give all of us thrill of pride in England and a stiffening of our purpose and resolution. To the docks and its dockers the sight of Troopers leaving England has no doubt become merely commonplace but the band seemed to draw them from their tasks and one assuredly felt that they shared our emotions as they waved us a safe crossing and safe return.[19]

Although they were on their way, the ships sat in Southampton Water for the afternoon, waiting for darkness and their destroyer escorts before they could begin the crossing – due to begin at 0130hrs. The men whiled away the hours watching flying boats take off and land and enjoying the excitement and novelty of their first foreign trip. Despite problems, the fact that they had the ship to themselves also meant they were able to prepare a hot meal on board. That evening, the Dukes' band formed the core of an impromptu concert and even the threat of U-Boat attack did little to sour the atmosphere of a group of young Territorials off to summer camp.

It was a marked contrast to the way most soldiers had experienced the crossing. Aboard the *Tynwald* on the previous trip, Don Clark of the KOYLI estimated that 2,000 men had been crammed aboard and the ship was so full that he and around 100 others had volunteered to travel aboard the naval escorts.

As the evening drew in, Clark suddenly heard sirens all around him as the ship came to action stations and launched a barrage of depth charges against a suspected submarine. These first few minutes of wartime action thrilled him and he was still excited the next morning when the convoy reached harbour.

For 137 Brigade, the crossing was uneventful and they woke next morning to find a solitary French seaplane escorting them on the final leg of their journey. Bandmaster Doyle immediately got his band together for a reprise of 'Land of Hope and Glory' and as a salute to their new allies, '*La Marseillaise*'. Whatever they were expecting, the war diary of the 2/6th Dukes recorded almost with disappointment that the 'civil population in Cherbourg

'*40 Hommes, 8 chevaux.*' The novelty of travelling by cattle truck soon wore off.

received the battalion with calm. There were no demonstrations.'[20] After a hot breakfast and with around six hours before their train was due to depart, the men were told they would be provided with a hot meal at noon and allowed the morning to go into the town. The regimental history records of the 2/6th that 'high tribute must be paid to the splendid character and bearing of the troops during their service in France. The only serious crime occurred at Cherbourg. On arrival a soldier was arrested for sending an uncensored letter in the civil post.'[21] When Don Clark had arrived the day before, his group had the whole day to spend in the town before their train and recalled that the older soldiers headed off to the local brothels whilst the younger men sent postcards home before visiting the local bars where they soon became involved in a street battle between a party of Highlanders in kilts, French sailors apparently intent on finding out what was worn underneath and the combined force of the military police of both nations. As Clark made good his escape, thunderflashes were being let off as the fight escalated.[22] The good character of the men of 137 Brigade may have owed something to the presence of large numbers of annoyed policemen roaming the town.

Movements staff at Cherbourg now issued the brigade with their orders. At 1406hrs, Brigade HQ, 2/5th West Yorkshires and 2/7th DWR would depart by train for Blain, a village about twenty miles northwest of the port of Nantes, and would arrive at 0830hrs – a journey of over eighteen hours aboard cramped cattle trucks with only a packet of

La Côte — La Presqu'île

TÉLÉPHONE : De jour : 3.44 et 6.21
— De nuit : 6.21

Revenant des lignes pour un repos mérité, des troupes anglaises défilent, musique en tête, dans les rues d'une ville ...quelque part en France

Left: The DWR in St Nazaire. *Right:* The DWR arrive at St Nazaire, as reported in the local press.

sandwiches and a blanket for comfort. If the journey was uncomfortable for those in the trucks, the men assigned to act as anti-aircraft defence had it even worse in shallow trucks mounted with a Bren gun and spread along the length of the train. Open to both the elements and the smoke from the engines, which, the West Yorkshires' unofficial diarist reported, 'slowly transfigured the unfortunates concerned into a fair semblance of particularly insanitary chimney sweeps' they faced a gruelling trip, as did the unlucky men allocated trucks that had recently been used for carrying coal who 'expressed the view that they would have appreciated a little more of the previous cargo having first been removed'. After a journey through Bayeux, Caen, Le Mans and Angers, the men 'tumbled, unshaven and stiff ... onto the lineside' at Blain. Here, the 2/5th were to part from the Dukes to begin training in the grounds of the nearby chateau. The 2/6th DWR had set out separately for Nantes and the 2/7th were now destined for dockyard work at St Nazaire. 'We were shocked to receive the rumour that we still had to face a five-mile march to our quarters; but as it turned out this was probably only started by an enemy agent in the hope of lowering our morale, for we were presently relieved to see our long lost Transport Officer bustling down the train to guide us to our own trucks in the village.'

Arriving at their newly built camp in the grounds of the Chateau Pont Pretain in the warm glow of a Loire afternoon, the discomfort of the journey was soon forgotten. A summer of hard work and training would be interspersed with time off in the local towns and villages. As the brigade began its journey, the government had announced that the price of a pint of beer would rise by 2*d*, instead of the expected 1*d*. Here, French beer cost just 4*d* a litre. For the West Yorkshires, at least, 'we came to the entire agreement that this was, after all, the life'.[23]

NOTES
 1 Beauman, Brigadier A.B. *Then A Soldier* London: Macmillan 1960 pp96–7
 2 Ibid p101
 3 Ibid p101
 4 Ibid p105
 5 Ibid p104
 6 WO167/853
 7 *The Iron Duke* the magazine of the Duke of Wellington's Regiment (West Riding) Vol XVI No 45 Feb 1940 p5
 8 Rex Flowers. Unpublished memoir.
 9 WO 167/853
10 WO167/736
11 Edgar, D. *The Day of Reckoning* London: John Clare Books p37
12 WO167/853
13 Ibid
14 Edgar Op cit p40
15 Laidler, J.C. *A Slice of my Life* privately produced memoir held at Wakefield Local Studies Library
16 Alan Forster (4459370 Pte. A. Forster) account produced by his nephew, Mr Bill Forster and accessed at www.wwiimemories.com/alanfoster.htm
17 Flowers, op cit
18 Gawthorpe, Brigadier J.B. '137 Infantry Brigade: A formation of the TA in the first year of war' In West Yorkshire Regimental Journal Ca Ira Vol XII June 1948 p223 19 WO167/737
20 Ibid
21 Barclay, Brigadier C.N. *The History of the Duke of Wellington's Regiment 1919–1952* London: Wm Clowes & Son 1953 p198
22 Clark, D. *A Personal History of the 1940 Normandy Campaign* Imperial War Museum document 99/16/1
23 WO 167/853

Chapter Five

Seeing the Wood for the Trees

By the time the men of 137 Brigade arrived, the Lines of Communication (L of C) in France were vast, firmly established and yet still growing. Ports and depots across the country acted as tributaries to feed men, stores and equipment into the steady stream heading north to the Belgian border but each port needed men to load and guard supplies and each new depot needed labourers to build it and still more men to run it. Convinced that the lack of movement by the Germans proved this would be another war of stalemate, Churchill himself had insisted on the despatch of three super-heavy artillery batteries whose immobile guns had to be installed in concrete emplacements served by their own light railway to bring up ammunition, adding a further burden to the already controversially overdue effort to complete the British defence line. In any modern army, the logistics 'tail' far outnumbers the combatant 'teeth' arms but the number of depots grew in order to stockpile supplies for a long war and the roads and rail links serving them had to be expanded, requiring ever more troops to be diverted from front line duties. The logistics tail was beginning to wag the dog.

Part of the reason for this was the lack of interest shown

Winston Spencer Churchill.
Churchill became Prime Minister
on 10 May after Lord Halifax
declined the position.

General Viscount Gort VC. Acknowledged as a brave soldier in the First World War, even his admirers regarded him as a poor strategist unable to meet the demands of commanding the BEF. His appointment owed much to the deep animosity between Gort and Hore-Belisha and was a means of getting him out of Whitehall.

by Gort and GHQ in the activities of the 'grocers'. As Beauman pointed out, there is no peacetime equivalent of the L of C so when war broke out, the names of men deemed 'suitable' candidates for the roles of movement, billeting or general administrative officers were required to be sent to the War Office so that the organisation could be formed from scratch. Few commanding officers were willing to see their best men go and the names put forward tended to be the young, the inexperienced, the inefficient or those whose faces simply did not fit in the mess for whatever reason. Two centuries of fighting wars far from home had taught the army that logistics were vital, yet in dismissing General de Fonblanque and his deputy as 'Mr Fortnum and Mr Mason', Gort and his staff were showing the traditional disdain 'fighting' men held for the unglamorous, albeit vital, task of keeping the army in the field. Only a few – among them 3rd Divisional Commander Montgomery – recognised the true importance of the L of C.

So great was the belief that the Germans would be held in a stalemate along the Franco-Belgian border that despite having time to consider and issue instructions regarding the correct shoulder from which to hang a helmet, Gort does not appear to have given any thought to the need for any protection of the supply lines in the event of a German breakthrough. General Ironside, as Chief of the Imperial General Staff, had witnessed German manoeuvres in 1937 and had been greatly impressed by their emphasis on mobility and air power. Accordingly, before Gort and Dill left on 10 September, Ironside met with them.

> I told them of all my strategic ideas, and I then made an appeal to them to see that their men and transport did not expose themselves to air attack. Anywhere behind the fighting line is the battle line. Nowhere is anybody safe. All must dig in and disperse themselves. This is particularly necessary amongst the Army Service Corps and the Army Ordnance Corps.[1]

Once in France, though, Gort turned his back on them – immersing himself instead in trivial issues. 'I had no confidence in his leadership when it came to handling a large force' wrote Corps Commander Alan Brooke.

> He seemed incapable of seeing the wood for the trees … his brain was geared to details the whole time. He wandered about scratching the barks of the trees and you could never get him to come out and look at the wood as a whole. The important points, such as the system of defence to be adopted, lines of advance into Belgium, relative advantages of remaining on the frontier as opposed to advancing to meet the Germans, all such and many others he left entirely to his staff, whilst he dealt with details such as platoon log-books, carrying of sandbags, booby traps …[2]

The workings and development of the system that would provide him with everything he would need for the coming battle were simply not of any interest to him.

It soon became clear to de Fonblanque that the men sent to man his supply depots could not work 24 hours a day. There was a need for a force to take on the tedious duty of guarding the stores to relieve the storemen and clerks of this extra burden and so, since November, a number of individual Territorial infantry units had been fed into the system to act as guards at designated 'Vulnerable Points' such as HQ buildings, depots and airfields as a token gesture to deter the rising incidents of pilfering. On 7 November 1939, the 1/5th Sherwood Foresters had arrived along with the 4th Border Regiment and were soon followed by the 4th Buffs. By February 1940 they had been joined by the 14th Royal Fusiliers and the 9th West Yorkshires. This last, designated a garrison battalion and deployed around Arras as an infantry unit was known – with good reason – as a 'veterans battalion'. Its commanding officer was by now on his third war and none of his men were below the age of 35 – many were revisiting battlefields they had already seen in the previous war. Private Gordon Smith, for example, already held the DCM and the Belgian *Croix de Guerre* for his actions in 1918 when he was killed in action near Calais after escaping the encirclement of Arras at the age of 55. In March, another veteran battalion, the 12th Royal Warwicks, arrived and found themselves deployed across Normandy with companies in Caen, Cherbourg, Rennes and Le Mans and in no position to even consider attempting to continue their training programmes. Far behind the expected front line, little thought was given to the idea that airborne troops or Fifth Columnist saboteurs might stage a pre-emptive strike and so no attempt was made to create any form of static defence positions. In fact, most guard duties were deemed routine enough to be performed by 'stick guards' armed not with rifles but with pick-axe handles.

The German invasion of Norway began in early April and by the time 46th Division arrived in France, their comrades in the first line battalions of the 49th Division were already in full retreat there. News slowly filtered through of parachute drops behind the lines but still no thought was given to the possible need to defend depots miles away from the front. From time to time, alerts were put out about possible saboteurs – on 24 April, for example, the 2/6th East Surreys were told that two 'very young' Germans in British officer uniforms had landed by parachute near Arras and stolen a car. A few days later, pieces of cut-up army greatcoat were found under a nearby hedge. The excitement soon blew over and was forgotten under the pressure of providing a company each day to work on the docks at Fecamp, another to guard the chemical warfare dump and others to Bolbec and Froberville on tasks ranging from working in the bakery to the groundwork for a new base hospital.[3]

Troops of the 49th Division return from Norway. The first line 49th Division had been given priority over the duplicate 46th Division for men and equipment but had been quickly overwhelmed by the German attack through northern Norway.

Of more concern to the new arrivals were the practical problems of doing their jobs. At their Chateau d'Empremesnil base, the Surrey's water supply was declared 'fit for neither drinking nor washing' and battalion vehicles had to be adapted to ferry water from the village to the camp for chlorination. Rain had left the 'whole place a sea of mud' which meant they were unable to dry their boots, which were rapidly disintegrating. There were 'no spares whatsoever'. A week later, the war diary complained 'Boot question acute. 600 pairs of good boots handed in prior to bn's departure to this country and now authority received to draw 20%.'[4] Surrounded by the main forward supply depots for the BEF, an infantry unit was unable to find boots for its men.

Despite the seemingly impressive build up of war materiel, the army in France was still desperately short of even the most basic equipment. When Gort visited the Territorial 42nd (Lancashire) Division, part of his III Corps, he claimed, 'I never believed it would be possible to see such a sight in the British Army. The men had no knives or forks and apparently lacked mugs. They were eating their meat with their fingers and placing it on the corrugated iron table tops.' It all demonstrated, he complained to Ironside, 'a lamentably low standard in elementary administration'.[5] Having, like so many others, seen L of C work as a dumping ground for incompetents and virtually ignored it for the past six months, Gort now complained in righteous indignation that it was not working effectively and blamed Ironside for its failures, using it as yet more evidence that he had diverted resources from France to support the Norwegian campaign. In fact, Ironside had been fighting a political battle to avoid just that but by now had fallen victim to the fallout from Hore-Belisha's resignation after the 'pillbox affair' and the widespread whispering campaign against him by elements of the BEF. In reality, the shortages of many items owed much to the British Army's deliberate policy of stifling initiative on the part of junior officers.

In marked contrast to the German policy of encouraging its men to adapt plans on the ground as they saw fit in order to achieve set goals, the British followed a very prescriptive battle plan that meant units moved only when told to do so. So ingrained was this that on a 1935 visit to the site of the Battle of Tannenburg, General Dill had asked his guide how the Germans 'had achieved such success despite the notorious disobedience of the junior officers' and failed to realise that they had won *because* junior officers had not blindly followed their limited orders and had instead seized on local successes.[6] Nothing, for example, prevented the officers of the 42nd Division from begging, stealing or borrowing what they needed from other sources except the need to account for them formally through the quartermaster (QM) ledgers but this in itself was enough to deter any individual action.[7] Against this background of rigid adherence to the rules, the digging divisions found that along with the shortages of basic items they had come to expect, they could obtain neither additional weapons nor ammunition for the training they had been promised. They were not, it was argued, designated as front line troops and therefore did not require a war establishment of equipment. In the inflexible logic of the official mind, what they had arrived with was clearly what they were required to have – no more, no less.

In early May, with little hope of any real training and even less expectation that they would need it, they went to work. Around Rouen, two of 12th Division's brigades – 35th and 36th – were fully occupied in building railway sidings and developing a rail centre at Abancourt and its third, 37th Brigade, was sent to build accommodation and huts at sites around the city whilst HQ based itself at Gamaches. Further north, 69th and 70th Brigades of the 23rd Division had been allocated work on airfield construction around St Pol and Bethune, just behind the BEF line. To the south, 46th Division had been sent into Brittany with 137 Brigade around the ports of Nantes and St Nazaire to work on unloading supplies and building new railway sidings whilst its other brigades – 138th and 139th – set to work in the area of Rennes, again on railway construction and handling ammunition supplies. The routine varied from unit to unit but among 70 Brigade, the 10th and 11th Durham Light Infantry battalions took turns between the first and second shift each day. Rifle companies worked for four days, had two days of training and one for rest whilst specialists like signallers spent just two days labouring and four training on their speciality. It was badly needed. Of the 2,000 men who made up 70 Brigade, 1,400 had not been trained on the Bren gun and 400 – one in five – had not completed rifle training.[8] In the brigade's other battalion, the Tyneside Scottish, Laidler and his fellow recruits were only now entering their fifth week of basic training and in the entire battalion, only one man, Captain John Dempster, had ever actually fired the Boys anti-tank rifle.

Despite the news from Norway, for the digging divisions the war seemed a long way away and especially among those fortunate enough to be able to spend time in the local towns and bars in the evenings, apart from the need to wear khaki denims and to march to and from work, for many there was little to distinguish between their army and civilian lives. Disappointed after their initial eagerness to train to fight, the men soon settled into their routines. Enjoying the prospect of a long, hot summer camp and the promise of a return home in a few months, they accepted their lot and set out to make the best of the sunshine and cheap alcohol. Rex Flower would recall with fondness his days spent working under the direction of the Royal Engineers, watching lizards scampering around as the men ate their sandwich lunches, of visits to local towns and drinking white wine sweetened with sugar and the wonder of seeing fireflies in the hedgerows at

night. Also at Rennes, Sergeant John Brown, a former solicitor's clerk from Wakefield noted in his diary how, at the end of one very hot day, he and his friends walked to a nearby village for supper and were joined there by Lieutenant Rawlings. After a good meal, the group split a bottle of champagne before walking home under the light of a crescent moon and starlit sky, playfully making sparks fly as their hobnail boots struck the rough road surface. It was a world away from the grim reality of life in the industrial mining towns of the West Riding and the nearest thing to a holiday most had ever had.

It was Thursday 9 May 1940.

Sergeant John Brown. A former solicitor's clerk from Wakefield, Brown acted as Quartermaster in the KOYLI and Beauman Division and kept a diary of his experiences.

A Fort Eben Emael attacked 10 May leading Allies to move up to the Dyle Line

B Main German thrust breaks through 13 May

German map of the Low Countries and Allied deployments, 1940.

NOTES

1 Ironside Diaries quoted in Karslake p43

2 Bryant, *Turn of the Tide* p80

3 Edgar, *Day of Reckoning* p45

4 War Diary 2/6th East Surrey Regiment (WO167/829)

5 Colville, *Man of Valour: Field Marshal Lord Gort* p177–8

6 von Senger und Etterlin. *Neither Fear Nor Hope* 1963 quoted in David French, *Raising Churchill's Army* p45

7 This lack of willingness to act without orders showed itself tellingly during the Arras counter attack of 21 May when tanks of the 4th Royal Tank Regiment were delayed on the D60 road because the level crossing barrier was down and, without radio contact with a senior officer, it took some time before the troop commander summoned the courage to break it down. See Richard Holmes, *Army Battlefield Guide* p192

8 Rissik, *The DLI at War* p8

Chapter Six

The Matador's Cloak and the Revolving Door

At 1930 hours on 9 May, as Sergeant Brown and his comrades sat down for supper in Rennes, in Germany Hauptman Walter Koch received a coded message – 'Danzig'. With that, the specially trained men of Assault Group Koch made their way to two airfields near Cologne and boarded a fleet of gliders, ready to take off at 0430hrs the next day on the mission they had been preparing for since shortly after the war began. In the pre-dawn gloom the men sang as they bumped across the airfield, drowning out the rattling noises until silence descended as they rose behind their Ju52 towplanes. By 0450hrs, 42 unmarked gliders were airborne and under strict radio silence followed a route marked with light beacons until they reached the Belgian border.[1]

The Belgians had maintained strict neutrality since the outbreak of war, refusing to even allow Allied officers to visit the country to plan defensive strategies. Its army of 22 divisions stood by behind a line of fortifications along the Albert Canal which included the fortress of Eben Emael – a state of the art defence work widely considered impregnable to ground attack. Although the French commander Gamelin had dismissively claimed that it could hold out for five days at best, memories of Verdun were still fresh in German minds. They believed it could delay their attack by at least two weeks by denying them the vital crossing points nearby that would lead them into the so-called Gembloux Gap where their tanks would be most effective. A ground assault, they reckoned, could cost around 6,000 casualties and take up to six months to reduce the fort completely. The Germans – on paper at least – were outnumbered in men, tanks, artillery and even aircraft and their plan relied entirely on speed. They could not afford any sort of delay. Instead, Koch and his men had been training since November for a special mission. They would land on top of the fort itself and alongside three nearby bridges and seize them in a lightning attack just minutes before the ground assault began. Using newly developed hollow charges to blast open the steel casemates, they were able to land on the roof of the fort and put most of its guns out of action within minutes.

The German attack came at the worst possible moment for the British. On 8 May, Captain Martin Lindsay, one of the first staff officers to return from the disastrous retreat from Norway, travelled to London and had lunch with Clement Attlee, the Labour leader of the opposition in Parliament. Although a pre-war Tory candidate, Lindsay was furious at the government's handling of the affair and what he saw as its failure to support the army. By that afternoon, the matter had been raised in the House by Herbert Morrison,

June 28th, 1940   *The War Illustrated*   689

The Nazis Show Us How They Took Eben-Eymael

German parachutists working under the protection of their own machine-guns paralysed the Belgian infantry defending the approaches to the fort. They also bored holes for mines in the massive concrete walls and eventually blew up the fort. Nazi soldiers are seen, left, by the partly destroyed fort.

On May 11 the German troops finally attacked the fort, after a terrific onslaught had been made by Nazi 'planes, which bombed and machine-gunned the garrison. The heroic struggle ended in a Nazi victory and the capitulation of the commander with 1,000 men. Some idea of the intensity of the attack can be gauged from the photograph below, which shows part of the damaged wall of the fort.

MOST powerful and modern of the forts of Liége, Eben-Eymael covered more than 200 acres and had an armament of two 12-centimetre guns (about 4·7-in.), over 30 of 6·5 and 7·5 cm., besides a large number of machine-guns, etc. Of its impregnability Belgium's military experts were convinced, and yet only a few hours sufficed for its capture by the Nazis. At first it was said that their parachutists descended on the cupola and threw hand grenades into the interior, but these photographs, reproduced from the German publication " Die Wehrmacht," prove rather that it was the severity of the aerial bombardment, combined with the mines laid by the parachutists, which broke the garrison's resistance, thus enabling picked storm troops to take the fort by assault. A Belgian soldier wounded in the defence of the fort confirmed the main outlines of the story.

The loop-holes in the thick concrete walls of Eben-Eymael were shattered as a result of mine explosions which went off with such force that the guns were broken out of their mountings. On the right, we see Hitler surrounded by some of the captors of the fort, who are proudly wearing the Iron Crosses awarded by the Fuehrer for their exploit.

Report on the attack on Eben Emael.

As featured in the report opposite, Hitler meets some of the 78 airborne troops who captured the seemingly impregnable Fort Eben Emael on the first day of the war in the west.

who demanded the resignation of Chamberlain and others associated with his appeasement policy. Chamberlain arrogantly accepted the challenge and called 'on my friends to support me in the lobby tonight'.[2] Reducing the serious debate to a matter of personal loyalties, Chamberlain destroyed any chance he had of retaining his position. With a good standing amongst members of all parties, Churchill, who himself shared much of the blame for what had gone wrong, spoke loyally in support of Chamberlain but had already been advised that he should not be too convincing. Harold Macmillan, then MP for Stockton-on-Tees had quietly told him, 'we must have a new Prime Minister and it must be you.'[3]

That night, despite the open resentment of the Conservative Chief Whip, almost every Tory MP in uniform – at least one in tears – filed into the Opposition lobby to vote against their own government. Quintin Hogg (later Lord Hailsham) voted in protest at the failure of the War Office to provide for his men's training or equipment. Another, Captain Roy Wise, explained simply, 'I voted on behalf of my men.' Ten minutes after the division bell rang, the votes had been counted – 281 against the government, 200 for. Amid stormy scenes, Chamberlain picked his way through the outstretched legs of his former colleagues and followers but despite this show of scorn he clung to power for two more days and even as German troops crossed the border into Belgium, he sought an alliance by asking Attlee to accept Labour seats in Chamberlain's cabinet. Attlee, whom Chamberlain had once called 'a cowardly cur', rejected the offer, saying 'our party won't have you, and I think I am right in saying that the country won't have you either'.[4]

Labour's preferred choice as replacement (and that of King George VI) was the Foreign Secretary Lord Halifax, and both he and Churchill were summoned to Downing Street at 11am on the morning of the 10th to meet with Chamberlain, who offered Halifax the post. After some thought, Halifax refused to accept the leadership, saying that as a member of the House of Lords he did not feel he could serve both houses adequately and would have difficulty commanding the respect of a coalition government. At 1800hrs that day, Churchill attended the King at Buckingham Palace and accepted the post of Prime Minister.

As the government at home collapsed, the British Expeditionary Force began to respond to the invasion. A French Warning Order had been issued at 0545hrs, three hours after bomb-

General Maurice Gamelin.
Commander in Chief of the French
forces, and by extension of the BEF,
Gamelin remained out of touch
throughout the campaign, reliant on
dispatch riders leaving his HQ on an
hourly basis to relay commands to his
troops in the field.

ing raids on Dutch and Belgian targets had begun and 20 minutes after the first gliders landed on Eben Emael. It took another 30 minutes before Gamelin gave the order to put Plan 'D' – the advance to the river Dyle – into operation.[5] After months of preparing for this moment, the BEF responded with an air of excitement but also with some trepidation. As there had been no period of alert beforehand, the men were unprepared and Gort was unsure of what to do. As a result, the 12th Lancers, spearheading the advance into Belgium, did not finally receive permission to enter the country until 1300hrs when, fortified by champagne drunk whilst waiting at the border, they roared across with their bugler sounding the charge.[6] The 'happy go lucky' French plan was under way.

Even his harshest critics could not deny Gort's personal bravery. He had won his VC as a young battalion commander with the Guards at Bourlon Wood and had traded on this throughout his career. Now, with the prospect of battle looming, he eagerly rushed forward to meet it. Unfortunately, Gort had never commanded any formation larger than a brigade and his lack of experience at his current level, along with his obedient Guards background, meant that he was happy to yield to the French High Command on all important matters. General Spears, Churchill's representative in France, later recalled that as early as November 1939 the French had been happy with Gort's appointment:

> The impression I received was that the British Commander-in-Chief was willing and anxious to please, and doing everything he was told. No-one quite said so, but I felt the French regarded Gort as a sort of friendly and jovial battalion commander.[7]

Accordingly, Gort was happy to comply with the plan to move the Allied forces forward into Belgium and to meet the Germans along the Dyle line. Even had he not been, his right of appeal to the British government would have been severely affected by the problems at home. Now, the whole Anglo-French front left their prepared positions and swung into Belgium, the right of the line hinging at the town of Sedan near the Ardennes. Watching from home, General Sir Henry Karslake, another victim of Hore-Belisha's cuts,

A British artillery unit enters Belgium.

noted the movements on a map set up in his study. Quietly, he took down the map. His son, Basil, notes his reaction:

> 'The war is over', he said. 'Gort and Gamelin have committed the one strategical error that even the most junior officer is impressed on avoiding; they have brought their fighting line parallel to their Lines of Communication. If the Germans attack here,' he pointed at Sedan on the general map of France that lay on his desk, 'and manage to thrust their way westwards, they will cut off the fighting troops from their supplies … I can understand Gort making such an error; he is just spoiling for a fight, to wave his sword and win another VC, but I am surprised at Gamelin.'[8]

For the Anglo-French plan to be effective, speed was essential and all emphasis was on getting the men into position as quickly as possible, even at the risk of travelling in daylight. Captain Sir Basil Bartlett, serving as a Field Security Officer, was on the Belgian border watching British troops move forward:

> They were travelling at a good speed, but were too closely spaced, I thought. They'd suffer heavily if the Germans took it into their heads to bomb them. There are so far no reports of sabotage on the route.[9]

A few days later, on the 14th, Bartlett's diary noted 'the weather remains brilliantly fine. The Germans are allowing the BEF to move into its battle positions almost without interference.'[10] Elsewhere, a staff officer of the British Air Forces France wrote on 13 May that a

British troops are welcomed into Belgium, 11/12 May 1940.

'strange, and I feel, very suspicious feature, has been the extraordinary lack of any German bombing of the BEF and the French armies in their advance through Belgium during the last four days. It looks almost as if the Germans want us where we are going.'[11] Intent on completing the advance, Gort and his staff simply took advantage of the lack of air opposition and chose not to question it.

Fall Gelb (Case Yellow), the German plan for the conquest of the west, called for an attack by Army Group B into the Netherlands and Belgium in what appeared at first to be almost a replay of their 1914 campaign with only slight modifications – indeed panzer

German troops inspect an abandoned French tank.

expert General Heinz Guderian had condemned it as such when it was first presented. Copies of the original plans had fallen into Allied hands a few months earlier when a German plane had crashed and the wreckage was discovered by Allied troops. It seemed to confirm the idea that this war would be a carbon copy of the last one. The Allied reaction and troop movements to counter what was then seen as an imminent threat was carried out in full view of German reconnaissance planes and confirmed what they already suspected would happen. The new plan called for something different.

The attack on Belgium has been described as 'the matador's cloak'. Army Group B, with 30 divisions, three of them armoured and two motorised, was intended to draw the bulk of the Allied armies away from their prepared positions and into Belgium. Once the Allied move was complete, Army Group A under von Runstedt would make its move. With 45 of the best equipped divisions in the German Army, including seven armoured and three mechanised, von Runstedt could call on almost 2,000 tanks to put into action what Erich von Manstein described as a 'revolving door'. As the Allies left their positions, the true attack would come through the Ardennes and across the river Meuse to thrust across France, sever the Lines of Communication and destroy the Allies in detail in a pocket along the coast. To achieve success, von Manstein told his men they must be across the Meuse by the 13th at the latest.

Having planned to extend his left flank too far forward, Gamelin had also heavily reinforced his right by placing 39 divisions and 10 tank battalions behind the allegedly impregnable Maginot Line and its existing garrison of 10 divisions, now faced with the 19 infantry divisions of General Leeb's Army Group C and ready for the unlikely scenario of an attack via Switzerland. This left very little with which to guard his centre. Along a 100-mile stretch of border opposite the Belgian Ardennes, Gamelin placed just ten weak divisions of the 9th Army under General Andre Sorap, of which only one was ready for front line duty. Three light cavalry divisions, each with one armoured and one horsed brigade provided a screen in front of them. Even Sorap had complained about the poor state of his forces and in particular the very poor discipline among his men – conscripts demoralised by a dangerous combination of boredom and bad living conditions.

German paratroopers meet with a 'Brandenburger' Special Forces agent during the invasion of the Low Countries. The work of such agents created a widespread fear of fifth columnists.

A JU 87 Stuka formation. The lack of air attacks on the advancing Allies was noticed but disregarded. In fact, the Germans chose not to bomb the Allied convoys to encourage them to move into the trap being set for them.

The Ardennes had been dismissed as impenetrable to tanks despite their having long been the route of invading armies, a misunderstanding of Petain's actual assessment that the Ardennes were 'impenetrable provided special dispositions are made there'.[12] A system of emplaced positions covering the area could make it extremely difficult to move forces through the forests and valleys but with no liaison between the French and the Belgians in the preceding months both thought that the other had the matter in hand. Despite information gathered by sources including Swiss Intelligence that their plan lay there, Gamelin had decreed that the Germans would not attack through the area. Even if they managed it, he said, it would take at least ten days – ample time for the French to react.

At the same time as Army Group B's attack to the north got under way and drew the world's attention, the tanks of Army Group A rolled across the Luxembourg border. The Luftwaffe deliberately remained absent from the skies over the Ardennes to avoid highlighting the advancing army and its route. There were no journalists with the troops as trucks carrying fuel and relief crews drove alongside the tank columns, changing crews and refuelling on the move to maintain momentum. Nothing to indicate that behind the reconnaissance troops stretched a 250km queue of over 41,000 vehicles. Here and there isolated Belgian units fought back. At the village of Bodange, a single company of Chasseurs Ardennais held up the 1st Panzer Division for six hours but they were only a thin screen, not a defence line. By the afternoon of 12 May, Guderian was making plans to cross the Meuse at Sedan.

JU 87 Stuka attacks.

German artist's impression of a river crossing in France.

The attack was to begin at 1600hrs on the 13th. The Germans were seriously short of artillery with only a third the number the French had opposing them and each German gun was limited to around a dozen shells, the remainder stuck in the traffic jam along the narrow roads behind them. Instead, the attack would be preceded by a massive aerial bombardment. The bombing began at 0800hrs and was followed by wave after wave of aircraft. Sedan was only a ten minute flight for the Stukas operating from a forward airstrip at Bastogne under the command of Wolfram von Richthofen, nephew of the Red Baron. With orders to target any enemy positions they could find, they returned again and again in the 'rolling raid' Guderian had requested.

Despite the devastating effect of the raids, the French were in strong bunkers and their heavy batteries had escaped the worst of it. From their positions they were able to prevent the German infantry from crossing the river in assault boats by artillery and machine-gun fire. Then, near Wadelincourt and acting on his own initiative, Sturmpionier Walter Rubarth led a small group across using the shelter of a ruined bridge and began systematically working their way along the line of defences. After destroying the first bunker, they raised a swastika flag over it as a signal to their comrades. Taking out the first line they then moved back to the second line trenches, by now finding Frenchmen assuming that the Germans were across in force and surrendering to them without a fight. As the breach opened, more troops crossed.[13] By 1900hrs, panic was spreading through the French defenders, stories reached HQ of tanks already across the river, although in reality it would take another twelve hours before pontoon bridges could be built to get them across. As more Germans crossed the river, the defenders broke and ran. In some places officers and NCOs tried to stem the rout only to have their entire unit flow around them and escape. Others claimed to have had orders to retreat but few could say where these orders had come from.

The German bridgehead was tenuous. Their tanks could not yet cross, and their artillery was low on ammunition. A counterattack could still hold them. Pushing ahead, Colonel Hermann Balck of the 1st Motorised Regiment ordered his men to keep attacking French positions in the dark. Aware of the risks of being cut off, Balck also knew the importance of keeping the French off balance. It was then that General Huntziger, the French commander of the Sedan sector, made a fatal decision. At 2030hrs he ordered the heavy gun batteries to withdraw. The 3rd North African Infantry Division, the best troops he had available to him, were told to move away from the Sedan area. These two movements were seen as confirmation that the battle was lost and the panic spread even further. Pockets of resistance continued but soon afterward Balck signalled, 1st Panzer Division's HQ: 'Schützenregiment 1 has at 22.40 taken high hill just to the north of Cheveuges. Last enemy blockhouse is in our hands. Complete breakthrough.'[14] The Sedan front had collapsed.

When the news reached Gamelin in the early hours of the 14th, he broke down in tears. The attack in the north had worked perfectly. In their eagerness to meet it, neither Gamelin nor Gort had thought to leave behind a reserve. Nothing now stood between the Germans and the sea. Except three divisions of untrained labour troops.

NOTES

 1 See Lynch, *Silent Skies: Gliders at War* Pen & Sword 2008
 2 Collier, *1940: The World in Flames* London: Penguin 1980 p74
 3 Ibid p74
 4 Ibid p76
 5 Blaxland p69
 6 Sebag-Montefiore p60
 7 Spears p56
 8 Karslake p53–4
 9 Captain Sir Basil Bartlett, *My First War* London: Chatto & Windus 1940 p48
10 Ibid p57
11 *The Diary of a Staff Officer* London: Methuen & Co 1941 p9
12 Glover p31
13 See Brian Moynihan, *Forgotten Soldiers* London: Quercus 2007
14 Sebag-Montefiore p94

Chapter Seven

'More gallantly than advisedly'

News of the German invasion of Belgium was met calmly by the men of the L of C. In Rennes, Sergeant Brown's diary mentions in passing the news that the Germans had attacked and records that he and a party from the KOYLI attended a BEF concert that evening, although supper was poor. As yet, the war seemed so remote that it was not until the 12th that orders came down for everyone to draw a steel helmet and respirator from stores. For Brigadier Beauman, the first news came not from GHQ but via a servant who had heard about it on the BBC news. The main change in his work was

that the skeleton rear HQ at Arras and its attached units were now to be incorporated into his district as another sub-area under the control of Colonel Usher and guards at vulnerable points were to be stepped up. GHQ, he wote, 'had never contemplated that the L of C area would have any tactical importance in case of active operations' and so when Gort and his staff followed the BEF into Belgium, Arras simply became another base area.[1]

Two days after the battle began and eager not to miss the fun, 46th Division's commander, Major-General Harry 'Squeak' Curtis, contacted Gort by phone and in Richard Holmes' words, 'more gallantly than advisedly' offered the services of his division as a combat ready force. The

Paul Reynaud, French Premier from 21 March to 16 June 1940, Reynaud telephoned Churchill on 15 May. In tears he told Churchill that the battle was already lost.

enthusiastic and extroverted former 60th Rifleman's description of his men as ready for action was duly noted.

The German advance through Sedan had been so successful and fast-moving that General Henri Giraud, who had only just replaced Corap as commander of the French 9th Army, was captured accidentally by a field kitchen detachment of the 11th Panzer Regiment who found him hiding in a shed where they were about to set up their cookers.[2] Taken by surprise at their own progress, von Runstedt, on direct orders from Hitler himself, called a temporary halt on the 16th along the line of the river Oise to allow his infantry a chance to catch up with the tanks fearing that any setback on the southern front could be an encouragement to the already fragile French political leadership and increase their resolve to stay in the fight.

By then, though, the French Prime Minister Reynaud had declared the war lost. The breakthrough at Sedan signalled a collapse in the collective French will. Even far away in Brittany, Brigadier Gawthorpe's liaison officer,

> ... a tough, experienced officer of a French Colonial regiment, said on hearing over the Paris radio that the Germans had struck at Sedan, '*Sedan, c'est fini.*' How right he was and how significant of the atmosphere in France.[3]

In a telephone call to Churchill at 0730hrs on the 15th, a tearful Reynaud told him that the Germans had broken the front at Sedan and 'were pouring through in great numbers with tanks and armoured cars ... We are defeated; we have lost the battle.'[4] Churchill Immediately flew to France to discuss the situation. In a famous encounter with Gamelin, he recalled how he had asked in his indifferent French "'*Ou est la masse de manoeuvre?*" General Gamelin turned to me and, with a shake of his head and a shrug, said: "*Aucune.*"'[5] Churchill declared himself 'dumbfounded' that there were no strategic reserves available but Gort was as guilty as Gamelin in that respect. Blinded by their own preconceptions of how the war would play out, the BEF and the French armies had been drawn into the German trap and now their entire southern flank was wide open.

Through French sources Beauman began to hear disturbing reports about the situation around Sedan. 'I could not as yet conceive that there was any serious threat to my district, but to be on the safe side I decided to form a mobile reserve consisting of one infantry battalion with small detachments of artillery and engineers.'[6] The 7th Battalion, Royal West Kent Regiment (7RWK) of 36th Infantry Brigade, 12th Division were chosen for the task. 'This came as rather a shock,' wrote Captain Newbury, commanding the battalion's 'A' Company, 'the bn being untrained and short of many LMGs [Light Machine Guns] – ATRs [Anti-Tank Rifles] – mortars – signalling apparatus and entirely without carriers.'[7] Having been relieved of their guard duties by another 36 Brigade unit, the 5th Buffs, the battalion were placed on 30 minutes notice to move from the area around Fleury-sur-Somme, although they would not actually receive any transport until the following morning. Beauman had decided that the trucks currently held in storage would simply fall intact into enemy hands if he did nothing to protect the L of C. So 37 3-ton lorries arrived at around 1030hrs to take his new 'flying column' to a new position at Quevauvilliers where they were joined by four 25-pounder guns that had been returned from 51st Division for servicing and were now manned by gunners taken from the General Base Depot at Forges. A section of sappers from 218 Army Troop Company Royal Engineers from Dieppe completed the new formation. The remainder of the brigade, the 5th Buffs and 6th RWK, were now told that they were

Mobile troops. Equipped with trucks from supply depots, Beauman formed the West Kents into a 'flying column' to respond to the speed of the German advance.

detached from the division and placed under the command of GHQ. They would be given their orders soon.

As 7RWK's column moved, Beauman was summoned urgently to Arras and told that a large armoured force was heading west towards Cambrai. There were no French reserves available and the decision had been made to form a defensive line with whatever was to hand. The first step would be to concentrate the three labour divisions north of the Somme in the hope of slowing the Germans and allowing the BEF to move troops to its southern flank. In the meantime, Beauman was to follow the plan originally devised to have the Northern District of the L of C take over the area of the Franco-Belgian border as troops under GHQ command moved forward. He now had to find a protection force for thirteen as yet incomplete airfields as well as dozens more HQ buildings and installations against sabotage and parachute attack.

On his way back to Rouen, Beauman was called into the HQ of the 2nd French Region at Amiens to check the latest news. His French counterpart assured him that the situation was under control and there was no real cause for concern. As they spoke, Beauman glanced out of the window. Outside, French staff officers were hurling packs of secret documents onto a bonfire in the garden. 'They evidently did not share his complacency.'[8] Worried, Beauman began to plan his defence of his over-extended command.

Even before Beauman had been briefed, orders had already gone out on the 14th to the units of the 12th, 23rd and 46th Divisions to make ready to move, although where and why remained unclear. Curtis' wildly optimistic claim that his men were ready showed just how out of touch with his command he had become. The War

Establishment of an infantry battalion had been set at 21 officers and 752 other ranks with 50 Bren guns, 22 Boys Anti-Tank rifles, 12 2-inch and 2 3-inch mortars. None of the digging divisions came close to these numbers. Among the battalions of 137 Brigade, for example, the West Yorkshires numbered 26 officers and 562 other ranks.[9] They were equipped with a rifle and bayonet per man, 10 Bren guns and 11 Boys rifles but no mortars of any kind. The story was repeated in other brigades. When the 2/6th East Surreys received orders to move to join the 51st Highland Division in the Saar for work behind the lines, frantic scrounging by the Quartermaster produced a total of 20 Bren guns with 500 rounds per gun. Without any support from either divisional HQ or HQ L of C, the best he could manage was just twelve rounds of ammunition for each of the eight Boys rifles the battalion now held. Maps, compasses, binoculars, grenades, revolvers and other vital equipment were non-existent. By now, though, they were all that stood between the Germans and the complete destruction of the Allied armies in Belgium.

Although farthest from the front, it seems Curtis's claims had been taken at face value. The first members of the digging divisions to be called forward were HQ 46th Division and 138 and 139 Brigades from the Rennes area. Leaving behind 138 Brigade's 2/4th KOYLI to follow on later, the two brigades entrained for Seclin on the 15th expecting to be put to work in the rear areas of the BEF to free up refugee traffic; but after a full day's train journey, the brigades arrived to find their orders had changed. They were now to become the front line as part of 'Macforce', an improvised formation formed by Gort under the command of his Director of Intelligence, Major-General Mason-Macfarlane to protect the right rear flank of the BEF. After a chaotic advance, they took up positions along the river Scarpe on the 20th only to find that the river was less of a barrier than they had hoped – the water was found to be just two feet six inches deep.[10]

In accordance with Plan 'D', HQ L of C began their move forward from Le Mans on the 16th, heading for Mantes on the river Seine but arrived to news of the German breakthrough and little information about whether the advance had been stopped. Unwilling to risk further disruption if the Germans continued their advance, de Fonblanque chose instead to cancel the move and recall his staff to Le Mans. At the same time, demands were coming in that as much of 12th Division as possible be made mobile and sent to GHQ. For the time being, after consultation with the divisional commander, Major-General Roderick Petre, it was agreed that one brigade should be made mobile and sent to the Serquex area whilst the remainder of the division travel to Abbeville by train.[11]

Next to move were elements of 23rd Division from their positions around St Pol. On the 13th, 10th Battalion Durham Light Infantry (10DLI) of 70 Brigade, 23rd Division had received orders to head south to guard airfields around Abbeville. So short of transport were they that it took the combined transport of the entire division to move them by road where, for three days before they handed over to 12th Division and returned to Nuncq, 'little of moment took place beyond parachutist scares, the local French Headquarters in Abbeville having apparently got parachutists on the brain.'[12] As they returned to the division on the 17th, a request arrived at 'Brassard' – the British Rear HQ at Arras – from the French commander-in-chief, General Georges, asking for the division to take up position along the line of the Canal du Nord south of Arleux.

Oddly, given that Churchill himself was aware of the true situation almost 48 hours earlier, this came as a shock to Lieutenant-Colonel Robert Bridgeman, then in command of the depleted HQ. London had not bothered to pass the information on and

A Boys Anti-Tank rifleman.

The British Vickers Light Tank Mk VI, armed only with a machine gun. These tanks were not intended for the assault role the French demanded of them.

Brassard had comfortably assumed that the area was under French control. Only now did Bridgeman order an 'intelligence appreciation'. It took just 20 minutes for what he later called the full 'horror of the situation' to become clear.[13] Out of his depth, Bridgeman contacted Gort's forward HQ. On the orders of Gort's Adjutant General, Lieutenant-General Sir Douglas Brownrigg, Petre was urgently summoned to Arras from Abbeville on the 18th and handed responsibility for the area's defence with another of the composite forces that were springing up. It was, noted Petre, 'difficult to understand clearly the composition of this force'.[14] As best he could understand it, 'Petreforce' would comprise the 23rd Division, 36 Brigade of Petre's own division and the Arras garrison made up of the 1st Welsh Guards, the veteran 9th West Yorks and a variety of support units, few of which he would be able to contact directly as none had radios and most would be some distance from his HQ. In the panic and confusion infecting Brassard by now, no-one thought it necessary to inform 12th Division HQ that Petre would not be returning from what he had assumed when he left was a routine briefing. For the next two days, all coordinated command of the entire division was lost.

In response to Georges' request, the 23rd Division under Brigadier Kirkup began their move on the 17th. The division comprised the 69th Brigade of the East Yorkshires and Green Howards and 70th Brigade with the 10th and 11th DLI along with their former 12th battalion now re-designated as 1st Tyneside Scottish (1TS) but instead of a third brigade, the division also included two battalions of the Royal Northumberland Fusiliers – the 8th RNF as a motorcycle equipped unit and the 9th as a machine-gun battalion – although before their arrival in France this latter had not even seen a British machine-gun and had trained on two captured German guns from 1918 from the regimental museum.

As directed, 69 Brigade deployed along the line of the river Scarpe whilst 70 Brigade, after fighting their way through crowds of refugees, finally reached the Canal du Nord. It had not been an easy journey; the roads were so densely packed with refugees that at times the convoy had to drive across country. For the Tyneside Scottish, whose transport consisted of two 30 cwt, seven 15 cwt and one 8 cwt trucks and 'a motorcycle of uncertain temper',[15] the move had been even further delayed by a wait for commandeered civilian transport which, when it finally arrived, included a bus whose bronze plaque proclaimed it to have been used to transport the French Army to the Marne in 1914. The CO and a recce party having taken one of only two maps available, 2/Lt Cohen, the battalion's intelligence officer performed a near miracle in keeping the convoy together and reaching the canal by 0300hrs on the 18th.

Lieutenant-Colonel Swinburne, commanding 1TS, now faced a daunting task. Military doctrine of the day held that a fully armed and supported division could be expected to hold no more than about four miles of front. With around fourteen Bren guns, eight Boys rifles and a few 2-inch mortars per battalion, the division could call on the support of no more than a dozen guns, most of which had no sights and could only fire at targets they could see. There were no anti-tank guns of any kind beyond the Boys rifles. With these meagre resources, the Tynesiders alone were to cover a front of around ten miles from Berthincourt to the Cambrai–Baupame road.[16] For Company Sergeant Major Baggs of 1TS, his new position near the village of Hermies was only too familiar; he had fought there in March 1918 during the great German offensive as had Brigadier Kirkup. History, it seemed, was repeating itself.

The canal they found would not prove much of a barrier. Dry in places, its banks crumbling, there were more potential crossing points than Swinburne's 660 men could

A few battalions, among them 23rd Division's 8th Royal Northumbrian Fusiliers, were equipped as reconnaissance troops and mounted on motorcycles. The role was abandoned after the fall of France.

adequately cover and so 'C' Company of the reserve 10th DLI was placed under his command. A consignment of Lewis guns had just reached them to bolster their fire-power but few among them had any training and scratch teams had to be put together to undergo a rapid course from the older NCOs. With no hard facts to work on infor-mation came in drips from retreating French troops and from refugees but as the sense of panic among the fleeing civilians grew, rumours of saboteurs, enemy agents and disguised parachutists became ever more rampant and the response to any suspect activ-ity increasingly harsh. On the 19th, CSM Baggs recalled, an alleged spy was brought before Colonel Swinburne and their French liaison officer. Without ceremony or trial, the man was taken out and shot by Provost Sergeant Dick Chambers, one of hundreds of French and Belgian civilians who would die on often the flimsiest of evidence in the coming weeks.[17]

Swinburne was in no mood to take chances. Earlier that afternoon, where the canal formed at least some form of obstacle, he had ordered the bridges blown and found one remaining. An engineer had prepared the bridge but it was crowded with refugees and clearly distressed, requested a couple of men be sent across to stop the traffic. Swinburne refused, 'whereupon he burst into tears (he was very young and junior), much to my horror, and I had to push down the plunger myself, much as I hated to do it with people still on the bridge. But orders are orders, and sentiment comes nowhere in war.'[18]

Despite the constant air activity around them and the sight of dead civilians on the roadsides after raids, for the young men of Recruit Company the war was still a strange adventure. 'Smithy', the awkward young recruit who had joined with James Laidler a few weeks earlier, was intrigued by a large metal object he found after an attack by Stukas. Proudly carrying it to his officer, he declared; 'Look what I've found, Sir.' As everyone around dived for cover, he was told in no uncertain terms to get rid of it. Calmly, Smithy turned and threw the unexploded bomb over the canal bank. Later, he was found walk-ing around without his helmet or rifle and asked by his officer what he would do if he was suddenly faced with a German: 'Kick him in the privates with me clems [boots].'[19] Bemused, the officer let him on his way. Unknown to any of them, Smithy had less than a day left to live.[20]

Meanwhile, 7 RWK had travelled to Doullens and from there had been ordered to Clery-sur-Somme to block the road to Peronne, arriving in the early morning of the 18th despite confusion on the roads that had intermingled 7 RWK's vehicles with those of other units. The sense of confusion was not helped, Captain Newbury noted, by the fact that 'information was practically non-existent and even the direction of the enemy was vague'.[21] That day was spent blowing all bridges in the area except the canal bridge on the main Clery–Peronne road. One bridge at Allaines to the north had not been completely destroyed and a road block had been established to defend it. At 1000hrs, a truck carrying another 35 Bren guns and fifteen ATRs arrived from GHQ stores still packed in grease as increasing air activity signalled the approach of the Germans. An air attack was beaten off by RAF fighters during the afternoon and first contact with enemy ground forces for the digging divisions came at around 1730hrs when Captain Gibbs of 'C' Company came under fire about 1.5 miles east of the town. By 1900hrs, tanks and motorcycle troops could be seen approaching and they were engaged by the four field guns. As the Germans pushed forward, a motorcyclist was killed at a road block on the Albert road but was closely followed by three tanks who began to spray the area with machine-gun fire. A volley of return fire from the Boys rifles had little effect – it emerged that they had been provided half charged training ammunition by mistake[22] – but good work by

Sergeant Drummond with the battalion's only 3-inch mortar appeared to set one tank alight and the others withdrew, seemingly facing heavier opposition than expected. At 2030hrs reports circulated of a drop by ten parachutists but no further attack came that night, although aircraft dropped flares at regular intervals. 'We had evidently held up the advance' noted a satisfied War Diarist.[23]

By now, Petre had decided not to leave his force exposed in isolated pockets but to bring them back to a position along the La Bassee Canal north of Arras where the German offensive of 1918 had run out of steam. Orders went out to try to fall the units back into a coherent line. For 7RWK, the next day remained relatively quiet as they began to consolidate their position. Realising that the battalion was in an isolated position, Petre considered moving them back to link with the flank of 70 Brigade in place of the promised French forces which had failed to materialise but decided that 'in view of the unsatisfactory nature of the CANAL DU NORD this would merely be putting further unsuitable troops into danger'.[24] Instead, the battalion was ordered to withdraw to Albert and turn it into an anti-tank locality. This would involve their taking up position in buildings at the far side of a built-up area so that the Germans would be channelled into streets and unable to make use of artillery and air support for fear of hitting their own men. Still with a pre-war mentality, many commanders found it difficult to bring themselves to destroy private property and the tactic was not popular but in Albert it was also unsuitable. The river was found to be a dry ditch and 'subterranean in town'. Instead, Lieutenant-Colonel Clay was given permission to withdraw farther to make use of high ground outside the town on the road to Doullens. He chose this option, arriving safely by 0600hrs on the 19th. Then, at 0130hrs on the morning of the 20th, they were ordered back to Albert. In six hours time, they would be destroyed.

The yawning gap between 7 RWK and the right of 70 Brigade had been occupied during the 18th by their former comrades in 36 Brigade, 6 RWK and 5 Buffs under Brigadier Roupell VC. They, along with the rest of 12th Division, had been ordered to Abbeville on the 17th with 36 Brigade travelling in trucks as part of the L of C mobile reserve whilst 35 and 37 Brigade entrained. Because of the difficulty in arranging transport and moving it through the already congested routes, it was not until the following day that the division were at last fully able to move. Even as they prepared for the trip to Abbeville, new orders placed 36 Brigade under GHQ and directed them to Doullens to await further instructions, the two battalions finally setting out at 2230hrs. On arrival, the battalions found a deserted town. Major Arthur 'Tim' West of the Buffs would later recall finding meals on tables and fires still lit as though the whole town was an enormous Marie Celeste. With just four Bren guns per company and fourteen Boys rifles in the entire battalion, the men set about building road blocks and worked under the impression that a few tanks had broken through but not in any real force, pausing only to watch the flow of retreating French troops pass through the town. They began to dig in on the Doullens–Arras road towards the village of Saulty with the town now forming the right flank of a ten-mile front held by the RWK, with the Buffs holding another six miles on their left. According to the latest reports from Arras, the 23-mile gap between their left flank and the right of 23rd Division was held by French forces. The reports were wrong. Nothing stood in the way of complete encirclement. That night a communion service was held in a cafe for the few men able to attend.

Behind them, the remainder of 12th Division was in chaos. With the 2/6th East Surreys detached for duties around Le Havre, 37 Brigade's remaining battalions, 6th and 7th Royal Sussex Regiment, had been warned off for a move to Abbeville 'to check any wandering

German units which had broken through' and were to 'hold a hollow square position with 7RS on the right.' As they prepared to move, each man had 50 rounds of ammunition and the battalion held 12 Bren guns, each with 12 filled magazines, 4 Boys rifles and 4 2-inch mortars without sights. Few believed they were going to war and 'a number were under the impression they were going on a scheme'.[25] After the inevitable delays the train carrying the 7th RS, members of a Field Ambulance and a group of engineers set out at 0430hrs on 18 May. Without warning, the train was redirected by GHQ and at around 0800hrs the men learned they were now headed for Amiens, but not why. Unknown to the battalion – or indeed to its motor transport still heading for the original rendezvous – it was now en route to Lens.

Passing through Abancourt, the train passed that containing their sister battalion who had set off earlier but had been held up by a derailment. The 7th, now travelling on the adjacent track, continued past. Noticing that the other train had mounted Bren guns to provide anti-aircraft protection, Lieutenant-Colonel Gethen of the 7th now ordered his men to do likewise. As the 'beautiful hot summer's day' wore on, most of the men had taken the opportunity to take off their boots and were dozing as the train approached Amiens that afternoon. Then, at about 1515hrs, a large explosion rocked the train. Hastily detraining and scrambling into cover, the men watched as an air raid struck the station of St Roche just outside Amiens itself. Sergeant Glover and Private Sexton, manning the AA machine gun, fired back but the damage was already done. The engine was wrecked, the driver killed and the track ahead had been torn up. A bomb had hit the front of the train, causing around 60 casualties, mostly among the battalion's officers. The Quartermaster and both interpreters were dead and the CO, Adjutant Major Cassels and Medical Officer Captain Mannington were amongst the wounded.[26] Behind them, the train carrying the 6th was shunted into a siding where it sat for six hours before continuing on its journey.

As the raid ended, a party began to retrieve what it could from the wreckage. For the young soldiers, the sight of maimed comrades came as a sudden shock as they watched the wounded being gathered together by the medics aboard. An anti-aircraft gun stood by to give cover if required but when an aircraft appeared the crew were unable to distinguish any markings before another bomb blew them off their feet. As the men dispersed into nearby woods, successive waves of bombs fell all around. That night, Gethen and Cassels 'kept discussing methods of getting on to Doullens as the railway was u/s [unserviceable]'.

The next morning, iron rations were being distributed when a mobile canteen arrived on the scene. After breakfast, the battalion moved about a mile away into woods alongside the Amiens–Rouen road. No orders were given to dig in but some men managed to scrape some sort of cover with the few tools to hand. The day was spent watching Stuka attacks on Amiens where two more trains were hit as they reached the station during the day. A further move was made after aircraft seemed to be bombing the woods nearby, and the men collected gardening tools from the farms and cottages they passed. As night approached, a group of around 30 mounted Belgian cavalrymen passed the position and warned the guard that the Germans were around 30km away. When the message was passed to Gethen, he ordered the guard commander 'not to take any notice of rumours'. Later that night, Lieutenant Bowyer was detailed to begin gathering stragglers and 'by the use of troops with bayonets', collected around 80–100 French soldiers but found that the only French officer they could find refused to issue orders, saying he had been told to reform his own unit. With that he and the stragglers left. Concerned about the effect on morale, Gethen told his men that the French were untrained recruits and of no use to them.

That night Gethen, who had been hit in the head during the bombing and appears to have been concussed, became increasingly adamant that he had no orders to go back the way they had come so could only either continue the journey or stay where he was. On the basis of information from the French staff at Amiens, who despite the evidence to the contrary continued to claim that the Sedan breakthrough had been contained, he chose to stay put. His decision doomed the battalion.

Unable to reach their destination because of line damage outside Lens, the train carrying 6th RS was forced to return along the same line, again passing the 7th and eventually coming to a halt in a siding south of the Somme and about ten miles from Amiens where its engine was removed. Unsure what to do, it would stay there for two days before the CO, Lieutenant-Colonel Wannup took the decision to take the train back down the line. The only other alternative was an uncertain march westwards and the colonel knew his men were not up to it. They had few rations and their training had not prepared them for the distance they would need to cover. A recce party was able to make contact with a skeleton railway staff at St Just-en-Chausee and arranged a new locomotive. At 2200hrs on the 20th the battalion gathered its kit and set off once again into the darkness. By then, the routes were often blocked and the battalion found itself directed to Paris where, on the orders of the military attaché, it was sent to Nantes to resume the labour work so recently vacated by 137 Brigade. Of all the digging division units, theirs was the luckiest. They would still be working on railway construction as the last ships from the northern ports were heading home but all would safely return to England.

Behind them, 12th Division's 35 Brigade – three battalions of the Queens Royal Regiment – were having an equally frustrating time. Its move to Abbeville should have been simple. Its 2/5th battalion were already working on airfield construction in the area and could easily reach the city by road. The other battalions, the 2/6th and 2/7th, were working on the rail hub at Abancourt and were only a short march from the station there. In any case, the two battalions arrived at Abbeville by noon on the 18th. Their role, apparently, was to act as a reserve with confusingly contradictory orders to take up position 'within four miles of Abbeville. The positions are not to be tactical, but areas to be allotted with regard to the fact that the brigade may have to defend Abbeville.'[27] This last was a surprise since the Germans were still widely thought to be over 100 miles away. Unsure of whether they were to prepare defences or not, they set to work building roadblocks east of the Somme in line with the plan for a hollow square with, they believed, 37 Brigade working west of the river.[28] Perhaps the worst equipped of all, 35 Brigade could muster just five Boys rifles and a total of 35 rounds per battalion.

In its panic, GHQ had been issuing orders to various units and calling them forward piecemeal. For the already overworked railway transport officers (RTOs) this added yet another layer of confusion to that already caused by the lack of radio contact and reliance on a telephone system that had been temperamental even before the bombing and saboteurs started their work on it. Air strikes on the lines constantly meant changes of plans and perhaps the local RTO at Abbeville mistook the brigade for elements of 46th Division. Certainly the risk of mistaking 12th Division's 37 Brigade for 46th Division's 137 Brigade – also expected through at any time – was all too real. Whatever the truth of the matter, Abbeville's RTO issued new orders for the 2/6th and 2/7th to 'proceed to Lens'. The order was questioned but he remained insistent. A call to Arras over a very poor line confirmed it. With the Brigade commander travelling by road with the 2/5th and not yet arrived, without radio contact with anyone at Divisional HQ (who themselves knew nothing of either the divisional commander's whereabouts or indeed those of any of their brigades) and completely unaware of 37 Brigade's earlier movements, 12th Division's senior officer on site saw no alternative but to send them on their way. Having been so close to Abbeville, the men had not brought any rations and there were none now to be had as they began the long journey to Lens, arriving there at 1900hrs only to find nothing in place for their reception. After angry scenes in the RTO's office, contact with GHQ was made. The order 'proceed to Lens' had been a mistake. It was actually that they should 'proceed to Doullens' to join 36 Brigade's right flank.[29]

By now it was too late for them to reach Doullens and instead the tired and hungry men were forced to camp out in a local park until 0600hrs the next morning when they began a slow journey back to their starting point. A move south brought them to Arras where, by chance, Petre heard of their plight and arranged a train to take them back via St Pol, the direct line having already been bombed, but he could do nothing about finding rations. By the time they finally reached Abbeville at 2000hrs that night, they had not eaten for two days. Meanwhile the 2/5th had been spared a nightmare rail journey but had faced instead a long, hot march when their transport failed to arrive. Reunited, the three battalions took up position as a screen northeast of the Somme around the villages of Drucat, Vauchelles and Bellancourt.

Sunday 19 May had been a frustrating day for HQ 12th Division. Petre and his senior staff officer had been called forward to Arras late on the 17th, arriving there at 0030hrs only to be given some information but no orders. He returned to his HQ as it prepared to move forward and set up in the village of Fressenville as they had been directed to do. Reaching Fressenville at 0900hrs, Petre had just 45 minutes to settle in before he received another summons to Arras. This time, he was given command of Petreforce and so stayed at Brassard. Unfortunately, the fact was not communicated to his own HQ so that by Sunday afternoon, 12th Division had literally lost its commander and seven of its nine battalions – only the whereabouts of the 2/6th East Surreys at Le Havre was certain and the 2/5th Queen's were known to be in the area of Abbeville but the rest had simply disappeared.

Farthest away and last to be called forward, 137 Brigade did not begin their move until late in the afternoon of the 18th. The previous evening, Brigadier Gawthorpe was dining in the mess of the Duke of Wellington's Regiment when a call was put through from General Curtis at Arras. Soon afterwards a signal arrived confirming that the brigade was to move forward the following day, collecting the 2/4th KOYLI en route. The 2/6th DWR would set out from St Nazaire whilst two trains would collect the 2/7th DWR and the 2/5th West Yorkshires from their camp at Blain. The DWR history claims that Gawthorpe was told that the brigade was to be used as a defensive screen[30] but, in keeping with the general air of confusion, Lieutenant-Colonel Taylor of the 2/7th DWR reported later that he knew they were 'untrained and practically unarmed … [and] understood that the Division was to undertake work in L of C in continuation of the pioneer tasks which we had already been employed upon in Nantes Sub Area.'[31]

In fact, the brigade had been earmarked as part of the proposed 'Polforce' being set up under 46 Division's commander in the vicinity of the town of St Pol. Whatever the truth, the brigade busied itself in preparing for the move. One vehicle per company was to be loaded onto the trains. These were to be driven to Nantes for loading. The remainder of the transport was to set out by road as soon as possible. The West Yorkshires' vehicles, under Second Lieutenant Richard Camrass, a former solicitor from Dewsbury, set out as planned. It would be many weeks before he was seen again, having had the unnerving experience of finding his own obituary in the local evening papers.[32]

After frantic preparations the 2/7th DWR and West Yorkshires paraded at 1700hrs on the 18th and, led by the DWR band, marched to the station where the locals turned out to cheer them on 'in spite of the misery and apprehension one could see in their faces.'[33] Whilst the DWR managed to have a train to themselves, the West Yorkshires were to share their packed train with Brigade HQ and attached engineer, pioneer and ordnance units as the three train convoy headed north. Their train finally pulled out of Blain station at 2100hrs and was followed an hour later by the Dukes. 'As darkness fell', wrote Major J.K. Parks of the West Yorkshires, 'it was noticed that cars, with headlights burning, were travelling in large numbers along the main roads southwards, though it is doubtful whether the full significance of this was realised by the men bumping along in the famous "*hommes 40. Chevaux 8.*"'[34] At 0430hrs on the 19th, the two battalions reached Le Mans and halted for breakfast. As they ate, the men watched trains crammed with refugees pass by in the opposite direction.

About the same time as the Dukes and West Yorkshires set out, the 2/4th KOYLI set out in pursuit of the rest of its brigade. Their journey from Rennes was so slow that men jumped off the train to answer the call of nature and then caught up and climbed back aboard, the KOYLI had little idea what awaited them although Lieutenant-Colonel Hodgkinson had heard through unofficial channels that they were en route to Arras, possibly for airfield defence.[35] Rex Flowers and a few friends had found a small map of France torn from a diary and were able to follow their progress via Laval and Argentan before finally reaching Rouen after 20 hours on the train. There, the KOYLI train was to join 137 Brigade's convoy north.

With dusk approaching, Amiens was already under attack and when the train carrying the 2/6th DWR was forced to pull back into Rouen it was realised that the main line north was now blocked. Without informing the battalions, RTOs made the fateful decision to change their destination from St Pol via Amiens to Bethune via Abbeville. The trains were switched to the coast line. They would travel via Dieppe, which had been designated a Red Cross port under the terms of the Geneva Convention. It was to act as the main medical centre and, protected under international law, there were no anti-aircraft defences. The decision to re-route troop trains violated its neutrality. German reconnaissance aircraft had spotted the movements of troop trains. Dieppe was now a legitimate target.

In the marshalling yards of Rouen, 137 Brigade and the KOYLIs made themselves as comfortable as possible for another night on the train. To the north, their sister battalions of 138 and 139 Brigade dug in as part of Macforce. Along the Canal du Nord, 69 Brigade were in position. To their right, 70 Brigade had received orders to begin to pull back to a line closer to Arras. 20 miles away, two battalions of 36 Brigade were heading for their new positions around Doullens. HQ 12th Division was desperately trying to establish some sort of contact with its brigades but failing. Barely equipped, poorly trained and with no news of the war, no direct communication with HQ or even between their own companies, the men of the digging divisions tried to make sense of what was going on.

And then the Germans blitzkrieg hit them full force.

NOTES

1 Beauman p 121
2 Freiser, *The Blitzkrieg Legend* p256
3 Gawthorpe, *Ca Ira* Vol XII June 1948 p223
4 Churchill, *The Second World War* Vol 2 p50
5 Ibid p56
6 Beauman p123
7 War Diary of 7RWK. WO 167/765
8 Beauman p124
9 War Diary 2/5th West Yorkshires. WO 167/853
10 Report on Macforce. WO197/118
11 Beauman papers. Report on L of C dated 25 June 1940
12 Rissik, *The DLI at War* p35
13 Sebag-Montefiore, p129
14 Report on Petreforce. WO197/118
15 *Tyneside Scottish, Harder than Hammers* 1947 p7
16 Ibid p8
17 Baggs, C.H. Imperial War Museum documents 94/49/1
18 Swinburne report in Sebag-Montefiore p133
19 Laidler, J. *A Slice of my Life.* Account held at Wakefield Local Studies Library p3
20 Believed to be 2759795 Private James Smith, whose age is given by the Commonwealth War Graves Register as 20 years old. Laidler states that he had lied about his age and was, in fact, just sixteen when he was killed on 20 May
21 War Diary 7RWK. WO 167/765
22 Blaxland p116
23 War Diary 7RWK. WO 167/765
24 Report on Petreforce. WO197/118
25 War Diary 7th Royal Sussex. WO 167/837
26 Estimates vary between 60 and as high as 100 according to sources. These figures are taken from the War Diary WO 167/837
27 Karslake p70
28 Glover p50
29 Karslake p69
30 Barclay, *The History of the Duke of Wellington's Regiment 1919–1952* p249
31 Taylor Report dated 2 Jun 1940 to Commander, X Brigade L of C in Gawthorpe papers IWM Document 78/44/1
32 *Ca Ira* Vol X No1 Sep 1940 p44
33 Barclay p249
34 Major Parks. Original manuscript in West Yorkshire Regiment Archive and edited account in Ca Ira Vol X No.4 June 1941 p181
35 Wylly, Col. H.C. *History of the King's Own Yorkshire Light Infantry* Vol V 1919 through to 1942, subtitled 'Never Give Up' 1950 p114

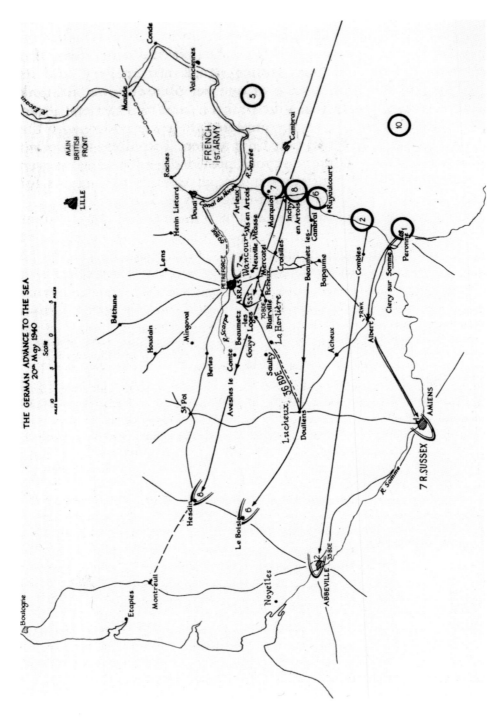

Sketch map of the German advance, 20 May 1940.

Chapter Eight

'Very brave, but very, very stupid'

0500hrs

As dawn broke on the morning of 20 May, a small truck belonging to the French 513th Battalion drove steadily along the road between the villages of Beaurains and Agny, just south of Arras. Corporal Marcel Binet and his three men, Victor Duquesnoy, Rene Ducrocq and Noel Odent, had all made the trip many times since the previous October. Mounted in the truck was a Hotchkiss machine gun and their role each night was to travel these roads as a mobile anti-aircraft patrol. As the sun rose, they began to head for home. They never made it. Tanks of the 7th Panzer Division found them and all four died in a hail of fire.[1]

As Binet and his men died, a few miles to the south the men of 70 Brigade were beginning yet another move. Petre had decided to pull his units back to form a stronger line north and west of Arras with the intention of falling back behind the La Bassee Canal line to the north. After days of marching, countermarching and attempting to dig in without tools, wire or effective weapons, the men had had little sleep and were exhausted. Their orders were now to head for the village of Thelus, north of Arras and a long night march began but Brigadier Kirkup then arrived with new orders. The situation was thought to have improved. Instead, they were now to head the other way, south to the village of Saulty, where they would be able to make contact with 36 Brigade, but since this meant another 20-mile march the Brigadier decided that they should rest up and send the battalion stores ahead of them. Then, using the trucks in a shuttle service, they could leapfrog each other to their destination. For the time being, 10DLI stopped at Mercatel, 11DLI at Wancourt and 1 Tyneside Scottish at Neuville-Vitasse, all places well known to older members of the regiment from the previous war. In Neuville-Vitasse, the Tynesiders found a group of 140 Pioneers and Ordnance Corps troops under the command of Staff Sergeant Perkins. The group had not seen an officer for over 24 hours and had not been told what they were expected to do. Between them, they carried 28 rifles and another 20 men carried boxes of Bren gun magazines but had no way to use them. They were taken under command. At around 0300hrs, the men finally had chance to grab some sleep.[2]

0600–0700hrs

The 7th RWK, having been given the option of choosing their own position, had established an anti-tank locality outside Albert. They then received orders to go back into

Lieutenant Colonel R. Gethen, 7th Battalion
Royal Sussex Regiment.

the town because, HQ insisted, the situation had 'materially improved' although when asked how, no answer was forthcoming. Having seen the effects of bombing in a built up area, Colonel Clay had his doubts but began the move at the insistence of his brigade commander, Brigadier Roupell. At 0200hrs they set out again, arriving around 0600hrs in the centre of town and parked in the cover of some trees. Within minutes, Stukas appeared and began their attack as the men ran to take up position.

To the north, the remainder of 36 Brigade had arrived in their positions around Doullens in the early hours and were now scraping out fighting holes along the railway line and putting up temporary roadblocks. To the west, 35 Brigade were still trying to find orders and the 12th Division's last two battalions, 4th Buffs and 2/6th Queen's – again without reference to divisional HQ – were told to prepare for a move by truck via Abbeville to Boulogne.[3] To the south, Colonel Gethen and his men of the Royal Sussex sat tight, waiting for instructions. Below the Somme, 137 Brigade had resumed its seemingly interminable trek north and was approaching the outskirts of Dieppe, where bombing attacks directed against the railway yards had already begun during the night.

0700–0800hrs

At around 0630hrs, German motorcycle troops had begun ordering civilians out of the village of Beaurains, warning them of the risk of heavy fighting in the area. Realising that the Germans intended to take Arras, the Chantrel family and others turned instead to the road south towards Mercatel. By 0645hrs, Madame Pruvost saw tanks heading rapidly towards Agny. By 0650hrs, the first refugees passed on the information to the men of 70 Brigade.

At 0700hrs, Colonel Swinburne gave orders for his men to begin the march. At intervals of 25 metres between sections, 100 metres between platoons and 400 metres between companies they would move tactically, leapfrogging by companies as they headed via Mercatel, Ficheux and Beaumetz to Saulty and the transport would operate a shuttle service, collecting the head of the column in each run. Even as they set out, German air activity was heavy. The confused orders had left 10DLI in Lattre but 11DLI had lost its HQ company which they assumed was still heading for Thelus, the original rendezvous. Two more companies were at Ficheux having rested there for the night. By now, the brigade was spread over a considerable area and a flight of Fairey Battles were seen attacking ground targets

German Panzer Kampfwagen II.

somewhere to the north, flown – although they didn't know it – by air force reservists from the Northumberland area.

In Albert, runners came to Colonel Clay with news that German tanks and motorcycles had been seen. One brought a report of 30 in one direction, another of 20 on the other side. Almost at once, tanks and armoured cars were advancing from all sides, appearing to have encircled the town already. The left forward company barricaded itself in a nearby house and held out as enemy artillery began to systematically destroy the building until the final few survivors surrendered. According to the historian Gregory Blaxland, 'the situation had become forlorn within two minutes of its developing.'[4] It was no wonder since another administrative error somewhere along the line had not corrected the problem at Clery – they had been issued the wrong ammunition. Two companies, caught as they attempted to get back onto their transport, were gunned down with barely a chance to fire back. Others took cover where they could and fought on, but neither the anti-tank rifles nor the guns made any impression.

By 0730hrs, tanks had reached the main square and Clay gave orders for his men to try to fight their way out to a rendezvous in the woods outside town, where around 250 later gathered. Separating them into small groups of around 20 men each, he told them to escape as best they could but with only two maps in the entire battalion, it was a long shot. Eventually, around 70 men under Captain Newbery reached Boulogne, many of them men who had become separated in the move from Clery days before. The rest were either killed or captured. The German war diary speaks of having encountered 'a troop of English artillery without ammunition on a field exercise'.[5] As Rolf Hertenstein, newly commissioned as a lieutenant in the 4th Panzer regiment of 2nd Panzer Division, later recalled, 'the British didn't even have their live ammunition ready! They had only blanks, because they hadn't expected us to advance so fast.'[6]

0800–0900hrs

To the north, 70 Brigade continued their move. At around 0830hrs, Colonel John Bramwell and the remaining elements of 11DLI were waiting in Wancourt for the transport to return when German tanks suddenly appeared. With no more than small arms available, the fight was short but vicious and Bramwell and his men surrendered only after hand-to-hand fighting in the village street. Reports of enemy tanks had by now reached Colonel Swinburne but he dismissed them as 'doubtful'. To the west, 137 Brigade was inching its way towards Rouxmesnil Junction outside Dieppe, held up by 'considerable rail congestion.'

By 0900hrs, all resistance in Albert ended. A desperate attempt by Lieutenant Brown to reach 36 Brigade HQ on a hijacked motorcycle failed but an engineer officer managed it in a stolen car. In their isolated pocket of resistance, the 6th RWK and 5th Buffs made ready; the only signs of the enemy were the three men dressed as pilots and a young woman carrying a small suitcase stopped by local villagers and handed over to the British, who passed them on to HQ.[7]

0900–1000hrs

At just after 0900hrs, Colonel Swinburne ordered Second Lieutenant Stordy to take two sections by truck to secure the right flank at the junction of the road to Ficheux. Taking a Bren and a Boys rifle, Stordy set out in the lead truck and took up position around the home of the Cagin family on the junction of the Bucquoy and Ficheux roads. At the same time, Lieutenant MacGregor was tasked with a reconnaissance towards Saulty and there he made contact with the left company of the Buffs.

Although the excellent 25pdr field gun was in service, many artillery units were equipped with the 18/25pdr gun, the venerable 18pdr of First World War fame re-bored to take the new ammunition. Those guns available to the Lines of Communication troops often lacked any sights and were supplied from repair depots.

Troops train with the .55in Boys Anti-Tank rifle. Virtually useless against tank armour, very few men trained to use the weapon and all feared its notorious recoil.

With everything apparently going to plan, Swinburne then set out in an 8cwt truck escorted by Second Lieutenant Cohen and three men to establish contact with brigade HQ, just three kilometres away at Barly. Behind him, seven trucks carrying HQ company and the AMPC and RAOC men followed along the road towards Ficheux. About 0915hrs, as the trucks drew near the Darras farm, machine guns of the 3rd Company, 8th Motorised Battalion of 8th Panzer Division opened up from their ambush.

Private Ross, in one of the trucks behind Swinburne, recalled:

We'd only travelled a short distance when we came under heavy machine gun fire. Our driver was killed and the lorry left the road after it had just passed in front of a farm, where there was a stable. One of our vehicles was on fire. Another with the water tank headed towards the fields. The enemy fire was coming from the South West … QSM Swordy, our oldest NCO, set up some defensive positions [but] we only had rifles and a single anti-tank weapon. As we had some casualties leaving the lorry, I received the order to set up a first aid post. I went behind the stable when all of a sudden, a fire broke out. There were a number of pigs with their skin on fire who were running in all directions. I then decided to take the wounded to the other side of the road towards a cattle trough. Piper Eadie and myself improvised a stretcher and carried those who couldn't walk to this new position.

Nearby, Private Malcolm Armstrong had also been in the convoy:

In my vehicle [39-year-old Private Arthur] Todhunter had been shot in the head. I was at the rear of the vehicle crouching down and shouting to him to get out which he couldn't do as he was already dead. There was panic everywhere. I went round to the left and saw a small tank approaching. We were given the order to fix bayonets to attack. Surprised, I noticed that the cannon turned towards me but I escaped death when he changed direction, fired and one of the other lads fell. With Private Albert Foster, who was killed later, we advanced along the side of the Pronier Farm. I was going to go in when a bullet or

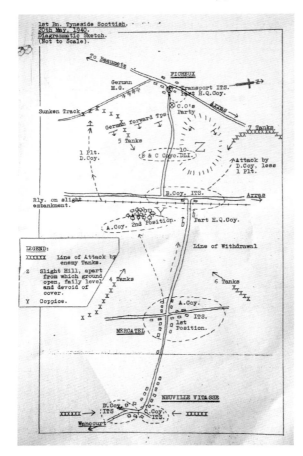

Left: A sketch of the position of 1st Battalion Tyneside Scottish on 20 May 1940.

Below: Sketch map of actions, 20 May 1940.

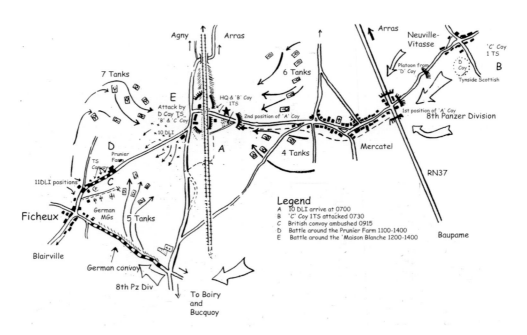

something similar struck my rifle and I dropped it. As I bent down to pick it up I was again saved when something just missed me. I then ran to an area behind this building and saw a dozen of my comrades mown down by machine gun fire. I quickly lay down behind them and was wounded by mortar fire. I put on a field dressing and, as there were Germans everywhere, I surrendered.[8]

The opening fusillade had hit the windscreen and engine of Swinburne's vehicle and set it on fire. Cut off from his battalion, he began making his way forward in the hope of reaching brigade HQ but found himself surrounded. He was eventually captured two nights later in the village of Avesnes-les-Comtes. Two men of the 11DLI he had found during his escape had been killed by fire from a French armoured column on the 21st.

Behind him, his battalion was in chaos. German infantry, tanks and armoured cars were closing in from all sides. In open ground, without cover or heavy weapons, the Tyneside Scottish stood little chance. The battle quickly deteriorated into a series of individual engagements. Company Sergeant Major Baggs later recalled that within minutes he had fourteen killed and six wounded as he and his men were caught in the open by enfilade fire. After struggling into the scant cover of the railway embankment, the Germans were able to bring up two tanks and blasted them out of their position. With no other option, Baggs surrendered.

Elsewhere, the Tynesiders were determined to go down fighting. At the Pronier Farm, Provost Sergeant Dick Chambers was seen to charge an enemy tank and was killed as he tried to fire through the slits in the turret. Company Sergeant Major Newton calmly strolled around his men's positions describing how 'interesting' the situation had become and how he had been wounded in this same area in the first war. Company Sergeant Majors Morris and Parmenter both took over Boys rifles whose crews had been killed and kept up what fire they could until they too were overrun. Lance Corporal Laidler carried with him regimental bagpipes that had been used in action at La Boiselle on 1 July 1916 when the pipers had led the attack, only to be gunned down. A junior NCO, only recently promoted, was heard giving textbook fire direction commands for targets just yards away – completely unnecessary but with a great effect of maintaining discipline – whilst two new recruits, wounded and manning a roadblock, refused to accept treatment and remained at their posts until overrun.

As fighting continued through the morning, exhausted men were seen to fall asleep even under fire. It was a one-sided battle, all the more so when a number of the Lewis guns that had been hurriedly issued on the Canal du Nord were found to be marked 'DP' – for drill purposes only and incapable of firing a shot. Despite these handicaps, though, Private James Laidler and his comrades of Recruit Company were determined to prove themselves. In a day of doomed courage, theirs was a story that epitomised the plight facing the digging divisions. 'Their ammunition expended', the Tynesider's history records,

a section of recruits with under eight weeks' training calmly obeyed the order to fix bayonets and meet the attack of an enemy AFV that was approaching them – a futile but heroic gesture. Surrender never occurred to them.[9]

In all, four Military Crosses, one Distinguished Conduct Medal, four Military Medals and twenty Mentions in Despatches were won but they came at a high price – reports vary, but estimates suggest that no more than 80 men escaped death or capture and that most of those captured surrendered only after being wounded.

An artist's impression of fighting in an unspecified French town.

Nearby, 11DLI had also been hit badly by both Rommel's 7th Panzer Division and SS Totenkopf and had almost entirely been killed or captured. A wounded sergeant managed to reach 10th battalion in Lattre to warn them and report that the 11th were now heading towards Hauteville. Colonel Marley of the 10th set out to make contact but, by sheer chance, was held up by a flock of sheep long enough for a message from HQ to reach him – Hauteville was in German hands. There was nothing Marley could do but try to gather together as many stragglers and survivors as he could. By the time night fell, of two battalions, 'C' Company of the 10th and the 140 AMPC men, just 233 all ranks had been accounted for.[10]

1000–1100hrs

Fighting raged around Ficheux all morning but elsewhere things remained relatively calm. At 1000hrs, HQ 12th Division put yet another call through to Arras but could find neither information nor orders. The decision was made by Petre's remaining staff to hand control over to Brigadier Wyatt, now redundant after his 37 Brigade had become hopelessly lost. Although Wyatt took command at 1030hrs, his first and most pressing need was to find anyone to issue orders to – it would be another 24 hours before contact could be made with the scattered remnants of the division and before some units received their first clear instructions for nearly four days.

At the moment, the German push was directed south of Arras, leaving 69 Brigade unscathed in their positions to the north east of the city. With almost nothing now in their path, the panzers pushed on towards the sea. Only three isolated pockets of resistance remained.

1100–1200hrs

Outside Amiens, Colonel Gethen and the 7th Royal Sussex remained stranded and the Colonel himself, possibly as a result of his injuries the day before, was becoming increasingly erratic. Just before 1100hrs, refugees reported that the Germans were just five miles away. When Sergeant Doidge reported this to the Colonel, he angrily replied: 'Don't talk rot, the Germans are not even 40 miles away' and went out to tell the guards that they 'could not trust a Frenchman' and that 'Jerry was 100 miles away.'[11] Not convinced, Doidge did as he was told.

From their positions outside Doullens, 36 Brigade had watched as German bombing became increasingly heavy throughout the morning. A gunner officer had reached them at 0930hrs with news of the loss of their sister battalion at Albert and a few lorries had managed to travel the Albert–Doullens road but none had thought to stop to warn the Quartermaster of the 6RWK, who was distributing rations when German troops found him.

In reply to the German attacks, a flight of RAF Blenheims are reported by some sources to have appeared overhead, trying to bomb concentrations of tanks reported earlier but who, by now, had moved on. (Georges had ordered a maximum effort by bombers but Ellis, however, notes that the only RAF raid of that day took place at around 1830hrs, so the flight overhead is likely to have been French aircraft or possibly misidentified German planes returning from a raid.) They were seen as a welcome reminder that 36 Brigade was not entirely alone, although they were certainly beginning to feel that way as the flood of panicked French troops through their positions continued. None could be persuaded to stay and in the end it was easier to simply let them through. At La Herliere, a woman was seen to tear down a propaganda poster in full sight of the fleeing troops. 'We will be victorious' it had read, 'because we are the stronger.'[12]

Still on their trains, 137 Brigade finally learned their destination was now Bethune. As news came through that the Amiens line was threatened, an alert railway worker had redirected the train carrying Brigade HQ and the West Yorkshires on to the coastal route towards Boulogne as it steamed through Abbeville. Behind them, though, bombing had hit the water replenishment facilities near Eu and the rest of the convoy was quite literally running out of steam as it fell farther and farther back. There was still a long way to go.

1200–1300hrs

It was a hot day, one of many. For Fred Clapham of the DLI, one abiding memory is of the discomfort this brought to any movement.

> [W]e were all wearing army issue woollen 'long johns' [and] our crotches were all sore with constant rubbing of the garments and perspiration. Consequently we were, after a few days, all marching with our legs as far apart as we could, officers included, and really looking at the blokes in front it must have looked quite comical.[13]

With the sun at its hottest, for the tired men of 36 Brigade any movement became an effort as they sat and waited. At noon, Brigadier Roupell visited the Buffs. There was little real information he could give them but, painfully aware of the fate of one of his battalions already, gave orders for them to retreat as soon as their position appeared untenable and to head for St Pol, 20 miles to the north.

The Buffs were hit first. Even as Roupell left just after midday, the Germans laid down a barrage of artillery fire in front of them, following it with sustained machine gun fire. Close behind it came motorcycles and armoured cars and by 1230hrs, attacks were coming in from both the east and the south as elements of 1st, 2nd and 6th Panzer Divisions all slammed into 36 Brigade. Almost immediately, the two forward companies were overwhelmed.

The Kents were hit soon afterwards. Roupell had asked them to hold as long as possible to give the Buffs time to disengage but by 1230hrs, tanks and infantry were already moving towards them in extended line. Without any means of communicating other than using runners, individual company commanders were left to guess at what might be happening. As the Germans pushed into gaps in the line, even runners had little chance of making it through. The two battalions fought on alone, neither knowing what the other was doing.

At around 1300hrs, the Buffs were ordered to pull back, but German infiltration by now made it almost impossible for units to communicate. One despatch rider from the left flank at La Herliere, for example, made the ten-mile journey into Doullens after having two bikes shot out from underneath him, narrowly dodging three tanks and killing two

Germans with his revolver.[14] Perhaps unsurprisingly, many messages did not get through to everyone and among those failing to make it was that to withdraw. Lone pockets of the Buffs held out, it was later found, for up to two hours, but with one Boys rifle for every two miles of front, there was little they could do but harass the enemy and delay the inevitable.[15] Nevertheless, their defiance had not gone unnoticed. The German war diary notes that 'ground could only be gained slowly and with continual fighting against an enemy who defended himself stubbornly.'

Meanwhile, to the south, General Guderian's 2nd Panzer Division had taken Amiens with so little difficulty that he took time out to visit the cathedral before deciding to push on to the sea. In the city, the Germans discovered four American volunteer ambulance drivers, Jack Clement, George King and Gregory Wait under the leadership of Donald Q. Coster of Montreal. All four men had paid their own expenses in order to work for the Red Cross in France and had made a last-minute dash into Amiens to try to evacuate the wounded but were now sheltering in the cellars of the Chateaudun Hospital as it took a direct hit in one of the many raids that morning. Now all was quiet. 'I can't tell you what an eerie feeling it was – this utter silence after an hour of inferno,' Coster later wrote.

> You could hear this silence – almost see it – with a tiny muffled noise underneath which was your own heart beat. At last it was broken by the clopping of heavy boots overhead. For terrible long minutes we held our breath, waiting for a grenade to be thrown down into our shelter. When none came, I suddenly decided that if I was to be killed I wanted to be above the ground. So I climbed up the stairs to the exit.[16]

Suddenly, Coster and his comrades found themselves in German hands and placed in charge of the 'German-American' hospital with orders to deal with civilian casualties.

What impressed Coster most of all was the sheer scale of the operation. 'You may have seen photographs of a Panzer column. But you haven't seen the endless stretch of it. You haven't seen its speed – roaring down the road at 40 miles an hour.' He wrote of watching tanks and armoured cars, vehicles with anti-aircraft guns mounted, trucks full of troops, guns of every calibre, trucks carrying boats and rafts and others filled with fuel for the tanks. Above all, though, he was impressed by the planning – every driver, it seemed, appeared to know exactly where he was going and drove through the streets as though he knew each one already. Within a short time, Amiens was secure. The next objective would be the Channel coast. From here, only one battalion now stood in Guderian's way – and they didn't know he was coming.

At noon, six Royal Army Service Corps lorries arrived at the 7th Royal Sussex position around St Roche. Their drivers had heard that Gethen's battalion were 'in a tight spot' and, acting without orders or any NCOs amongst them, had driven over to help. Gethen, still determined to stay put, ordered them to pick up their rifles and join his men. Quietly, during the afternoon, the drivers left.

1300–1400hrs

Although Guderian and his division were by now just a few miles away from St Roche and the stranded 7th Royal Sussex, Colonel Gethen refused to accept the reality of his situation. That morning he had visited the town and offered his help to the French commandant, only to be refused and told by two officers who claimed to have driven from there that there were 'no Germans between us and Sedan'.[17] So when, at around 1330hrs, Sergeant Doidge reported the sounds of artillery fire, Gethen insisted it was the French firing practice rounds. Soon afterwards, a report came in that the town had fallen. Gethen, still believing what the French staff had told him, immediately threatened to court-martial anyone who said the Germans were in Amiens. When a foot patrol led by Corporal Barnes of 'B' Company went there and saw for themselves, Gethen insisted that it was 'all lies' despite Barnes being supported by a captain of the Royal Engineers. Instead, he ordered Doidge to tell the men to take off their equipment and relax. Wisely, Doidge chose not to relay the command.

1400–1500hrs

At about 1400hrs, the first machine gun fire was heard. Recalling the French commander's assurances of the day before, Lieutenant Jackson dryly commented that it was 'fast moving from Sedan to Amiens overnight.' Ordered to charge their magazines with five rounds, many men could not believe an attack was imminent. After that, the regimental history describes a battle that was 'brief and suicidal'.[18]

Tanks had approached the forward companies and sprayed them with fire from their main and secondary armament. With only one Boys rifle and ten rounds of ammunition for it, there was little the men could do in return and they were quickly overrun. From then on, the battle became a confused series of clashes in fields of standing corn that would continue into the evening.

1500–1600hrs

Unaware of the unfolding disaster, 137 Brigade's slow journey continued as they passed through HQ 12th Division's area without any contact between them. All day they had seen trains heading south at intervals of just 500 yards crammed with refugees and fleeing French and Belgian soldiers, many making cutthroat gestures as they passed. Everywhere, traffic seemed to be getting heavier and, as the writer of the Dukes' history put it, 'one wondered whether one would be taking such a detached interest if these events were happening at home.'[19] Several men would later recall this detachment and describe how watching through the open doorway of their dark cattle trucks made it feel as though they were looking at a newsreel on a cinema screen. Still believing themselves to be heading north for labour duties, events outside seemed to have little to do with them.

Throughout the afternoon, the three trains carrying the KOYLI, 2/6th and 2/7th Dukes had picked their way northward, stopping repeatedly for air raids. At one stop, Colonel Llewellyn of the 2/6th managed to speak to the stationmaster and the two armed policemen guarding the station building. Although determined to stay at his post, the stationmaster warned that the pumps used to provide water for the engines had been put out of action by saboteurs and that news from other stations indicated that the Germans were not far away. After a brief conference on board the train, Llewellyn ordered that ammunition should be made ready and that officers should pay close attention to the terrain around the train at all times.

The track from Dieppe travels north to the line of the Somme and then turns right for a long, straight run alongside the canal into the city. As the trains moved along this open and exposed route around mid-afternoon, the German air forces hit Abbeville with a vengeance. Aboard the KOYLI train, Rex Flowers knew nothing of what was going on outside.

We were still in ignorance of the true situation. We were idly watching a squadron of planes approaching, they were not very high. We thought that they were ours! What a laugh, we never made the same mistake again. If you classed all planes as enemy ones, you

Above: Luftwaffe aircrew confident in their domination of the skies.

Left: Luftwaffe bomber's eye view of an Allied convoy under attack.

were never wrong … The planes came nearer, very near, voices could be heard, shouting. I could see plainly to my horror, the planes had got black crosses on them! I could hear now, what they were shouting, 'it's Jerry, it's Jerry!' They were very low, I cannot give an estimate except they were very low indeed. There was no opposition you see. The train stopped with a jerk and we were all ordered off. We did not need any prompting. We all jumped off to the left into a small field. One chap, [Lance Corporal Sam Hunt] I can see him now, jumped off to the right, straight into the River Somme. He got out alright, but got his leg well and truly pulled. Even more so a bit later, he took his wet trousers off and put some long johns on, of all things. I shall never forget that sight.[20]

Trapped between the canal to their left and the marshes to their right, there was little to laugh at as the battalions detrained and took cover where they could until the raid passed. As they gathered themselves together, the driver of the first train reported that he needed to uncouple the engine to get water in Abbeville station. He was never seen again. For now, the KOYLIs were completely stranded.

About a mile behind, the two trains carrying the Dukes had also stopped. The bombing missed the train itself but Colonel Llewellyn vividly recalled 'seeing parts of cows and tree trunks falling from above.'[21] As they watched the raid develop, several men, not having seen flak bursts before, reported seeing parachutists and alarm quickly spread among the ranks. Around 40 aircraft were spotted in a raid lasting around half an hour but just when it seemed it was over, another eighteen appeared and more bombing followed, creating widespread panic among the refugees.

When at last it seemed it was over, the KOYLI attempted to regroup around the train but found their ranks having to open to allow streams of refugees past. Sergeant Brown, the memory of his night out drinking champagne in Rennes a distant memory, watched in horror as a young girl of about eighteen ran through the ranks laughing hysterically, behind her a woman in mourning clothes led by her mother, both looking 'broken in spirit'. Yet all around, he noted, was a fine summer's day, the sunshine and birdsong contrasting sharply with the smoke and the wave of battered humanity pouring out of the city.

1600–1700hrs

On the other side of the city, 35 Brigade watched the bombing from their positions east of the Somme. Still without definite orders, the brigade could clearly see and hear that things were going wrong but had no idea of where the enemy were supposed to be. Worse, they had no idea where 37 Brigade were. Since it was supposed to be holding their southern flank, 35 Brigade was now open to encirclement. Their first indication came at 1630hrs when a small party of the 2/6th Queen's set out on foot from Drucat to deliver a message to the 2/7th near Vauchelles. En route they were found by a German patrol. One man was killed but Sergeant Toster was able to get word back to Colonel Bolton that the enemy had arrived. Already, the two battalions had been cut off from each other.

By then, the advance elements of the 2/7th, astride the Doullens road, were already under attack. Having been given orders not to set up tactical positions, the 2/7th had occupied buildings and set up roadblocks but lacked the means to make either secure. The six rounds per Boys rifle were soon used up and, yet again, the Germans were able to bring their tanks up and spray the battalion with machine gun fire. At 1415hrs Brigadier Wyatt had ordered him to 'Carry out recce for withdrawal of one battalion across the Somme to protect right flank, also to consider manner of withdrawal of remainder of brigade across river.'[22] Realising that the situation was hopeless, the CO decided to withdraw across the Somme – a move that had previously been agreed with the brigade commander, Brigadier de Cordova.

Sending a despatch rider with the orders, Bolton watched as his first two companies began to fall back before leaving to reconnoitre a crossing point over the Somme. In fact, only one company had received the order. What he had seen was his two companies withdrawing on their own initiative into the relative protection of the village of Vauchelles. Since the village lay off the main road, the two and a half companies who had made it into cover were simply bypassed and rounded up by tanks and infantry the next day. About 100 men were able to escape and cross the river with the CO.

To the north, Colonel Bolton and his men sat tight. Their position, too, lay off the main axis of advance and they were ignored. That night, using his privately purchased compass – the only one available to the battalion – he managed to extricate almost all his men across a bridge some miles upriver, losing only one platoon who acted as rearguard.

1700–1800hrs

The Royal Sussex had been destroyed as a fighting force in minutes but isolated pockets held out. Second Lieutenant Sevenoaks had been leading a platoon on patrol when the attack came and had chanced across Colonel Gethen driving a car, who told him to get back to the battalion. They had tried, but ran into a tank after a short distance and had taken cover in a thicket as the battle raged. They were still there.

Just as among the Tynesiders, there were many acts of courage. After firing smoke bombs – the only mortar ammunition they had – Colonel Gethen ordered his men to fix bayonets. As the smoke cleared, they advanced across a ploughed field, directly at the enemy tanks. Major Miller, OC 'B' Company, was seen charging a stalled tank and firing through the gun slits before he was cut down; it was a futile gesture. Just before 1800hrs, word spread among the survivors that they should try to escape. No-one was certain where the order originated although one man reported being told by his officer that he should 'go while the going's good – it's suicide here.'[23] One by one they began to edge away. Private Burtenshaw later reported seeing Colonel Gethen, his head covered only by a bandage, watching his battalion die. As he went forward at around 1730hrs to try to get an idea of what was happening, he was confronted by a line of enemy tanks just 100 yards away.

To the west, Wyatt had finally heard about the fate of the West Kents and Buffs and decided to pull 35 Brigade back. At 1715hrs, a message was sent; 'Enemy reported at 1200 hrs today in vicinity of Doullens with AFVs. 35 Brigade will withdraw across the Somme and take up positions on west bank covering roads Abbeville – Blagny and Abbeville – Eu. Right flank will be refused to cover approaches from South.'[24] The message crossed with a report by de Cordova timed 1755hrs 'reporting indications of enemy approach', shortly followed by another stating 'enemy AFVs in area'. As communications broke down, a brigade officer was sent to try to contact Divisional HQ but returned at 1945hrs with the news that he had met German tanks in Abbeville and had not been able to contact Brigade.

Brigadier de Cordova ordered a withdrawal across the Somme, little knowing that the order had already gone out and that, by now, his battalions were no longer fit to carry them out.

1800–1900hrs

Along the Somme Canal, the crew of 137 Brigade's second train had also absconded. As the official history of the Dukes noted;

> in consequence a senior warrant officer was put in charge of the engine driver and fire-man of the Dukes' train and they were informed that they would not be allowed to leave. They became very excited, but eventually bowed to the inevitable and proved to be a couple of stalwarts who did magnificent work.[25]

Other sources make it clear that 'the inevitable' involved the Regimental Sergeant Major and a large bayonet with the support of their French liaison officer and his pistol. Colonels Llewellyn and Taylor conferred. It was unclear what was happening and, not having been briefed properly, they had no idea of where Brigade HQ and the West Yorkshires had gone. Taylor briefed Captain Gerrard and the battalion's liaison officer, Thomas de Strahlborn, for a recce into town.

Up ahead, Colonel Hodgkinson had left a guard on the KOYLI train and led the rest of the battalion and the attached engineers along the tracks towards Abbeville, planning to cross the canal using the wooden bridge at Pont Laviers and establish positions on the northern bank. At that point he had heard no reports of ground fighting and it was still hoped that they could skirt the bombing of the city and pick up the St Pol road on the other side to continue their journey. Even under ideal conditions it was an optimistic plan since there had been no opportunity to undertake many route marches in training but now, with the men tired and hungry after their long journey, their water bottles almost empty and the ballast of the tracks making progress slow and painful, problems began almost immediately. Packs and boots rubbed skin raw and the heavy air presence made it necessary to take cover every few minutes. Sergeant Brown, leading a platoon from HQ Company, also noted the rumble of gunfire to the east and mentioned it to Lieutenant Aykroyd who calmly told him it was anti-aircraft fire. As he looked to the east, however, Brown noticed a lot of firing, but few bursts of flak like those they had seen earlier. He also saw French units quietly slipping away in the river of refugees pouring across the Pont Laviers bridge and bringing with them rumours of tanks already in the city. It soon became clear that the plan was not going to work. Reluctantly, the battalion turned back towards the train.

1900–2000hrs

After an hour's standoff, a German tank suddenly lurched toward Gethen's position and he was forced to surrender. He was made to accompany the tank around the battlefield, ordering his men to give up the fight as around twenty tanks broke cover. As Gethen later wrote from his prison camp;

> It would appear that the battalion's action amounted to a bluff, which succeeded in delay-ing the enemy advance in this area for at least six hours and probably till next morning. They could have cleared our position in five minutes had they known the real situation.[26]

To the west, the sound of artillery fire was joined by that of small arms and machine guns as the Dukes' recce party found Abbeville in chaos with British and French soldiers all reporting a ground attack in progress. After hearing the report, Colonel Taylor went forward himself and found 'the station was in flames and I saw sailors who had been ordered to get back to Rouen under their own arrangements. A French officer said that the town had been evacuated by Allied troops; machine gun and artillery fire were heard quite near.'[27] It was clear to Taylor that his men were in a very poor defensive position where they were and, at another trackside conference, he persuaded Colonel Llewellyn that the two battalions should pull back down the track to a position on higher ground. A message was sent to the KOYLI second in command to explain the plan but with the battalion still dispersed across the canal he could only acknowledge it and say he would wait for his commander's decision.

'With the help of M Strahlborn who again showed great energy and zeal', Taylor reported a few days later, 'the drivers and guards of the train, who had strongly expressed their intention to leave, were finally persuaded to link the two trains together and withdraw along the same line to a more suitable tactical position.'[28] Work began immediately.

2000–2100hrs

The last resistance of the Royal Sussex fell just before 2000hrs when the final positions were overrun. Lieutenant Jackson, wounded four times in the battle, was congratulated by his captor and offered a lift in a staff car to get treatment. He refused and stayed with his men. It was a tense time. Major Cassels, the battalion second in command, had been shot out of hand for his reluctance to raise his hands in surrender and, aware already of the Nazi attitude towards Jews, Lieutenant Cohen faced an uncertain future.[29]

At the 'German – American' hospital in Amiens, Coster and his men were told to bring in the casualties from the fighting and assigned a driver to take them out to the scene.

> It was a real battlefield. Fortunately it was too dark to get the full effect. A company of young Tommies had attacked the main column of the mechanised Germans. Like mosquitoes attacking a locomotive – and been wiped out. Amongst all the dead and terribly wounded British, we didn't come across a single German casualty; if there had been any, they had already been removed to maintain morale. The story was current that Germans who fell were at once flown back to Germany to hide them from their own comrades.[30]

After a fitful night's sleep, Coster was sent out again the next morning.

> Under a hot, cloudless sky lay a wide field of high grass, simply covered with the English dead and wounded, and wounded and dead cattle. The British boys had been massacred by the tanks, as they had no artillery, only a few light machine guns to supplement their rifles – about as effective against a tank's armour as a pea-shooter. Their only hope had been to score a lucky hit through a gun slit. Here as last night we didn't find a single dead or wounded German. Out of possibly 300 British, we picked up maybe 25 or 30. The rest had all been killed. Many of the wounded had been run down by tanks, their bodies flattened like pancakes. Others, caught by the cross machine-gun fire of the encircling tanks, had been almost cut in two before they fell. Every fourth or fifth bullet from these guns is a tracer which burns through the body like a white-hot poker. It was hard to locate all the wounded in the high grass; the hot sun was overhead when we got the last of them up, and I don't have to remind you what that means in a battlefield.

The work of recovering the Sussex's dead and wounded continued for days. Coster would particularly remember the behaviour of Captain George Cook of HQ Company who had lain on the field for two days before being found. Despite several wounds to his arm he walked himself to the operating theatre, passing a group of French soldiers on the way. Hearing the French complaining about the war, the lack of facilities and the lack of food available in the makeshift hospital, an exasperated Cook asked Coster 'What are we expected to do – sail our English fleet right up the bloody Seine to cheer these chaps up?'

2100–2200hrs

The Dukes' trains began their slow journey back along the track at 2120hrs with enthusiastic volunteers working the second engine. With two trains coupled together, the strain on the couplings was enormous and there were frequent breaks. Colonel Llewellyn would recall how the couplings would then be repaired only for the sudden jerking movement of the train to break another almost immediately and that they could move only at a snail's pace, all the while very much aware of how vulnerable they were. As darkness fell, the risk of air attack lessened but progress remained slow. The lack of water and the incline they were attempting to reverse up threatened to burn out one engine and the fires had to be drawn, leaving just one engine to pull the whole train. Then, close to the crossing point of St Marc, another sudden jerk ripped the floor of the mess truck out completely, dumping the passengers and their kit onto the tracks. The line ahead was blocked by the wrecks of trains hit by bombing and others that had run into the back of the bombed trains. This was the end of the line. It was midnight.

2200–2359hrs

12th Division's last two battalions, 2/6th East Surreys and 4th Buffs, had been ordered by Arras to move from Rouen to Montreuil where they were to protect GHQ at their planned new location but reached the Somme too late to get across. Instead they reported to 12th Division at 1900hrs and were sent to guard the crossing of the Bresle, the next river south of the Somme. Soon afterwards they were joined by some light anti-aircraft guns which had escaped from Abbeville airfield and had crossed the river at Port le Grand. By late that night, they were the only planned positions holding the northern flank of the Lines of Communication.

At Amiens, Lieutenant Sevenoak and his platoon emerged from their thicket and began to trudge south, hoping to reach British lines below the Somme.

Around Ficheux, stragglers made their way back towards Arras, among them Private Thomas Dabner. Dabner would be captured the next day and ordered to drive a truck filled with wounded men at the rear of a German convoy. That night, seizing his chance, he skidded around a road junction and drove off at speed, later delivering the wounded to a British hospital.

At Doullens, Brigadier Roupell and his staff were picking their way through the woods to evade their attackers. A German patrol had reached brigade HQ early in the evening and had been held back by a single sentry, but it was now a matter of personal survival for what remained of 36 Brigade.

To the north, 137 Brigade HQ and the 2/5th West Yorkshires steamed on towards Boulogne whilst the KOYLIs prepared to begin the long walk back to Dieppe and the Dukes set up all round defence, now at least with some idea where they were thanks to a copy of *Bradshaw's Railway Guide to Central Europe* donated by a officer's batman.

Coster noted the comment of one of his patients when asked about the German panzer columns; 'Beautiful to watch, but terrible to receive.' In the last eighteen hours, the untrained men of the digging divisions had had their first taste of combat and had been slaughtered. 'Not even during the murderous engagements on the Somme or at

Left: British POW after the battle. The German caption simply says he is 'a survivor'.

Below: A makeshift cemetery at the Prunier Farm for casualties of the Ficheux battle.

German troops in the ruins of Amiens.

Passchendaele', wrote Basil Karslake of the loss of the Royal Sussex, 'had any unit suffered such casualties.'[31] Accurate figures are hard to come by. The dates of death of many casualties could only be estimated later as sometime in May or even June. Some died of wounds days or even weeks later, others in captivity later in the war. The best estimates suggest that around 131 men of the 7th Royal Sussex are known to be buried in Commonwealth War Graves, along with a possible further 38 men marked as unknown who may well be linked to the Amiens action. What is known is that 701 men were embarked on the train and only 70 could later be accounted for when the battalion regrouped. For the 6th West Kents, 75 men returned to England, 503 men were posted as missing.[32] Of the Buffs, 80 got back, leaving behind 525 of their comrades.[33]

Elsewhere, 70 men of 7RWK under Captain Newbury reached Boulogne. They and the 50 men of the rear party left in Rouen were all that could be found. Of the Tyneside Scottish, over 100 men were known to have died in the fighting along with 50 of the attached 10DLI company and an unknown number of the RAOC and AMPC troops – around 450 men of the battalion were lost. Of 35 Brigade's 2,400 men, almost half were lost – 1,234 made it to Rouen. By midnight, 12th Division had been destroyed as a formation; 23rd Division had lost one of its two brigades and 46th Division had been scattered across France, all cohesion lost. In contrast, the BEF's fighting in Belgium over the past ten days had cost the entire force some 500 men.

They had achieved all that had been expected of them – although that wasn't much – and had bought a few hours for Gort to strengthen his southern flanks. For the Germans, the resistance they met was both surprising and pathetic, their histories referring almost sadly to what they called 'the children's division'. Clearing the field at Amiens, Coster noted how German troops responded sympathetically to the wounded. '"Very brave," one of the Germans remarked to me, "but very, very stupid."'

Notes

1 Coilliot, A. *Mai 1940: Un Mois Pas Comme Les Autres* Arras 1980 p68. As Coilliot explains, the date of death for these men is given as 23 May but this is almost certainly the day of discovery. German war diaries show that 7 Panzer Division were in this area at 0500hrs on the 20th and firmly in occupation by the 23rd. No offensive Allied action took place in this area after 21 May.

2 *Harder Than Hammers*. See also Rissik, *The DLI at War*

3 Blaxland p127

4 Ibid p119

5 Ellis, *The War in France and Flanders* p80

6. Rolf Hertenstein, Interview with Mulcahy, R. 'Blitzkreig's Beginnings' in *World War II* magazine March 2006 p55

7 Coilliot p72

8 Accounts supplied by Adrian Noble, whose father, Lieutenant Noble, served with 1TS

9 *Harder than Hammers*, p15

10 Archivist and Librarians' General Series 1200/21(B), pp113–114. W.D./B.E.F./131/7/E, 70th Bde., May. Quoted in Ellis p79

11 War Diary 7th Royal Sussex. WO167/837

12 Blaxland p121

13 Shaw, F. & J. *We Remember Dunkirk* Oxford 1997 p162

14 Blaxland p122

15 Ellis p80–81 notes that the 'German War Diary says they met for the first time "English troops who fought tenaciously (a battalion of the Buffs) ... The battle for Doullens claimed the whole attention of the troops. In spite of the use of numerous tanks it was only possible to break down their resistance after about two and a half hours."' Archivist and Librarians' General Series. 1200/21(a), p32; A.L. 748; A.L. 2012. See also Glover p55.

16 Coster, D.Q. *Behind German Lines* In *Readers' Digest*, November 1940

17 Glover, p56

18 Martineau, GD. *A History of the Royal Sussex Regiment* Chichester 1953 p232

19 Barclay, *History of the Duke of Wellington's Regiment* p250

20 Flowers. Unpublished account

21 Barclay p201

22 Summary of operations by units of 12 Division May – June 1940 WO 197/98

23 War Diary 7th Royal Sussex. WO167/837

24 Summary of operations by units of 12 Division May – June 1940 WO 197/98

25 Barclay p250

26 Report prepared at Oflag IXA in August 1942. WO167/837

27 Colonel Taylor's report to HQ L of C dated 2 Jun 40. Gawthorpe papers IWM 78/44/1

28 Ibid

29 Cohen survived captivity despite having proudly stepped forward when German officials demanded to know if any Jews were held in his camp.

30 Coster, op cit.

31 Karslake, p67

32 Chaplin, H.D. *The Queen's Own Royal West Kent Regiment 1920–1950* London, 1954 p32

33 Knight, C.R.B. *Historical Record of the Buffs (Royal East Kent Regiment) 3rd Foot 1919–1948* London 1951 p76

Chapter Nine

'We happen to be going that way'

Oblivious of the disaster behind them, 137 Brigade HQ and the West Yorkshires continued north via Etaples, Boulogne and Calais before turning inland to St Omer, which they reached in the early hours of the 21st after three nights aboard the train and having had very few rations during that entire period. 'By this time,' wrote Brigadier Gawthorpe,

> I felt it was desirable to be in touch with someone in authority instead of just in the hands of the French railway authorities, so I used the station telephone and got put through to Movement Control at GHQ … I gathered they were glad to hear of my whereabouts, but would have preferred to hear of an armoured brigade, which was being sought.[1]

Instead of the hoped for orders, Gawthorpe was told to make for Hazebrouck and to get in touch with any British HQ he could find there. Leaving the train, he then drove by car through Merville and Estaires and finally found his way to 46th Divisional HQ at Sailly-sur-la-Lys, an area Gawthorpe was familiar with; like many of the older men he had fought there many years before.

Gawthorpe found his Divisional Commander, General Curtis, in a reflective mood. He had been called forward earlier and 'his breezy greeting on arrival at GHQ, Arras, from the base area – "Well, where's the enemy? What am I to do?" – came like a gush of mountain air through the oppressive gloom of the vaults of St Vaast.'[2] Even his enthusiasm, though, was blunted by the role assigned to him. He was now to command 'Polforce', another improvised unit presented with the task of defending the right flank of the BEF and preventing the enemy reaching Dunkirk. By now, Curtis seems to have been regretting his flamboyant claim to have a combat-ready division at his disposal and it is noticeable that the official record has since been amended to read that his mission was to 'try defending' the line of the La Bassee Canal between Aire and La Bassee itself. This line was eventually extended to reach Watten in the north – a distance of around 40 miles and at the moment all he had been given to achieve this was one battery of 25-pounder guns and 'units of the division at present en route by rail to the Seclin area.'[3] Since those elements sent to Seclin had already been taken into Macforce, Curtis was left with 137 Brigade and the KOYLIs – if they could be found. With just one battalion under command, Gawthorpe found he was to expect reinforcements when they could be located but for now he was to hold the line just north of Bethune from Hinges to St Omer – a distance of 24 miles and with no fewer than eighteen bridges. With communications between brigade and battalion HQs limited to what could be achieved by a few officers on borrowed bicycles, it was immediately clear that the best they would be able to do would be to deny them the bridges and force the Germans to mount a river crossing operation – a delay of a matter of hours.

The West Yorkshires, in the meantime, had been taken off the train and told to take up defensive positions around the town with orders to hold it 'to the last man, the last round.'[4] Lieutenant-Colonel Pulleyn and the officers of the battalion began hastily making hand drawn copies of the only available map on scraps of paper to help organise the perimeter.[5] It was with some relief that they now found themselves told to reboard the train and head for Hazebrouck and on to Bethune where they arrived at 1500hrs to face their next problem. The battalion stores amounted to some seventeen tons of equipment but in the chaos behind them the battalion transport had been cut off and they had just two small trucks with which to shift it. Taking only the essentials and pausing to take cake, tinned fruit and cigarettes from an abandoned NAAFI canteen they set out to a position in woods outside the town where almost immediately they came under air attack. It was met with a barrage of small arms fire and they were excited to see one bomber burst into flames. Although secretly they suspected a nearby anti-aircraft gun had scored the hit, several rifle-men claimed it for themselves.

At 1700hrs the battalion received orders to take up a defensive position covering six miles of the La Bassee Canal between Hinges just outside Bethune and the Lillers–St Venant road bridge. Colonel Pulleyn and his second-in-command Major Parks set out at once for the village of Robecq leaving orders for Captain Dunscombe-Anderson and their French liaison officer, M. Taupin to bring the battalion to the village later. After a confused night march, HQ and two rifle companies reached their position just after mid-night but their two other companies got lost and wandered into Calonne, two miles away. It was not until dawn that they finally found the battalion again.

Their front now covered two main roads and several smaller bridges over the canal, all crammed with refugees. The canal itself was filled with French and Dutch barges and Gawthorpe considered what to do about them. Permission to attempt to burn the wooden boats was denied – in any case they would not be fully destroyed that way while they were in the water and there were not enough explosives available for a more thorough job. A further problem lay in the fact that the metal barges only had to sink a matter of two or three feet before settling on the bottom of the canal and forming pontoons for any attacker to cross. The only solution, it seemed, was to keep them moving and to prevent any tying up side by side and effectively bridging the canal. Having been allocated just two military policemen on motorcycles for the entire area, Gawthorpe realised that traffic control was beyond them and used them instead as dispatch riders, sending out infantry patrols to try to keep the canal as clear as possible.

By the evening of the 21st Gawthorpe was painfully aware that the West Yorkshires were desperately short of weapons and that further north several bridges along his sector were unguarded except for small parties of Royal Engineers preparing them for demolition. Promised that more troops were on the way, he was able to gather together a small force of experienced men from the leave transit camp at Don and these 'Don details' were quickly fed into the line to plug the many gaps.

The 22nd was spent putting the canal line into a state of defence as GHQ moved to the Hazebrouck area with the news that more troops from the regular divisions were on their way. The canal line was the first of many waterways between La Bassee and Dunkirk and only around St Omer was there a direct route that might allow the panzers to strike.

Map of the Canal Line sketched
by Brigadier Gawthorpe.

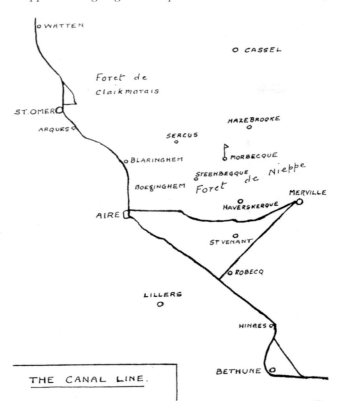

Three lorry loads of anti-
tank mines had been sent out
and all the bridges prepared
for demolition. Armoured
support had been promised
for the next day and French
troops were arriving to take
over. Better news came with
the arrival that evening of
four French 75mm guns
under Lieutenant Vibert and
a company of Renault R35
light tanks belonging to the
9eme Bataillon de Chars
de Combat (9th BCC or
Combat Tank Battalion).
Each carrying a death's head
badge modelled on that of
the German hussars who had
burnt down the family farm
of its commander, Colonel Gauthier in 1914, the tank battalion had also had a confusing
war having been sent north from St Omer to try to link with the Dutch at Breda and had
been directed to the North Sea coast at Ijzendijke on the 17th before turning back south.
They had been south of Ostend by the 20th and had arrived in the Lillers area late on
the 21st before being dispersed around Bethune. Elements of the 2nd Company under
Lieutenat Braillon had been assigned the Robecq region but were still under the command of the local French HQ and expected to head north again the next day.[6] Like the
British, the French were now improvising forces. General Tarrit of 1e DINA (Division
d'infanterie Nord-Africaines), whose men had been among the very few to hold their
ground at Sedan, was now in command of 'Groupement Tarrit' with his Moroccan and
Algerian riflemen taking position between the village of Cuinchy and the West Yorkshires'
flank at Robecq. They were supported by a small number of guns and elements of 22eme
BCC, also equipped with R35 light tanks. Commandant St Leger made a reconnaissance
with Captain Dunscombe-Anderson to see how the posts could be strengthened.[7]

As Gawthorpe struggled to fill the gaping voids in his defence line, the German advance
had passed to the south of Arras and was swinging northwards. Heading straight towards
him were three heavily armed divisions – the Wehrmacht's 3rd Panzer Division and two
SS formations, the SS-Verfugungsdivision (SS-VT – literally 'Special Reserve Troops' and
later renamed the 'Das Reich' Panzer Division) and the SS-Totenkopf (Death's Head).
Unlike the SS-VT, the Totenkopf had not been raised as a military unit but as a police
unit to provide concentration camp guards, and had already earned the distrust of their
Wehrmacht colleagues for their thuggish behaviour in Poland – instead of hunting down
resistance in the countryside as ordered they had spent their time swaggering around the

Colonel Recknagel, commander of Infanterie Regiment 54, 18th Infantry Division, whose men fought through the rearguard action of 139 Brigade, 46 Infantry Division on the Dunkirk perimeter.

Colonel Bohnstedt of Infanterie Regiment 51, the sister unit of Infanterie Regiment 54, also involved in the action on the perimeter.

towns bullying Jews. Under their fanatical commander, Theodor Eicke, recruits had been required to renounce their religion and swear loyalty only to the Führer and were well versed in Nazi ideology. Following much political manoeuvring, Eicke had had his unit assigned combat duties after a winter of intensive military training. Held in reserve during the first attacks, the Totenkopf were humiliated by rumours – fuelled by Rommel and his men – that the SS had turned and run in their first encounter with British tanks at Arras. Their response had been to murder 92 civilians in the town of Aubigny-en-Artois and another 45 in the villages of Vandelicourt and Berles-Montchel, both acts committed early on 22 May as they headed towards the canal line.

Also moving north that day were the remnants of those units by-passed by the Arras attack. Elements of the British 2nd, 44th and 48th Divisions were all beginning to arrive in the Bethune–La Bassee area and by nightfall, Gawthorpe's command had expanded with the allocation of troops from two Royal Engineer Chemical Companies, two RE Field Companies, three Belgian anti-tank guns, one company each of 9RNF and the Don Detail battalion, some artillery and a mixed group of RASC and anti-aircraft gunners reassigned as infantry. As he left a conference at Polforce HQ to head for St Omer that evening, his car came under fire from a German reconnaissance armoured car on the far bank. At St Omer, he heard that German tanks had been seen in the woods between the town and the port of Boulogne. The order went out to demolish the bridges. At 'D' Company's position outside Robecq, 33-year-old Private Robert Fenwick became the battalion's first fatal casualty – killed by a piece of flying masonry as the bridge exploded at 1945hrs. The company had been due to hand over their positions to 'B' Company at 2000hrs and there had been no warning that the bridge was about to be blown.[8] A few hours earlier, a patrol of six men had been sent out under Sergeant Wilbey and Lance Corporal Poller to bring in the pilot of a German aircraft shot down over the south bank. They had not returned. Then, at around 2100hrs, the first probing attacks began.

Treading more carefully after the counterattack of the previous day, the SS-VT were also in position near Aire. Hauptsturmführer (Captain) Johannes Muhlenkamp's 15th Motorcycle Infantry Company equipped with motorcycles and machine guns on side cars had reached the canal by that afternoon and were quickly followed by an artillery battalion and the division's three infantry regiments, the 'Deutschland', 'Der Führer' and 'Germania'. Once there, General Hausser ordered them to prepare for a defence to the north-east, with Germania providing defence in depth.

Orders now went out to 23rd Division's 69 Brigade to begin a move from their positions at Seclin south of Lille to the canal line from St Omer to Gravelines on the coast. After a long wait, they set out after dark but GHQ then decided that the need was greater in their old positions than at their destination. Frantic efforts by staff officers managed to find the convoy at Estaires, just behind the canal line at around 0300hrs and turn it around but by then brigade HQ had disappeared and was not seen again until after the evacuation. The 6th Green Howards never received the message and continued on their way with the divisional engineers, being placed under the command of Rustyforce when they alone reached Gravelines. After a six-hour journey that served only to further tire the exhausted men, 69 Brigade found themselves back where they started.

They were, though, luckier that their erstwhile colleagues of 9RNF. Late in the evening it had been decided to send a company into St Omer to bolster the French garrison. Armed with the best weapons that could be found for them, the trucks were waved into the burning town only to find themselves surrounded by the Germans. The entire company was captured without a chance to send a warning back across the canal. A convoy of five RASC trucks had also been sent with vague instructions to pick up troops for an anti-tank patrol which included the instructions to ram any tank they encountered. They too had disappeared.[9]

Shortly after midnight, isolated shots rang out along the line of the canal as SS patrols probed forward on either side of the West Yorkshires' line. As yet, only the lead elements of the 3rd Panzer Division were at the southern bank opposite them. To the north, Untersturmführer (Second Lieutenant) Schulze approached the outskirts of Aire at the head of a small motorised column containing his reinforced platoon of the SS-VT and a few anti-tank guns. He had been tasked with securing the Aire bridge and in the pitch dark-ness he took his troops into the town. About halfway along the street, Schulze found his path blocked by a vehicle and realised it was part of a column stretching down the road and creeping forward. Assuming that they were tanks of 3rd Panzer outside their sector he tagged along behind as they made their way through the town. The stop/start movement of the tanks infuriated him and, impatient to get on with his mission, he climbed aboard the nearest tank and rapped on the turret with his pipe only to be greeted by a torrent of French.

Wisely keeping quiet, he dismounted and ordered his men to unhitch the anti-tank guns and move them to the side of the street. They opened fire at point-blank range and gunned down the crews as they tried to seek shelter in the houses lining the street. Recovering well, the French fought back and destroyed Schulze's vehicles but without inflicting any German casualties. Leaving a trail of 20 burning tanks along Aire's main street, Schulze withdrew.[10]

Even as Aire came under attack, orders were issued to lift the anti-tank mines so that the British and French troops still on the far bank could withdraw, but it was too late. During the night, attacks were made against all the bridges along the brigade front. Inexperience showed as defensive positions were set up on the north bank of the canal but with few among the support troops now thrust into the front line appreciating the importance of placing defences on the far bank and approaches. Fear of being trapped when the bridges were blown was understandable, but the alternative meant the Germans had to launch only one attack to get across instead of encountering a defence in depth. It was a problem Gawthorpe had tried to tackle but with limited success.[11] All along the line, footbridges had been left standing to allow the last of the men trapped on the far bank to rejoin their comrades. It was these that the Germans now targeted, one being blown even as German engineers attempted to remove the charges.

At around 0500hrs on the 23rd, an unidentified officer of the West Yorkshires called to the house of the Durand family in the village of Busnes and told them to leave as they were in imminent danger from an expected German crossing of a nearby footbridge. As he pre-pared to leave, the family watched bemused as he placed his helmet on a broomstick and held it at the window before deciding it was safe to leave. He then borrowed their bicycle and pedalled off.[12] A short time later, a patrol led by Lieutenant McLean of HQ Company soon established that the enemy were in the village of Busnes opposite the West Yorkshire positions. By early afternoon, an armoured car was spotted approaching the now demol-ished bridge. It had been followed more armour and motorcycle troops and an attack developed on the right of the West Yorkshires as the armoured column advanced towards the Busnes–St Venant bridges held by HQ Company. At the same time, the defenders came under artillery, mortar and machine gun fire from their right rear. Also under heavy fire, the French holding the railway bridge on their right flank had fallen back and been fol-lowed by German infantry who clambered over the ruins of the partly destroyed bridge. In danger now of being outflanked, HQ Company began to withdraw towards the line St Venant–Calonne, suffering around ten killed or missing and two wounded.

German troops wait to cross the La Bassee Canal at Robecq.

German troops crossing the La Bassee Canal near Robecq.

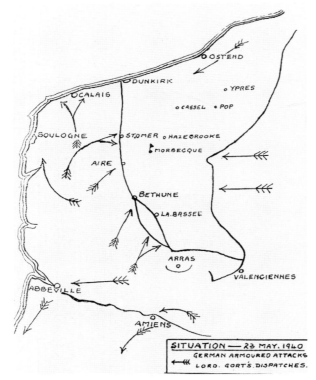

Above: British casualties after the battle for Robecq.

Left: Map of the situation on 23 May sketched by Brigadier Gawthorpe.

Further east, 'B' and 'C' Companies stayed in position. Although they were not yet under fire, they were acutely aware of the canal traffic still on the waterway and filled with people. Some were still occupied by their owners, others taken as temporary lodgings by refugees but any of these apparent civilians could be fifth columnists intent on using the barges to help the Germans cross the canal. All smaller boats had been systematically smashed but even as the engineers attempted to move the larger craft they had been driven back by machine gun fire.

Having advanced against only very light resistance, Eicke and his men were regaining confidence and he became determined that they would cross the canal and redeem themselves. The overall German plan was to push across the canal before the British could firmly establish their defence line and the Totenkopf had been assigned the limited objective of advancing to Bethune on the 23rd to reconnoitre potential crossing points to the north of town, but no more than this. Reaching the southern outskirts of Bethune that afternoon and without bothering to attempt any reconnaissance of the far bank, Eicke instead ordered an immediate crossing in battalion strength. It was only when his men reached the far side that they discovered how strongly the British were dug in. Just beyond the West Yorkshires' left flank were the regular troops of the Royal Irish Fusiliers from 25 Brigade who were able to force the Germans back under heavy fire. Only now did Eicke follow his instructions and order a reconnaissance in force along the southern bank with engineers stood by to throw a bridge across the canal if an opportunity arose.

By evening, troops of the SS-VT had penetrated into the Forest of Nieppe and were working their way into the villages of St Floris, St Venant and Robecq. Among the advancing Germans, a soldier named Homann later described 'a hail of fire' meeting them as they approached Robecq. Nearing the cemetery on the outskirts of the village, he recalled a 'furious barrage' from the tree line. Taking cover, one of his men found an abandoned machine gun lying on the ground.

'The dogs are perched in the trees', said my comrade. 'Wait? We will indeed.' Advancing, he calmly pulled the trigger, firing into the trees in the cemetery. A brown silhouette fell among the graves. 'Did you see', he asked with a hard laugh, 'he fell like a rotten apple; he won't bother us again.'[13]

By nightfall, the West Yorkshires were in danger of being surrounded. Enemy forces were in the woods to the west and pushing towards both brigade HQ at Morbecque and GHQ at Hazebrouck with some reports that they were already on the outskirts of the town. To the east, the Totenkopf were preparing an assault near Hinges. For now, 'B' Company in the middle were asked to hold as long as possible as the other companies tried to establish themselves in new positions near the airfield at Merville, where the only British planes left in France were evacuating. It was easier said than done – 10 Platoon were half a mile from HQ Company's old position and three quarters of a mile from 11 Platoon and Company HQ. They had fifteen men to hold a half-mile front. Lieutenant Moor sent five men out on a roving patrol all night but there was no further contact before the next morning.

During the day and into that night, Gawthorpe's command had grown. By midnight he was told that 2nd and 44th Division troops would reach him late the next day but that the Royal Inniskilling Dragoon Guards and 9RNF would be there before dawn. The 4th/7th Dragoons should be with him sometime during the day and 138 Brigade with the few surviving elements of 70 Brigade would come under command shortly. With those forces at his disposal, Gawthorpe decided he could use his reserves to counterattack at dawn before

French Char B1 tanks. Confidence in French military power was high, largely as a result of public displays of massed tanks like these. Capable of withstanding German anti-tank fire, in combat the B1 was hampered by a small fuel tank which frequently put it out of action before the enemy could.

the Germans could consolidate their crossing, the Inniskillings would lead with 9RNF occupying each position as it was taken. Equipped only with armoured cars, Gawthorpe praised the willingness of the Irishmen to attack as if they were the lead elements of a tank force despite being massively outgunned by the enemy, but warned them not to stay in any one position for more than three minutes to avoid drawing fire.[14]

At 0430hrs, just before the attack began, Polforce was alerted by a message that the French 5th Motorised Division's positions east of Aire from Isbergues to Guardebecque had been overrun and that the division was no longer in any state to mount a defence. This left the West Yorkshires even more vulnerable to encirclement. Behind them, the 250 men of the 6th York and Lancasters from 138 Brigade who had managed to complete their move as a formation, began a sweep through the area west of Merville but were unable to prevent a tank from entering Hazebrouck itself. A scratch GHQ defence force had been created using the few troops to hand and a number of 1917 vintage light tanks[15] but the motley collection of clerks and batmen managed to operate a 25mm anti-tank gun effectively enough to force a withdrawal by around 1030hrs.

Around the partly demolished Busnes–St Venant bridge, German motorcycle troops had begun pushing forward. 'B' Company's 10 Platoon attempted to move into position to cover the flanks but came under fire from three sides at ranges less than 75 yards. Almost immediately half the platoon became casualties and the remainder crawled under fire to Company HQ, itself now taking fire from the Robecq road running parallel to the canal. The acting Company Commander, Captain Wilkins, then sent two groups to try to reinforce 12 Platoon at the Bethune–Robecq bridge. The second got through to where 12 Platoon, a handful of French stragglers and the three light tanks now formed the strongest position they could. Having now lost contact with Company HQ, Second Lieutenant

Oversby and Sergeant Munton crawled back to try to find them, only to see Second Lieutenant Stansfield of 11 Platoon attempt to lead a party of men through a deep tributary of the canal. Caught in the water by a burst of fire, only one man made it across. There was no sign of Wilkins and the rest of Company HQ. The enemy were by now in Robecq and two of the French tanks made for the village. 'They had hardly reached the nearest houses when they both went up in sheets of flame' wrote Lieutenant Moor, describing how 'B' Company's exposed position 'became untenable only when half a dozen medium German tanks emerged from the village of Robecq and pounded down on the defenders with all guns blazing'.[16] Private Ken Dyson suddenly found himself 'looking at the wrong end of a double-barrelled machine gun mounted on a half-track'. Not far away, nineteen-year-old Douglas Fletcher, his mouth bleeding after the loss of his front teeth in hand to hand fighting, was lined up against the wall of a cafe with six others. An SS trooper was setting up a machine gun tripod when an officer arrived and took charge. He asked Fletcher his age and laughed at the reply. 'Now they are sending schoolboys' he said, adding 'but you are soldiers.'[17] Dyson and Fletcher were marched off to captivity in Poland.

The rest of 'B' Company fell back through 'C' Company's positions and together they closed around HQ Company at Calonne. Meanwhile, 'D' Company had inflicted five casualties on a motorcycle detachment and recovered a number of documents from a nearby pond where the German officer had thrown them before being hit. The Company Commander, Captain Wood, was satisfied with the action but couldn't help thinking about his close shave – a bullet was lodged in the respirator slung across his chest.

An intense air attack had started against the now abandoned airfield at around 0900hrs and, expecting an airborne landing, HQ Company deployed along the Hinges–Calonne road at the airfield perimeter. For around two-and-a-half hours they had been subjected to repeated strafing attacks and, at approximately 1500hrs, three light tanks appeared and began to fire into Battalion HQ on the road between Calonne and Merville. Attached anti-tank guns under the command of Captain Christopher replied and the three tanks were destroyed. One officer and two gunners had been wounded in the exchange but only then was it discovered that the attackers were, in fact, the French tank support they had been waiting for.

Early that morning, Eicke's men had managed to throw a bridge across the canal and were across. 'With the bravado of a reckless amateur', writes historian Charles Sydnor, 'Eicke – pistol in hand – led the attack.'[18] Despite being pinned down Eicke ordered three more companies to join the attack and began directing artillery fire support. Within an hour he had established a firm bridgehead on the north bank but found himself ordered back across the canal. Instructions had reached XVI Panzer Corps to break off its attack and prepare for an enemy armoured assault. The orders came as part of the controversial halt order intended to ensure that the rapidly advancing tanks did not overstretch themselves and leave the supply lines vulnerable to counterattack as well as preparing for the second phase attack south of the Somme.

Infuriated, Eicke began to pull his men back only to find British fire intensifying as they recognised the withdrawal. Artillery fire was brought in from north of Bethune and it soon became clear that an orderly operation was out of the question. Abandoning their kit, his SS troopers were thrown into a headlong race for the canal where they simply jumped in and swam for the safety of the far bank leaving behind 42 dead, 121 wounded and 5 missing men.[19] Once back across, Eicke found his Corps Commander waiting for him, having witnessed the debacle. Hoepner's already low opinion of the SS had only been confirmed by what he had seen and he is alleged to have called Eicke a 'butcher' to his face in front of Eicke's own staff.[20] For two days, a furious Eicke and his men sat in pouring rain south

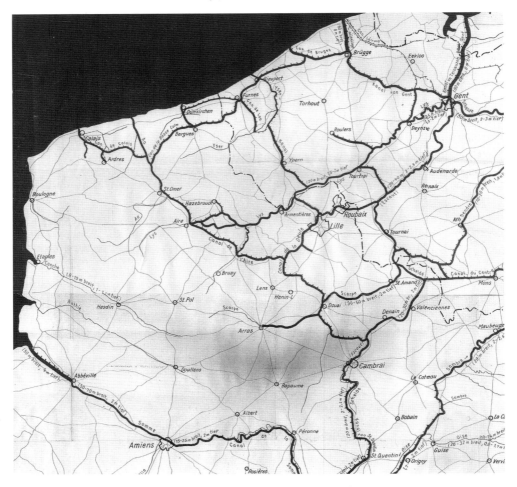

German map showing the waterways around Dunkirk. The difficulty in manoeuvring tank formations in this type of countryside has been put forward as one explanation for Hitler's infamous 'Halt Order'. (Courtesy Martin Marix Evans)

of the canal line waiting for the order to be lifted as British mortar and artillery fire kept up a steady bombardment. On his own initiative, he decided to send small teams across the canal to locate and destroy the mortar positions. One such team, led by Obersturmführer Harrer, crossed the canal and encountered a British dispatch rider on a quiet road. He was knocked off his motorbike with a shot to the shoulder. Harrer, barely able to speak English, asked if the wounded man spoke French. When the prisoner failed to answer, Harrer shot him in the head and the body was pushed into a ditch.[21]

At Gawthorpe's HQ, a man in a British officer's uniform had appeared and asked questions about the plans for the next day. '[As] I could not verify his credentials' wrote Gawthorpe, 'and liked neither his face, accent, attitude or anything else about him, I dropped him through a hatch into the cellar and put an armed clerk on guard.'[22] An hour later, a staff officer appeared to explain that whilst the man might be 'tactless and excited', he was genuine and he was released. The man had had a lucky escape. A great many suspected fifth columnists had already been executed on far flimsier grounds, the Grenadier

Guards executing as many as seventeen – possibly more – in a single day. Anthony Rhodes, an officer with the BEF spoke to one Field Security Policeman who claimed to have interrogated up to 100 suspects a day. He records one conversation between a colleague and the divisional provost officer when he asked if the provost really shot spies:

'Of course' said the provost officer.
'And you do it entirely on your own? I mean the trial and that sort of thing?'
'Of course.'
'But I suppose you take very good care that they really are spies, don't you? I mean –it's a sort of absolute power of attorney, isn't it?'
'It's absolute all right,' he said, grinning.[23]

In all, it is believed that overenthusiastic British and French troops killed civilians at a rate comparable to the 5,000 killed by the Germans in the 'Rape of Belgium' in 1914 – an action that saw them labelled as 'a barbaric, baby spitting horde for the better part of half a century.'[24]

The British, meanwhile, were using the pause to replace the West Yorkshires with regular troops. Around Hinges, the 2nd Royal Norfolks began taking over on the night of the 24/25th. In the late afternoon of the 24th, two platoons of 'A' Company were preparing to hold their position at Calonne as the rest of the battalion pulled back through them towards Neuf Berquin. At 1900hrs, a party of retreating Frenchmen told them that the Germans were only a mile away. At 1930hrs, the ominous sound of tracked vehicles grew louder and 'it seemed the small force was destined to have an exciting time.'[25] Then, around the corner came the carriers of the relieving force of 4th Brigade. Even as the

platoon commanders met, the Germans opened fire at close range, sending Second Lieutenant Clough and Major Parks diving for cover in an evil smelling ditch.[26] Patrols were sent out to track down the Germans but no contact was made. The carriers then set out towards Robecq and the sound of heavy fighting was followed by a column of prisoners being marched back.

That night, the exhausted men of 'B' Company had their first sleep for four days but there were no rations for them except biscuits and chocolate. By the light of a single candle stuck in a bottle, Colonel Pulleyn briefed his officers in a cottage in the village and told them that the battalion was to gather the next day

A suspected fifth columnist under arrest. Hundreds, perhaps thousands, of French and Belgian civilians were summarily executed – often on the flimsiest of evidence – by Allied soldiers during the campaign.

in Calonne and then move to take up position in reserve of the newly arrived 2DLI, who would be attacking St Venant as troops of the Welch Fusiliers counterattacked at Robecq.

Outside, German artillery fire was stepped up to try to disrupt the incoming forces and reports were coming in of 'at least one gas shell to St Floris'.[27] At around 0100hrs 21-year-old Albert Porritt was killed by a splinter and the company moved closer to the centre of the village for protection. Further proof of the difficult position the battalion was in came during the night when Captain Leslie Sykes, commander of HQ Company, was killed by sub-machine gun fire whilst on reconnaissance with his platoon commanders when they encountered an enemy patrol.

At dawn, fighting patrols were sent out and came back with a number of prisoners. Five light machine guns and three submachine guns were captured and thrown into the Lys canal. At 1000hrs the battalion was ordered to cross the canal and to take up positions facing the Forêt de Nieppe. Across a makeshift bridge of planks placed across a barge, they no sooner reached their positions than they were ordered instead to withdraw and to move to Merville and then to Estaires for a rest. As 'C' Company led the way through Merville, an artillery barrage dropped and its first shell fell in their midst causing several casualties, although fortunately none were fatal. The barrage lifted only when Stukas appeared overhead and screamed into the attack. Soldiers and civilians alike hid in cellars as the bombardment continued in relays, the battalion edging their way out of town in the brief intervals between until, on the far side, they were caught in a box barrage across the only two exits from the area. It is perhaps a mark of how the last few days had hardened them that Lieutenant Moor remarked that 'by a miracle the only fatalities were civilian.'

Strung out over several miles and harried all the way by air strikes, the battalion finally reached Estaires at dusk and settled into barns and farms around the village only to find that the promised rations had been sent on to Doulieu instead due to conflicting orders. For the past two days, the battalion had been placed under the orders of 25th Brigade by Gawthorpe but the battalion had assumed that this was simply because communication with 137 Brigade HQ had been lost. Now, as they withdrew, they once again fell under Gawthorpe's command but by now his plans had changed. Under the command of 138 Brigade, the remnants of 137 were to hand over to the incoming troops and withdraw to Doulieu for a rest and then move to catch up with Gawthorpe at Cassel.

The town of Cassel, perched atop one of the very few hills in Flanders, was an obvious target for a German attack. Control of it would dominate the approaches to Dunkirk and it was vital that it be defended. When Gawthorpe arrived, however, it was already in enemy hands and he 'could not get within four miles of it'. Instead, he was advised to steer to the east of it and to recce an approach from that side. With that in mind, he headed to the village of Steenvorde but on arrival there was greeted by a staff officer with instructions 'to take no further aggressive action ... report to III Corps headquarters at Teteghem, near Dunkirk, with all you've got.' When Gawthorpe protested that Dunkirk was on the English Channel, the officer was terse: 'We happen to be going that way.'[28] It was the first indication Gawthorpe had of a general retreat.

For Private Ernest Jones of the 2/5th, the 27th was not only a day of rest spent sheltering from the pouring rain, but also his 21st birthday, celebrated with his first hot meal for days and his last until he reached England. His battledress jacket was holed in two places where bullets had narrowly missed him, passing through his wallet and tearing a photograph inside it. Now, he sat with his friends watching Estaires burn. Unknown to him or his comrades, just a few miles away, the Totenkopf had finally resumed their attack, and had been given the task of securing the area around Hinges and pushing north to the line

Estaires–Neuve Chappelle. Against a defence so desperate that British troops ran out of ammunition but fought on with bayonets and entrenching tools, the military ineptitude of Eicke and his officers led to men being ordered to attempt frontal assaults on machine gun positions in the belief that brute force and ignorance could achieve as much as skill and training. In particular, Bertling, commander of the Division's 2nd Infantry Regiment, got his unit into such difficulties that the entire division had to be diverted to his aid. The 2nd Norfolks, who had relieved the 2/5th at Hinges, barricaded themselves into a farm to delay the advance of the Totenkopf's left flank. When the British ran out of ammunition and surrendered, the SS were once again embarrassed by their own incompetence and eager to take their frustration out on their prisoners. All the surviving Norfolks were gathered together against a barn wall and gunned down. Even including the victims of this atrocity, Eicke could only claim that his division had inflicted around 300 casualties on the British but his poor leadership of the Totenkopf had cost twice that many casualties among his own men – some 155 dead, 483 wounded and 53 missing.[29]

At dusk, orders came for the West Yorkshires to head for Kemmel and so the battalion set out on a long, uncomfortable march along crowded roads in heavy rain. Reaching the smoking ruins of Bailleul around midnight, their destination was suddenly changed to Berthen, which they reached at 0430hrs. Despite the weather, Pulleyn decided to take his men through the village and into woods on the high ground to the north, leaving the Lincolns of 138 Brigade and the Northumberland Fusiliers in their comfortable billets. Two hours later, though, he was proved right when an air raid struck Berthen with tremendous force and hit a church where ammunition had been stored, triggering secondary explosions that continued for some time in a spectacular display. One stick of bombs overshot the village and hit the edge of the woods where 'B' Company were sheltering, causing another six casualties including 20-year-old Sam Roberts, a former player for York FC who died of his wounds five days later. Throughout the rest of what Lieutenant Moor called 'an endless morning', the bombers returned time and again, plastering the area so that by midday, 'B' Company was down to fewer than 30 men. Two of the attacking planes were shot down and 'the crew of two who bailed out of one of them were rounded up and killed.'[30]

The survivors of 'B' and 'C' Companies threw up a defence line along the northern edge of the wood and remained there until 1630hrs when orders reached them to head for the coast. The main concern now for the battalion officers was whether their tired, hungry men would be able to make the 30 miles to Dunkirk on foot. A violent thunderstorm had broken out at 1500hrs, effectively preventing further air attacks so the men were at least able to move openly but felt far from safe.[31] 'It was now learned' wrote Lieutenant Moor, 'that German mechanised forces were closing in on all sides. The men's feet were by this time in poor shape and after Watou, Haringhe and Rousbrugge had been passed, with A/T weapons in position at the road side all the way, it began to appear doubtful whether the Bn would win its race down the narrowing corridor to the sea.'[32] Once on the main Pyres–Furnes road, however, they met with heavy traffic and were able to hitch lifts in small groups to the coast.

In its entry for 29 May, the battalion war diary notes 'whereabouts of the bulk of the battalion unknown having been scattered on march.'[33] 'Amidst the confusion of abandoned vehicles, flooded fields and disappearing officers', recalls Ernest Jones, 'we made our way to the coast.'[34] Some went to Dunkirk, others to the beaches north of the port, many simply left to fend for themselves. Pausing for the night of the 28th near a farm, Lieutenant Clough and Company Sergeant Major Clayton woke to find the battalion had moved on, leaving them to find their own way back. Private Jones was one of a group of ten men

The evacuation beaches. The 'Provost Jetty', created by driving vehicles into the sea at low tide, enabled ships to come close into the beaches at high tide.

The public shelter on the Place de la Republique, Dunkirk. It was here that Ernest Jones and Cyril Rigby took cover.

German artist's impressions of the British escape from Dunkirk.

who reached a square in Dunkirk where their officer told them to stay where they were and went off to find transport. He did not return and it was only later that Jones discovered he had reached home five days before his men.

Those who could be found were put to work directing traffic and putting the final canal line into a state of defence. Knowing that there was a real risk of panic, Gawthorpe himself stood on the beach directing troops in an effort to maintain calm; 'Right, you join your division over there … yes you're all going together but you can't go without tickets … Division's got the tickets.'[35] He was right to do so; already Dunkirk was filled with drunken, panicking troops.

In the square, Jones and his party took shelter from incoming artillery in an air raid shelter. As they waited, another soldier arrived, tripped, and his rifle went off, striking Jones' friend Cyril Rigby in the knee. They managed to get him to an American nurse who dressed the wound. 'Two hours later a passing ambulance convoy picked him up and we went to the quayside with him to be confronted by row upon row of ambulances.'[36] Told to make their way to the beaches, Jones and his friend 'Chuck' Skillbeck found a stores vehicle, changed into clean uniforms and made their way to the harbour's mole where, in groups of 50 at a time, they moved up to safety aboard HMS *Exeter*. Jones was never able to find out what happened to his wounded comrade.[37]

Offshore, the ships that had so recently brought the BEF to France were now taking them home, but the strain of facing the German air superiority quickly began to show. Many returned time after time throughout the next week under increasingly difficult

A German soldier inspects a 1917 vintage Renault tank brought into service to defend GHQ.

B Company, 2/5th West Yorkshire Regiment.

conditions; but not all felt the same way. The evacuation got under way on the night of the 26/27th but as early as the 28th, the *Canterbury* sailed only after direct orders and a naval party had been put aboard to 'stiffen the crew'. The next day, the captain of the *St Seiriol* had been put under open arrest and again a naval crew brought aboard so that she could return to Dunkirk after her first trip. On 1 June, after three trips, most of the crew of the *Tynwald* – the ship that had brought the West Yorkshires to Cherbourg in April – along with those of the *Malines* and the *Ben-My-Chree* all refused to sail from Folkestone and

Troops in the 'cinema queue' on the mole.

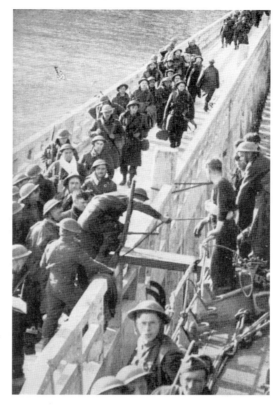

had to be replaced.[38] Each was capable of carrying up to 2,000 men at a time and indeed the *Tynwald*, under a navy crew, later loaded 4,000 men in half an hour on the night of 4 June[39] but for precious hours they sat idle throughout that night. When relief crews arrived the next day, they were met by jeering and the crew of the *Ben-My-Chree* had to be physically prevented from leaving by a naval party wielding fixed bayonets. As the navy dealt with the other ships, the *Malines* quietly slipped anchor and sailed for her home port, her captain later claiming; 'It seemed in the best interests of all concerned.'[40] Elsewhere, the coxwain and motor mechanic of the Hythe lifeboat were dismissed at the end of June for their refusal to sail.[41] For the men trapped on the beaches, time was running short.

At Gravelines, the 6th Green Howards of 69 Brigade held on to a four-mile front but were in no state to hold it for long. On 29 May, their commanding officer, Lieutenant Colonel Steel, informed Brigadier Norman, in charge of that sector:

> My battalion is a labour battalion of 20-year-old boys. They were sent out to dig trenches and are armed only with rifles. They have been put into an unsuccessful counterattack near Gravelines in which they lost heavily. They have been down to the beaches, and told they were going home. They were then brought back, and put on the ground where they are now. They will stay just as long as they do not see a German. At the first sight of the enemy, they will bolt to a man.[42]

Elsewhere, as the perimeter shrank, other labour troops found themselves being left to sacrifice themselves for the better equipped regulars. By 1 June, 138 and 139 Brigades formed the last line of defence under the command of General Curtis. With no reserve except the 70 remaining men of the 2/5th Leicesters, they held the line of the canal at Bergues. Hard pressed, a German bridgehead was established against 139 Brigade's front at Hoymille on 2 June that was only beaten back when, with incredible bravery, 550 men of the French 21st Divisional Training Centre attacked through a field flooded thigh deep. Only 65 men survived unscathed but the Germans were pushed back.[43] Bergues finally fell at 1700hrs and the survivors of the rearguard broke off contact, firing their remaining ammunition and setting up delaying mechanisms to fire rifles propped against barricades to give the impression that they were still manned as the defenders slipped away.

By 4 June, the BEF was gone. Now German attention turned south.

A German soldier watches an oil depot in flames at Dunkirk. The smoke had been a marker for retreating troops for the past week.

NOTES

1 Gawthorpe, '137 Infantry Brigade: A Formation of the TA in the First Year of War 1939/40' in *Ca Ira* Vol XII June 1948 p224

2 Blaxland p186

3 Report on 'Polforce.' WO197/118

4 Lieutenant R.A. Moor. Personal account.

5 Sandes, E.W.C. *Pyramid to Pagoda* p253–4. See also *Ca Ira* Vol X No 4 June 1941 p181

6 Stéphane Bonnaud. 'Le 9e Bataillon de Chars de Combat. Pt II' in *Histoire de Guerre Blindés & Matériel* No75 Fevrier/Mars 2007

7 The role of the North African units has been largely overlooked in France. They were composed of North African Arabs and '*pied-noirs*' – literally 'black feet' or Frenchmen born abroad. The colonial formations gained a reputation for fighting well but the Nazi ideology refused to consider them worthy of treatment under the Geneva Convention. A great many North and West African troops, along with smaller numbers of Vietnamese soldiers, were murdered after capture. 1st DINA would later hold the line alongside the remnants of 138 and 139 Brigades on the Dunkirk perimeter and, after evacuation to England, the 27th Algerian Infantry would be shipped back to France to take part in still more fighting throughout June.

8 Moor's papers. Fenwick's brother, Arthur, a 35-year-old corporal of the Royal Engineers, would later be a victim of the *Lancastria* sinking on 17 June.

9 Blaxland p194

10 Friesen, B.H. 'German Flank Guard Actions During the 1940 French Campaign' *Armor* Jan–Feb 1994

11 *Ca Ira* Vol XII Dec 48 p300

12 Anonymous and undated account provided via the mairie at Robecq.

13 Ibid. Report is described as having been published in *Signal* in 1941.

14 *Ca Ira* p302

15 Blaxland p190

16 Moor papers, see also Parks report op cit.

17 Whiting, C. & Taylor, E. *The Fighting Tykes* London 1993 p206–7

18 Sydnor, C. *Soldiers of Destruction* London 1989 p98

19 Ibid p99

20 Ibid p99–101

21 Later that day Harrer's group were themselves captured. In marked contrast to their own behaviour, Privates Schopfhauser, Radl and Gieck were given clean clothes, cigarettes and a hot meal. They were then provided with British greatcoats to avoid any attack on them by French civilians and marched to the coast. They were able to escape their captors during the chaos of the evacuation. See Sydnor p102

22 Gawthorpe *Ca Ira* p303

23 Rhodes, A. *Sword of Bone* 1942 Quoted in Hayward, J. *Myths and Legends of the Second World War* 2003 p37. Hayward refers to Appendix One of the 1942 edition which describes the handling of suspects. Later editions of the book carry no appendix.

24 Hayward 2003 p38

25 *Ca Ira* Op cit p267

26 The fire caused no casualties among the troops but is reported to have killed two women sheltering in a nearby house. No French record confirms this but the Loock family of Calonne suffered the deaths of 35-year-old Marie and her two children, five-year-old Maurice and seven-month-old Genevieve during a bombing attack on that day.

27 Moor papers – there are several instances of gas shells reported but it seems likely that these were flares misidentified by poorly trained sentries.

28 Collier, R. *Sands of Dunkirk* p32

29 Sydnor p104-108

30 Lieutenant R.A. Moor. Personal account.

31 The local priest of the nearby village of Boeschepe later erected the Chapel of the Sacred Heart in gratitude for what he saw as divine intervention to save his village. It can be found in the centre of the village alongside the D10 road.

32 Lieutenant R.A. Moor. Personal account

33 War Diary 2/5th West Yorkshires WO167/853

34 Shaw p173

35 Collier p41

36 Shaw p174

37 28-year-old Rigby died of his wound on 30 May and is buried at Dunkirk

38 Thompson, J. *Dunkirk: Retreat to Victory* 2008 p269. See also Lord, W. *The Miracle of Dunkirk* 1984 p223

39 Lord p259

40 Ibid p241

41 Reported in the *Halifax Courier* 27 June 1940

42 Sebag-Montefiore p365

43 Jackson, R. *Dunkirk* 2002 p142

Chapter Ten

'Heroic but thoroughly unsound'

As dawn broke on the morning of 21 May, the two battalions of the Dukes could hear the sounds of gunfire which soon died down and they could see armoured fighting vehicles in the distance, but their patrols had returned without any useful information other than that the line back towards Dieppe was blocked. At 0900hrs they were joined by Major King and his men of 271st Field Company RE who, by breaking up some of the train's trucks, improvised a ramp to unload two vehicles. One, driven by Captain Gerrard and the French liaison officer Thomas de Strahlborn set out towards Eu to attempt to locate any HQ still operational whilst in the other, Lieutenant Kenneth Smith, Intelligence Officer of the 2/7th and his 2/6th counterpart, Second Lieutenant G.W. Smith (no relation) accompanied by their French Cavalry Liaison Officer Stevenson and Privates Morris and Cocker drove off towards Abbeville to check the situation there.

At a level crossing just outside the town, the truck stopped and the three officers went forward on foot. As they reached the crossing, three Germans appeared on the line and opened fire. Calmly, Private Morris reversed the truck and turned it round as the officers sprinted towards him. A machine gun mounted on an armoured vehicle then opened up on them, killing Kenneth Smith and wounding Private Cocker but somehow Morris managed to get the bullet-riddled truck back to the battalion. With confirmation that the enemy were in control of Abbeville and air activity increasing by the hour, the two battalions moved to the cover of a wood about three miles from their now useless train. By this time the men had just a few bars of chocolate and some biscuits between them and foraging parties went out to see what could be found. All around them were deserted farms and unmilked cattle moaning in pain in the fields. The people had fled, taking their food supplies with them.

After another night in the open, Colonels Taylor and Llewellyn met again to discuss what to do. The enemy were clearly ahead of them. Brigade HQ was missing, presumed captured. No orders were forthcoming from higher authorities although Captain Gerrard had found out that most troops were heading back to Dieppe. As Llewellyn later put it,

> … to stage a forward attack without supporting arms seemed heroic but thoroughly unsound: to remain where we were and hope seemed equally foolish … The only other possibility was to withdraw to a line of general resistance, where communications and commands existed.[1]

Abandoned vehicles, Dunkirk beach. Many are civilian vehicles pressed into service at the start of the war.

Dunkirk harbour after the surrender.

Wrecked British vehicles and equipment block a street.

The two officers agreed that they should follow the tracks back to Dieppe and try to make contact with HQ Lines of Communication from there. The 2/7th would take the west side of the line, the 2/6th the east.

Carrying everything possible, the two battalions set out, with the 2/7th leaving last at about 1100hrs. Marching along the tracks was extremely difficult and made them an easy target so the men were moved into the farmland alongside the embankment but contact with the 2/6th was soon lost in the heavy woods and thickets that lined each field and the 2/7th carried on alone. The rear company took some machine gun fire but there were no casualties and the enemy made no attempt to follow them. They encountered the CO and 30 men of the 2/7th Queens who reported enemy armour in a village about a mile to their right. Soon after, the entire battalion took cover and watched the tanks go by. As the men paused, Sergeant Lees pushed on for another half mile to a wood he had spotted. Finding it to provide ideal cover from both air and ground attack, he reported back to Colonel Taylor, who ordered the battalion there immediately.

On the approach to the station of Woincourt outside Fressenville, the battalion encountered a mass of train wreckage covering both the up and down lines. Evidently one train had been hit by an air strike and another had simply driven straight into the back of the first, followed by another. The men were awestruck by the destruction in front of them.

A refugee woman and her children. The German blitzkrieg often deliberately targeted refugee columns in order to create chaos behind Allied lines.

Arnold Straw saw a cattle truck filled with people that had been crushed to a length of ten feet. Hanging from the front of one locomotive was the body of a woman wearing just a vest, the rest of her clothing blown off by the explosion. In the locomotive, the driver lay decapitated and in the engine's tender lay the corpse of a man, still clutching his dog's lead as it jealously guarded his body. Gently, it was taken from him and travelled with the battalion for the rest of their stay in France. For Straw, though, the worst memory was of finding the bodies of two young children of about four years of age.

Abandoned French equipment on the route of the retreat.

They were lying together, face upwards, and at first I thought they were sleeping. There was not a mark on either of them, their cheeks were still shining and rosy red, but there was a waxen sheen to them which gave them the look of two beautiful dolls.[2]

Food and wine were still on the tables and luggage piled high in the racks of the undamaged carriages and the men moved down the train, salvaging what they could. One train was found to have been carrying a French cavalry unit and their horses had been left behind when the men fled. Bandmaster Doyle, acting now as medical orderly, selected a grey mare for his own use and set the rest free. Behind that was a hospital train with the wounded still aboard. For the moment there was little that could be done.

On a blazingly hot day, the men were short of water and food and Taylor ordered a reconnaissance party to continue down the track to the station at Chepy-les-Valenes in the hope of contacting the railway authorities for help. There, by great good luck, they found Henri Pruvot, a French railway engineer from Rouen in charge of a recovery train attempting to restore order. Pruvot immediately agreed to help clear the track to recover the hospital train but asked the Dukes for help. Colonel Taylor was gratified to find no shortage of volunteers despite the circumstances and a work party of 100 men was gathered, together with others willing to mount an anti-aircraft guard.

For five hours, interrupted every few minutes by German aircraft passing overhead, the men worked to clear the wreckage. Aware of the impact it might have on the young soldiers, Armourer Sergeant Cavendish took the task of recovering the bodies on himself and laid out ten of the eleven corpses found. Without tools there was no chance of burying them but at least they could be left decently covered. Pioneer Sergeant Allaway, who had supervised the unloading of the trucks on improvised ramps, now turned his attention to working on the railway. Whilst the work was going on, M. Pruvot had directed a party towards the abandoned hospital at St Valery-sur-Somme and their truck returned laden with chicken in aspic and other treats – although as Arnold Straw bitterly recalled, these were not distributed as widely as he might have hoped. In the past two days, he had been given just two cigarettes; small comfort to the non-smoking Straw.

Finally, at nightfall, the hospital train was freed. A delighted Pruvot handed around a few bottles of beer to celebrate and told Colonel Taylor that if his men could squeeze aboard the few cattle trucks standing nearby, he would get them to Dieppe. 'We made the grade,' Taylor later wrote,

> … packed like herrings; few trains have been driven more frantically. On two occasions men fell out going around corners, and at one point the floor of a truck was pulled completely out. The driver of the train was running no risk of being overtaken by the Germans, he drove as if he were on the footplate of the 'Flying Scotsman'.[3]

After more delays, the battalion triumphantly reached Dieppe at 0730hrs the next morning, 22 May.

After the shock of the events of the 20th, the British forces south of the Somme were in complete disarray. HQ 12th Division and two of its brigade HQs had survived intact but between them they could only locate one battalion of the Queen's Regiment. Two of its battalions – 4th Buffs and 2/6th East Surreys – were nearby having been halted before they reached Abbeville and another – 6th Royal Sussex – sat in a railway siding south of Amiens. All could easily have been brought back under control had they had any signals equipment, as could the three battalions of 46th Division now cut off from their own HQ and it might have been possible to quickly reform them into a cohesive defence line along the Somme. As it was, the chance was lost simply because they were not aware of each other's presence. Instead, it was now left to Brigadier Beauman and his Lines of Communication staff to take on the role of managing both the defence and withdrawal of millions of tons of supplies with whatever troops were to hand.

After many delays, the 1st Armoured Division had finally arrived at Cherbourg the previous day, having originally intended to reach the BEF via Le Havre but being diverted because of the bombing of that port. They were even now on their way to Rouen, the tank crews fitting their machine guns to their vehicles as they rolled along on the flat bed railway trucks bringing them north. Until reinforcements could be sent out from England, Beauman needed to gather whatever he could. The arrival of even a poorly equipped battalion like the 2/7th DWR was welcome news.

On arrival, Colonel Taylor reported to HQ 12 Division and was directed to the Nissen huts of 101 POW Camp, set up south-west of the town overlooking the docks where his men finally had the chance to get their first meal for three days and a rest, before being set to work constructing roadblocks as part of Liddel Force, another composite unit manned by local AMPC units and the former patients of the BEF's VD hospital.[4] Their task was the defence of the coast road into Dieppe itself. For now, though, the Germans seemed content to stay north of the Somme.

NOTES

1 Barclay p203
2 Straw's account at www.bbc.co.uk/ww2peopleswar/stories/50/a2069750
3 Barclay p252
4 Colonel Taylor's report 2 June 1940. Contained in Gawthorpe Papers IWM Documents 78/44/1

Chapter Eleven

The Sixth Wheel

By the time the Dukes reached Dieppe, the British L of C forces were beginning to recover as best they could. Also cut off by the German advance and far to the east, the 51st Highland Division was attempting to rejoin them and facing a difficult task. The Division had been deployed in the *Ligne de Contact* before the Maginot Line at Waldweistroff when the German assault began there on 13 May. The Highlanders had fought well until a general withdrawal had been ordered on the 15th, and on 20 May they were removed from the command of the French Third Army and put in reserve as the first stage of the pre-

agreed plan to return them to the main body of the BEF. By the 23rd, the concentration of the Division at Etain was complete, ready for the next stage of a move towards Paris, but before the troops could continue, new orders arrived sending them instead to Varennes, about 30 miles from Verdun. Contrary to the terms of the Anglo-French agreement and without consultation, the Highlanders had been redeployed to the French Second Army who wanted them as a reserve for the fighting around Sedan. Following the new orders, Major-General Fortune arrived at Varennes on 25 May, only to find that six battalions of his men had been sent, without his knowledge, to Rouen instead. Infuriated, Fortune was then informed that it was no

General Maxime Weygand, who took over from Gamelin on 19 May as commander in chief of French forces. At nearly 70 years of age, his increasingly strident demands that his men fight to the death raised concerns that he was mentally unfit for the role.

longer possible for him to rejoin the BEF and that he and his men would now fall under the command of General Robert Altmayer's *Groupement A*, an improvised force later to become the French Tenth Army. They were to be deployed along the line of the Somme and would be in position by 2 June.

As the Highlanders made their way across France, the wavering Gamelin had been replaced by General Maxime Weygand and a plan to counterattack was taking shape. Gort had already set in motion an attack to be launched near Arras to relieve the garrison there and to threaten the German flanks. As this attack went forward, it was hoped that the French V Corps under General Rene Altmayer (brother of the Tenth Army commander), would attack northwards to link up and cut the German lines. Gort, fearful of his army becoming encircled, refused to commit large numbers of his badly needed men and instead sent a force of two reserve divisions – in reality little more than two battalions by now – and 83 tanks. The attack was a success in that it caused the Germans to hold back their lightning advance, now seen as potentially overstretching the force and exposing vulnerable flanks, thus contributing to the infamous 'stop order' issued by Hitler that saved the 2/5th West Yorkshires on the 24/25th. The anticipated French attack, however, never materialised. The liaison officer sent to find Altmayer reported that the general, who

> … seemed tired out and thoroughly disheartened, wept silently on his bed. He told me his troops had buggered off. He was ready to accept the consequences of this refusal [to go to Arras] … but he could no longer continue to sacrifice the Army Corps of which he had already lost half.[1]

Despite this, Weygand now proposed a similar scheme, but on a much grander scale. Eight British divisions, supported by the French First Army and Belgian cavalry, would spearhead the attack south to link up with the French armies below the Somme. Weygand spelled out his plan at a meeting at Ypres but Gort was not present. The only officer able to deal in detail with the joint plan was then killed in a traffic accident and the plan was doomed. With a command structure incapable of responding to the speed of the fighting, the collapse of the Belgian Army and the lack of support from his allies, Gort's confidence in the command and fighting abilities of the latter disappeared. From the highest levels, it seemed, the French authorities had accepted defeat and the fall of France was now inevitable. Despite the British government's orders to co-operate fully with the French, he decided that the time had come to use his discretionary powers and save the BEF by withdrawing to Dunkirk.

Many in the French High Command, keen to find a scapegoat for the failures of their own staff, chose to portray Gort's decision to evacuate the BEF as betrayal by 'perfidious Albion' and to use it as a bargaining tool as Churchill came under increasing pressure to commit more of Britain's last line of defence – the RAF's fighter squadrons – to the battle immediately. French fighter losses had been heavy, but in reality delivery of new aircraft so exceeded their losses that by the end of the fighting, the French air force was actually larger than at the start. These aircraft, however, sat unused far to the south. The need to keep France in the war was urgent, but Churchill had to consider whether the French determination to seemingly defend their country only to the last Briton could be allowed to outweigh the needs of his own people. In France, Fortune and his men would now become the sacrificial gesture needed to prove to France and the world that Britain would support its allies to the end.

General Jean Blanchard,
Commander of the French First
Army and later of the Allied armies
in the north east.

As German tanks reached Abbeville, the British 1st Armoured Division under Major-General Evans finally reached Cherbourg. Too late to reach the BEF, the leading elements of the division were rushed forward to Rouen, and on 23 May the Queen's Bays, one of the three cavalry units forming 2nd Armoured Brigade, received an order to seize bridges across the Somme – 'Immediate advance of whatever elements of your Division are ready is essential. Action at once may be decisive; tomorrow may be too late.'[2] Evans was aware of the risk of committing his forces piecemeal into an attack but had no way of contacting GHQ to question the order and no alternative chain of command except to contact Gort via London, a slow, unwieldy process. Pushed into the assault supported by troops supplied from the best battalions Beauman could offer, the Bays fought well but found themselves too thinly spread to achieve any real success.

General Georges decided to use the two British divisions to carry out Weygand's doomed plan to force a link with the northern group and the BEF. Two armoured brigades – the 2nd comprising the Bays, 9th Queen's Royal Lancers and 10th Royal Hussars and the 3rd comprising 2nd and 5th Royal Tank Regiment (the 3rd RTR having been diverted to support the defence of Calais) – were hastily formed up. The 2nd, on the right, would be under the command of the French 2nd Cavalry Division and the 3rd on the left under the French 5th Division. Evans argued with the French that his division was not equipped for assault, but for pursuit. He was ignored and on the morning of 27 May, the tanks began to roll forward. Although the Germans had been in position for a full week, no real reconnaissance had been carried out and the 10th Hussars, unable to communicate with the French gunners who had postponed their barrage for one hour, went forward unsupported into a sector supposedly held by lightly armed Germans only to find themselves shot to pieces by heavy and accurate anti-tank fire. Their tanks disabled, the Hussars pushed forward on foot armed with pistols and, in one case, just a crowbar.[3]

To their right, the Bays were caught on an open slope by well concealed guns and lacked the smoke canisters that might have provided some cover. The brigade commander, seeing the hopelessness of the situation, held back the 9th Lancers in reserve. The 3rd Brigade made better progress and advanced towards Abbeville and St Valery-sur-Somme.

Bomber crew view of burning oil
depots at Rouen.

General Alphonse-Joseph Georges,
Commander of the North-East
Armies. Georges had expressed
concerns about what he saw as
Gamelin's 'happy-go-lucky' plan
to move into Belgium from its
prepared positions along the
border.

General Sir Edmund Ironside.
Ironside had expected to act as
C-in-C of the BEF but instead
was given the post of Chief of the
Imperial General Staff. He was
moved to command Home Forces
on 26 May.

Having lost eighteen tanks, their commander, Brigadier Crocker, tried to organise a co-ordinated assault with French infantry but the promised support again failed to materialise. The 1st Armoured's attack ground to a halt with the loss of 65 of its tanks destroyed and another 55 broken down from the long and rushed move forward. It was out of action as a co-ordinated whole. General de Gaulle's 4th Armoured Division now launched its attack – Weygand's plan envisaged consecutive, never concurrent, attacks – and took over the assault with its heavier tanks now better aware of the enemy dispositions. Even this was not enough and the Division withdrew.

The disastrous failure of the counterattack at Abbeville was yet another indication of the problems facing the British. Twenty-four hours after the loss of contact with the BEF, word finally reached HQ L of C at Le Mans of the previous day's events. In near panic, General de Fonblanque issued orders for the immediate removal of all guns north of the Seine and the destruction of any that could not be moved, much to the dismay of Brigadiers Beauman and Shilstone. From the start of the war, the British had been acutely aware of their shortage of weapons. Even before the German attack began, efforts were underway to locate Belgian arsenals with a view to recovering as many anti-aircraft guns as possible if it looked as though the country might be overrun.[4] Perhaps it was with this in mind that the German success in isolating the BEF caused de Fonblanque to consider saving the guns as his top priority; but Brigadier Shilstone, commanding all anti-aircraft defences in the Northern District, chose not to comply, realising that it would leave the vital depots at Rouen and Le Havre completely defenceless in the face of a situation that was, as yet, uncertain. For now, it seemed that the Germans might be held along the line of the Somme, or the Bresle or, at worst, the Seine, but to do so meant developing a co-ordinated plan.

In Britain, General Ironside was made aware of de Fonbalnque's orders on the evening of the 21st and countermanded them immediately but recognised the evidence of the chaotic conditions prevailing across the Channel. In an attempt to rectify matters, he called on Lieutenant-General Sir Henry Karslake, another victim of Hore-Belisha's purge in the late 1930s and now in retirement at home. With orders to 'Get out all you can

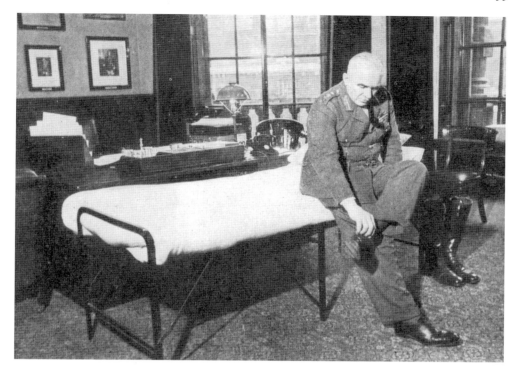

Ironside in his office, May 1940.

without alarming the French,'[5] Karslake sailed the next day armed with a list of priority stores considered essential to Britain's survival should France fall. The intention was that his arrival would relieve de Fonblanque of the operational management of the Lines of Communication and leave him 'free to concentrate on the very big administrative problems which will arise'[6] but when word of the change reached de Fonblanque at 0110hrs on 23 May, he is said to have torn off his insignia in disgust and exclaimed that he might as well serve as a private.[7] After this uncharacteristic outburst, he soon regained his composure and remained in France until sent home at the end of the campaign.

The priority now, Karslake thought, was to put together a scratch defence force to protect the most important depots so that the vital equipment could be removed and evacuated. This force could then also provide a defence line along the rivers to cover the withdrawal of advanced troops should a retreat be necessary. To that end he set about contacting General Georges – still in overall command of the British units – at the HQ of the French Northern Forces. He followed this with a meeting with Beauman at Rouen.

Beauman had already set about the task of establishing a defence force for the L of C, inevitably now called Beauforce. He had passed responsibility for the administrative tasks to his sub-area commanders and was preparing improvised units from infantry base depots and the AMPC. Ironically, these men, largely discounted by Gort and the BEF, were often experienced reservists and better trained than many of their front line compatriots. There was a large cadre of veterans of the First World War who had survived the great 'Operation Michael' offensive of 1918 that had almost pushed the BEF into the sea and morale was still high amongst such men. They also had confidence in their commander, who had first led a brigade at the age of 29 and had been one of the youngest generals in the British Army by 1918.

General Sir John Greer Dill. Dill succeeded General Ironside as Chief of the Imperial Staff on 26 May. His dislike of Ironside was such that he countermanded or ignored orders already issued by Ironside – particularly that giving Karslake authority to command the British Army in France – creating additional confusion in an already untenable command structure.

He had hoped for better than the treatment he received after the war and, like Karslake, had been retired early. In the current situation he had been given carte blanche by de Fonblanque to do as he saw fit and he had seen in the situation a chance to shine and perhaps to resurrect his military career, so it was a guarded meeting when Karslake first arrived. Karslake, though, was sympathetic and the two men quickly established a good working relationship as Beauman explained his use of the forces available to him to throw a screen north and east of Rouen with its left flank at Dieppe. Karslake agreed and suggested that the screen should be organised on divisional lines.

Karslake also took the opportunity to meet with General Evans of the 1st Armoured and soon realised that the common problem was a sheer lack of information. Immediately he ordered the formation of motorcycle reconnaissance teams under the command of officers from the Royal Tank Regiment to find out exactly where British and French units were and, if possible, German locations too. Without a staff, he made do with the help of only a small number of officers on the ground but managed to complete a detailed report for Ironside by midday on Saturday the 25th. The officer entrusted with delivering this report was taken seriously ill during the flight to the UK so Karslake himself returned that evening, reaching the office of General Ironside at around 2100hrs. There, it was agreed that Beauforce would be formally restructured as a division and two experienced brigadiers recently returned from Norway with knowledge of German tactics would be sent out to work under Beauman as brigade commanders. Karslake, meanwhile, would be given the role of Corps Commander and assume control of all British forces still in France under one unified HQ.

Unfortunately, Ironside was in the process of handing over his post and taking up the command of all Home Forces from Monday 27 May. His replacement, Lieutenant-General Sir John Dill, had returned the day before from a visit to Gort in France and was, presumably, very much aware that the BEF had lost contact with the forces south of the Somme

General James Marshall-Cornwall. Sent by Dill to act as liaison officer without the authority to issue commands, Marshall-Cornwall was heavily criticised for his failure to protect British interests.

and that French command and control was disintegrating. After the Germans reached the Channel coast, over 140,000 British troops – a number roughly equivalent to that of the entire Allied landing force on D-Day four years later – had been left leaderless. Any communication with Gort had to be sent via London but if Gort had shown little interest in the Lines of Communication before, at least now he had an excuse to be preoccupied. The remaining men were on their own.

Clearly, Ironside's decision to appoint a single commander to manage the British south of the Somme made sound sense, but for some reason some of the decisions made that evening were never ratified and chief among the orders that were never enacted when Dill took over was that giving Karslake any authority to assume command. Charitably, one might suggest that Dill chose not to follow this plan because he misunderstood the intention and thought it better that Karslake concentrate on the removal of stores rather than combat. Equally, it is possible that he decided to ignore it because he disliked Ironside and, by extension, any potential supporter of Ironside. There is even some evidence that he may have cancelled the order giving Karslake command in the knowledge that his own friend, General Sir Alan Brooke, would be part of the 'Second BEF' Churchill was already proposing should be raised and sent to Normandy. If Karslake had command there, Brooke could not be given it. Indeed, one of Brooke's first actions on arriving in France with the new BEF four days before the final collapse was to order Karslake home – sending the man perhaps best placed to advise him on the situation away within two hours of arriving on French soil and without bothering with any handover briefing.

Whatever the truth, Dill's decision to cancel Ironside's orders left the British in France without any centralised command. To compound the problem, Dill then appointed Lieutenant General James Marshall-Cornwall to head No17 British Military Mission with orders to work with the French Army HQ to

> … see every order issued to the British troops, and to report at once to the CIGS if I considered that their survival would be imperilled unnecessarily … [Vice CIGS Lieutenant General Robert] Haining added that it was the Prime Minister's intention that the British troops should continue to fight to the last extremity in order to give the French no excuse for abandoning the struggle.[8]

Major A.G. Syme, commander of Syme's Battalion, Beauman Division. Syme's Battalion is credited with a textbook defence of the sector alongside the DWR and KOYLI despite being made up of men of over 30 regiments, few of whom had worked together before.

Taking up his role on 29 May, he arrived in France on the 31st, completely unaware of Karlsake's appointment and later complaining that Karslake's actions in assuming command were 'injudicious'.

The divisional structure for the Beauman Division had been put in place by 28 May and orders formally raising it were issued by the War Office on the 31st. It is a measure of the confusion Dill had brought with him that the same day he himself ordered its disbandment and the evacuation of its personnel. Karslake was prepared to lose the now redundant HQ 12 Division but was reluctant to see the Beauman Division go. Obliged to comply with Whitehall, he immediately went to General Georges to discuss arrangements. Georges was astonished at the request. Although under no illusions about its origins and weaknesses, Georges pointed out that quite apart from its value in holding its present line, its removal would sent a powerful signal to the French that the British were once again heading for home at the first opportunity. As a result of George's intervention, Dill reluctantly backed down.

Formally constituted as the first British Army division named after its commander since the Napoleonic wars, Beauman Division consisted of 'A' Brigade, (formerly Beauforce) now under the command of Brigadier Green and comprising the 4th Buffs, 2/6th East Surreys, 4th Borders and 1/5th Sherwood Foresters; 'B' Brigade (formerly Vickforce) under Brigadier Kent-Lemon and formed around three 'Provisional Battalions' – the 1st, 2nd and 3rd but more usually known as 'Merry's', 'Davies' and 'Newcombs' Rifles respectively. 'C' Brigade (formerly Digforce) under Lieutenant-Colonel Diggle was made up of three AMPC battalions – 'P', 'Q' and 'R'. To this, he was able to add divisional troops from the three 46th Division battalions stranded south of the Somme and 'Symes Battalion'. This last was to prove a highly effective example of improvisation, welding soldiers from over 30 different regiments into a single fighting force capable of proving a greater obstacle to the German advance than much of the BEF had managed to accomplish.

Against Beauman and Karslake's rapid progress in reorganizing the L of C, thus far Dill had managed only to create a system in which General de Fonblanque was in command of the administration of the L of C with Brigadier (now acting Major-General) Beauman commanding the defensive screen and both were answerable to Karlsake who, in turn, answered to General Georges at French Northeastern Command HQ. General Evans, commanding the 1st Armoured Division, was meanwhile answerable to Gort's GHQ but could only communicate after considerable delay via London as all lines connecting the BEF to the south had been cut and thus was at the mercy of any more senior officer to himself. General Fortune, whose 51st Highland Division were still under French command but working their way back to the British sector from Paris, was answerable to General Ihler of the French IXth Corps but also both Fortune and Ihler were directly under General Altmayer of the French Tenth Army. All were also required to take orders from Whitehall which could conflict with any orders from the French, but would be forced to argue their case whilst agreement between London and General Georges could be met.

In all this, Marshall-Cornwall's role was ostensibly to act as a liaison officer at Altmayer's HQ and to co-ordinate British and French efforts but his role owed more to diplomacy than generalship. He reports that he focused his attention on the 51st and 1st Armoured as the 'only fighting formations' still in France and dismissed 'Beauman's so-called division' as simply misleading the French into believing it 'had some fighting value'. This appears not to have simply been a military assessment but a highly personal matter. Beauman writes of having been denied promotion to Major-General because one of his rivals had learned that a member of the selection panel was keen on shooting and so had rented a game lodge where he entertained the panel member for a month. The rival was duly supported by the panel member and promoted. 'Even if I had been prepared to sink to such tactics,' Beauman wrote, 'I could not have afforded them.'[9] In Marshall-Cornwall's memoirs, he writes of having added his uncle's name of Marshall in order to gain an inheritance. He was thus able to rent a mansion near Perth with '250 acres of good rough shooting, including a fringe of grouse moor.'[10] He also notes that this lasted for about two years before 'I was promoted to the rank of Major-General at the age of 47. This was an early promotion in those days.'[11] Having gained his colonelcy in 1918 as a result of his staff work in the intelligence field, Marshall-Cornwall felt that this gave him seniority so it is little wonder that Beauman, who ended the war as one of the youngest Brigadier-Generals after leading the 69th Infantry Brigade of the 23rd Division during fighting in Italy and before that serving almost continuously as an infantry officer from the outbreak of war, felt that he had been cheated by a technicality – he had not been given sufficient seniority for substantive rank. Throughout his memoir, he refers to Marshall-Cornwall only as the 'Senior British Officer' whilst Marshall-Cornwall in turn manages just two passing references to Beauman and in his post campaign report is highly critical of Beauman's willingness to allow his men to use their initiative. In particular, he notes that Beauman issued orders that his men would be

> … required to give the maximum resistance possible without getting encircled. Orders for your retirement are left to your discretion, but should not be given until the enemy is reasonably near or there is a definite danger of encirclement … This is a very different spirit from Haig's order of 12 April, 1918: 'Every position must be held to the last man … With our backs to the wall and, believing in the justice of our cause, each of us must fight to the end.'[12]

Although quickly deciding that the French had lost control of the battle and describing a meeting with Altmayer and the French Commander in Chief Weygand marked by Weygand becoming 'hysterical' and 'screaming' that positions should be held to the last, with men fighting with their teeth if necessary, it seems odd that Marshall-Cornwall then goes on to criticise Beauman for not taking this same suicidal attitude, especially since he says he was there to avoid British troops being 'imperilled unnecessarily' and, in any case, did not regard Beauman's men as fighting troops. His account is filled with similar apparent contradictions, stating for example, that the 51st Division was 'not under my orders, but I felt that it was under my wing'[13] – an odd comment given that he had been sent specifically to guard its interests but perhaps one seemingly calculated to distance himself from the division's eventual fate. Equally, he wrote to Evans that his own 'personal feeling and advice to you' was that Evans must be prepared to sacrifice some of his men 'to bolster up the French', even though this would involve Evans deploying his men in 'an illegitimate role, but I feel this must be accepted.'[14]

For their part, it seems that Generals Beauman, Fortune and Evans had little respect for Marshall-Cornwall or his abilities. Other than brief visits to the front as part of his staff officer duties, Marshall-Cornwall had no combat experience and had never commanded a formation in action. Beauman, for example, describes a 'stormy interview' at French Army HQ with Marshall-Cornwall.

> This officer had during his service held a long series of staff and military attaché appointments. As a result his knowledge of the handling and management of troops was not based on much personal experience and he appeared to think that they could be moved about like chess pieces regardless of fatigue and the state of their equipment.[15]

After threatening to report Beauman to the War Office, the matter was settled by General Altmayer, who 'proved much more reasonable'. Marshall-Cornwall himself refers to an incident in which General Evans 'explained to me forcibly' that his tanks were in need of maintenance before they could undertake further action – although accepting Evans was 'right to do so'. It is clear from both his own memoirs and from other accounts at the time that he could contribute little more than an extra level of confusion to the situation and was either powerless or unwilling to countermand French orders for fear of the potential impact on his career rather than his duties to the British troops whose fate he would determine. In his rather self-congratulatory memoirs, he dismisses Karslake as 'the fifth wheel on the coach' but, this being the case, he himself became the sixth wheel. What was really needed now was a driver, but that chance had been missed.

NOTES

1 Chapman, G. *Why France Collapsed* 1968 p186
2 Karslake p94
3 Blaxland p355
4 Correspondence between Lord Hankey and General Ironside March 1940. WO 208/92
5 Karslake p91
6 Glover p151
7 Karslake p93
8 Marshall-Cornwall, J. *Wars and Rumours of Wars* 1984 p139
9 Beauman, A.B. *Then a Soldier* 1960 p91
10 Marshall-Cornwall p92
11 Ibid p94
12 Ibid p156. See also WO216/116
13 Ibid p147
14 Ibid p152
15 Beauman p166

Chapter Twelve

'Houses covered in rambler roses'

After a few days rest, the men of the 2/7th DWR had largely recovered. They had mounted anti-aircraft defences around the camp and now were ordered to begin setting up road-blocks along the coast road. The Dukes were under the command of 'Beauforce' and deployed as divisional troops with the task of holding the line of the river Bethune, linking with the 2/4th KOYLI around Arques-la-Bataille. The KOYLI in turn were in contact with the 2/6th Dukes further inland but the two battalions were ordered back to Rennes by train on the 26th. Just before leaving the KOYLI handed over their motor transport to the 2/7th to add to that already provided by HQ L of C to create mobile patrols to try to cover the numerous side roads along Beauman's 57-mile front. From their camp on the hillside, the Dukes had a grandstand view of the sporadic bombing raids on the harbour and, whilst they were not attacked, the threat remained. Watching a heavy raid one day soon after their arrival, a batman suggested that his officer might like him to fetch a brandy. Asked why, the man replied 'I think it might do us both good sir.'[1]

With no sign of the expected German attack, the battalion continued to reorganise, moving men from HQ Company to strengthen the rifle companies. On 29 May a reconnaissance party under Captain Gerrard went forward and made its way back to the abandoned train, reporting that whilst much of the battalion's luggage had been ransacked, its band instruments were still safe. Immediately, Colonel Taylor approached Brigadier Beauman. '[T]hey were loath to leave without their band instruments which had been left in the train,' wrote Beauman later. 'The country was by that time infested by German patrols but I agreed a rescue attempt.' At 2300hrs, Taylor held a meeting to organise the recovery party. 'This was very difficult as everyone wanted to go.'[2] Finding that the officers' luggage had been looted, probably by French civilians, the party had more luck in finding the men's greatcoats and packs and, of course, the instruments. On the 30th, the battalion 'marched triumphantly back to Dieppe with its band at its head.'[3] A delighted Bandmaster Doyle was then given permission to beat retreat in the town square.

Over the coming week, the battalion laid mines on the coast road and sent out patrols but despite a sense of a gathering storm, there was little sign of enemy ground troops approaching. On 5 June, the newly formed 'A' Brigade of the now official Beauman Division moved up to the line of the river Bresle to mop up an enemy infiltration into the Haute Forêt d'Eu in support of the 51st Highland Division, but that night word came back that enemy tanks had broken through. Reports came in of German airborne troop

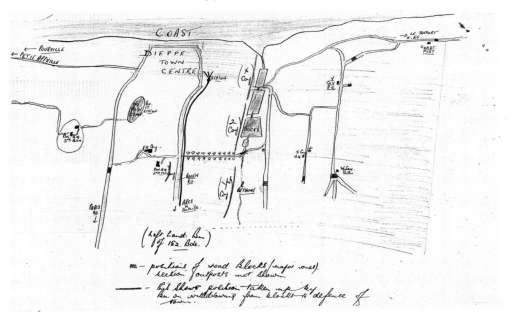

Sketch map of Dieppe.

landings but 'the only addition to the game register was a German parachutist who was shot whilst descending but not seriously wounded.'[4] Leading a patrol towards Eu on the 7th, nineteen-year-old Second Lieutenant Tom Birkhead was killed, the battalion's second combat casualty. That night, Taylor assumed command of all Dieppe's defences and decided that the evidence that the enemy were on the move and already across the Somme forced him to withdraw his forward companies from their exposed positions east of the town and around the grass aerodrome. Although their positions were sufficient to repel a raid, the main defences lay along the line of the river and the docks. That night, they withdrew. The landing strip was ploughed and any stores too heavy to move were destroyed.

The 51st Highland Division was nearing exhaustion after the Germans launched their new offensive, 'Operation Red', on 5 June. Dunkirk had fallen the day before and now attention turned to the south with a massive attack across the Somme. Around Abbeville there had been heavy fighting against 154th Brigade of the 51st. The 7th Argyll and Sutherland Highlanders had evacuated their remaining fit or lightly wounded men from their position in just four trucks, losing over 500 men as their isolated companies fought on after being surrounded for up to 48 hours before finally running out of ammunition. Although they yielded some ground, the Division had held firm despite the odds stacked against them. Having been given the impression that Marshall-Cornwall was acting in the role of corps commander, General Fortune wrote asking for permission to fall back to the Bresle if necessary. Marshall-Cornwall passed on the request to Altmayer, who was finally persuaded to agree although it went against Weygand's 'last man, last round' orders. Beauman then offered the 51st his 'A' Brigade as support and sent them forward to the Bresle, leaving the Dukes to garrison Dieppe. The move lost Beauman a third of his force, but also meant he was able to hand over responsibility for ten miles of front to General Fortune. Together, the two men discussed the possibility of a retreat along the coast to Le Havre but were worried about the ease with which they could be flanked by German armour.

General Victor Fortune. Criticised by the French as 'General Misfortune', the commander of the 51st Highland Division was placed by the War Cabinet in the impossible position of having to obey French commands as a political sop despite realising very quickly that the Division would be trapped as a result.

Regardless of the true facts around events, Weygand was already furious that the 51st had given any ground at all and, speaking to Churchill's representative General Spears, accused them of trying to make for the ports. He even managed to persuade the American Ambassador in Paris to tell Washington that the only breakthrough had come in the British sector and that 'the single British division in France, supported by the only British armoured force, had run from the Somme back to the Bresle.'[5] In fact, Rommel's tanks had broken through the French line as well but Weygand's claims would now make it impossible for Churchill to negotiate the extraction of the 51st without further international criticism.

Marshall-Cornwall then contacted London to report that French orders were placing British troops at pointless risk and asked that if the division could not be withdrawn, then two more divisions should be sent as soon as possible to reinforce them. Although the 1st Canadian Division was making ready in England, there was little hope of immediate relief. At worst, Dill thought, the division could be evacuated across the beaches but the potential political damage of withdrawing them now far outweighed their military value later. Nevertheless, Marshall-Cornwall argued that the division should be withdrawn from the control of the French and allowed to act independently to get their men to the lower Seine. His liaison officer was refused permission to cross the river by French troops and another was captured by a German patrol as he attempted to reach Fortune, who had already made the decision to send his guns towards Rouen.

It is unclear what Weygand's plans really were. The official British history records that by now the French Tenth Army Headquarters had moved south and all communication with their IX Corps had been broken. General Fortune was 'out of touch with everyone' due to the loss of his codes and much of his signals equipment. His only information so far about German progress had reached him when a dispatch rider arrived during the morning of the 9th with a message from Colonel R.B. Butler at the British garrison of Le Havre; he had been told by the French Admiral of the port that the enemy had entered Rouen on the 9th. On hearing this, General Fortune saw the IX Corps commander, who agreed that their withdrawal must now be changed from the direction of Rouen to Le Havre. Marshall-Cornwall, who appears by this stage to have turned his attention towards the defence of the Seine at Weygand's request, reported to London that the 51st had crossed

A German soldier watches as Rouen burns.

the line of the Bethune and that 'its withdrawal via Havre now seems the only chance.'[6]

The War Office then contacted the British Liaison Mission at General Weygand's headquarters with a report that 'Admiral commanding Havre had given orders to 51st Division to withdraw to that place. He has also asked for ships to evacuate approximately 60,000 French and 25,000 British from Havre to Trouville, Caen and Cherbourg. Is this in conformity with General Weygand's plan?' Dill had understood that the intention was to direct withdrawal on the lower Seine on either side of Rouen and this still seemed the most sensible move. Meanwhile, Fortune made contact via a dispatch rider sent to Le Havre who telephoned from there. 'I am now out of touch with everyone owing to the fact that I am not in possession of the recent code. All communications to me should be in clear or French code.' This was followed by a report of

> … Ninth Corps including 31 and 40 Divisions and two weak cavalry divisions moving west to Le Havre 51 Division on sea. Sending rearguard to reinforce French on line Fécamp–Lillebonne … My speed depends on French movement about 20 kilos a day. Tomorrow morning line should be Dieppe. Essential that air delay enemy movement mostly A.F.V. to south on Saint Saens–Bolbec road also his infantry advance from east. Air support requested to prevent unrestrained bombing. Naval support along coast also of great moral support. If enemy break through French or cut me off from Le Havre will attempt pivot on one of northern ports or in hope of evacuating a few men from behind bridgehead. My rearguard assisting French Fécamp–Lillebonne has orders to drive on Le Havre to attempt embarkation of as many men as possible.

As a result, by the night of the 9th the War Office knew that the 51st was withdrawing to Le Havre and the French Admiral there was asking for ships to be sent for evacuation.[7]

General Weygand, though, still clung to the belief that the IX Corps could carry out the plan to reach Rouen and next day signalled

> Orders of General Weygand dated 10 June. Fall back on the Seine below Caudebec inclusive. Protect your front in the direction Gournay–Rouen by occupying defensive position behind anti-tank obstacles. In cooperation with Admiral Le Havre reinforce bridgehead Fécamp–Lillebonne. Higher authority will prepare means of crossing [the Seine].[8]

The signal was sent via the Admiralty and the War Office with a request that it might be passed to the 51st Division for delivery to the commander of the IX Corps – itself demonstrating how little control Weygand now had of the situation if he had to rely on London to relay messages to his own troops in his own country. By that point, though, the Germans were within 20 miles of the city whilst Fortune faced a 45-mile journey. It was clearly hopeless.

In Tenth Army, Ihler believed it would take his men four days to reach Rouen by foot and it was now certain that the Germans would reach it first. The only possible route left for evacuation was therefore via Le Havre, 60 miles away. Fortune had the means to do it in 24 hours using his motor transport but he was all too aware that the French could not keep up. Gathering his men together, Fortune told them,

> Gentlemen I know you would not wish to desert our French comrades. We could be back at Le Havre in two bounds. But they have no transport. They have only their feet to carry them. We shall have to fight our way back with them step by step.[9]

As Fortune took the agonising decision to lead his men into almost certain defeat rather than abandon the French, he was already being made a scapegoat at Weygand's HQ. The French demands for '*défense à l'outrance*' was a dramatic gesture but no more than that. Without any effective control of their men, the French generals lost thousands of brave and loyal troops in countless last stands made irrelevant because their outposts could not provide mutual fire support and were simply surrounded to be mopped up later. In his desperation to keep the French in the war Churchill turned a blind eye to their incompetence and by refusing to accept Ironside's decision to appoint a single commander when he might have had a role, Dill allowed a situation in which Fortune was placed in the impossible position of being likely to find himself damned by his superiors if he saved his men but gave the Anglophobes in France more grounds for complaint, yet still providing them with ammunition to claim that it was he who had given way. In that light, it is hard to disagree with historians who claim that Weygand's action during this entire period were motivated by pure malice rather than any military sense; but pettiness was not solely a French vice. A measure of the state of Anglo-French relations by this time comes in General Spears' account of deliberately prolonging a telephone conversation with Weygand because he knew he was desperate to use the lavatory.[10]

Even in better circumstances, IX Corps was in no condition to complete the move. Before they were issued, Weygand's orders were out of date and he was ordering his army to withdraw into an area already under German control. Fortune and Ihler began to arrange the move to Le Havre, placing Brigadier A.C.L. Stanley Clarke in command of a screening force which, as it was formed at Arques la Bataille, was to be known as 'Arkforce'. He was to take under his command the remnants of 154 Brigade and 'A' Brigade together with elements of other battalions badly hit earlier, two French battalions and some 75-mm guns already on the position. General Fortune's orders added: 'Should it be apparent that enemy attack from the south or east on the IX Corps has made any organised evacuation from Havre impossible you will withdraw and evacuate at Havre as many of your force as you can, destroying all material and taking off such material as can be carried.'[11]

That night, the Corps began its retreat. The transport for the 51st passed through the Dukes by midnight on 8/9 June and the bridges behind them were blown, leaving a small fox terrier on the other side trying to get home. German probing attacks began to test the defences the following afternoon but suffered heavy casualties doing so. Brigaded alongside the 4th Seaforths and the 2nd Black Watch, the Dukes fell back along the coast until the night of 10/11th when they reached the village of Petit Appeville and found transport waiting for them. Following minor roads to reduce the risk of ambush, they arrived at dawn at the coastal town of Veules-les-Roses. 'The village, well named, looked very beautiful with most of the houses covered in rambler roses' wrote Taylor.[12] It did not look like a potential battlefield.

Unknown to the Dukes, 'Arkforce' were moving into position to cover the approaches to Le Havre between Fecamp and Bolbec, a front of around 20 miles; but at 1100hrs, a message reached Fortune that German tanks had already cut between him and Arkforce, a radio operator just having time to get the message out before being captured. Further reports indicated that panzers were at the coast near Cany. The closest port was still Dieppe but it was believed – wrongly – that the harbour was out of action and unusable. That left the fishing ports along the coast and, in particular, the port of St Valery-en-Caux, eighteen miles from Fortune's HQ. Signalling ahead, Fortune warned the naval detachments at Le Havre of his intentions and explained he had rations for two days. After jettisoning as much kit from their transports as possible, the division began to speed up its move.

By now, the Dukes had taken up position on the coast road at Veules-les-Roses with their left flank on the coast and the 4th Seaforths on their right on the Blossvale-Bourg-Dun road. As the remainder of the troops arrived, a thin screen formed around St Valery, its sides eleven miles apart. An hour after the message, the first bombs fell on Veules-les-Roses. It was a hot day and the strain of the operation was beginning to show. The men were tired and struggled to stay awake as they lay in their positions. At 1630hrs, a brigade conference took place with half a dozen German tanks visible just two fields away. Taylor was told that the division was now surrounded and that the intention was to evacuate across the beach as soon as the navy could get there. All vehicles were to be destroyed along with any spare stores.

The battalion was deployed with 'Y' Company on the right, 'W' Company in the centre and 'Z' Company on the left with 'X' Company held in support near Battalion

St Valery.

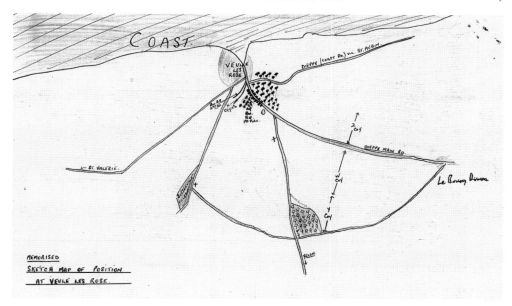

MEMORISED
SKETCH MAP OF POSITION
AT VEULE LES ROSE.

Sketch map of the St Valery area.

Headquarters in a sunken road on the outskirts of Veules-les-Roses. Heavy small arms fire began against 'Z' Company at about 1700hrs and was followed by a mortar barrage. At 1800hrs, a group of up to 40 tanks was spotted approaching along the main Dieppe road. Although they had no artillery or heavy machine gun support, the Dukes had been given two 20mm anti-tank guns which managed to get off one shot each before being destroyed.[13] Despite this, 'Z' Company were able to stop five or six tanks and the rest pulled back. During the attack, Captain R.H. Royds, commanding 'Y' Company, was hit three times just above the knee and had his arm broken by a bomb splinter but continued in command until two NCOs 'almost forcibly dressed his arm'. Managing to hide the relatively light leg injuries he was able to direct his men back to Veules after dark and was later prevented by the chaplain from venturing out to try to locate any missing men.

Elsewhere, Private L. Smith's section was pinned down by an LMG that had dismounted from the cover of a tank. Armed with a rifle and bayonet, Smith set out to find it. He failed, but as his Company Commander put it, 'it may be assumed that the gun crew retired rather than face cold steel.' In any case, there was no more fire aimed at his position. Lance Corporal Bill Gamble, in position at a roadblock, attempted to hold position against a tank attack with a Boys rifle until he was told that the battalion's entire supply of ammunition was gone. All across the battalion front clerks and cooks were acting as runners under fire and refusing to leave their comrades. In close fighting, Lance Sergeant J. Illingworth had killed several enemy soldiers when he was hit in the mouth by a spent bullet which broke his jaw and smashed his teeth into his mouth.[14] He refused to be evacuated and was later found trying to hide his injuries when he disembarked at Southampton. But despite their courage the end was coming.

Air activity had increased and Colonel Taylor refers to 'fireworks' being dropped. These are described as sounding like firecrackers and imitating the noise of heavy gunfire up to 20 minutes after the aircraft had passed over; the Dukes assumed that it was to undermine morale but in all likelihood it appears that what seemed to be the sound of gunfire behind

The basics of the evacuation of St Valery.

them may well have been simply that, rather than any special weapon. In any case, only two casualties are attributed to 'cracker bombs', both suffering slight burns.

At 1800hrs, Captain Hurst, the battalion's adjutant, reported a 'dogfight' overhead but noticed that none of the aircraft wore British markings and that a Henschel spotter aircraft flew over immediately and identified positions where troops had emerged to watch the air battle. Despite a few more probing attacks, Hurst says that by around 1900hrs, the battalion realised 'its leg was being pulled' and withdrew as many reserves as possible back to the sunken road. Crossing the open field towards the road, Arnold Straw came under fire and threw himself to the ground, only to find his knee landing in a pile of what he thought must be human excrement. Unpleasant, but the least of his worries. Once in the sunken road, most fire passed over the heads of the young men who were experiencing combat for the first time. Unable to fight back, many found this the hardest time of all.

Shortly after 2045hrs, the OC of HQ Company was organising listening posts when he saw a red flare fired in front of the forward positions. This was followed by three green flares around ten minutes later and immediately a heavy mortar barrage fell around him. Then, at 2110hrs, a fire so intense that one survivor likened it to 'somebody using a watering cart' opened up. Taking reports from company commanders, Hurst estimated up to 200 AFVs approaching. 'The outstanding feature of the German attack,' wrote one company officer 'was the incredible length of time such an enormous fire production can be maintained from AFVs. This gives rise to speculation as to the ammn position.'[15]

Among Peter Walker's company, sheltering in woods alongside 'Y' Company's position, the greatest number of wounds were caused by splinters from the shells as they burst among the trees, and minor wounds when the explosions blew chips off the trees with enough force to penetrate the skin. With the attack developing to their left and largely out of range, Walker's group took shelter in a slit trench. After days without sleep, one by one they drifted off to sleep, waking at dawn to find their position had been overrun. With further resistance useless, Walker and his friend John Marsland, together with Platoon Sergeant Major Douggie Harper and Captain Warton of 'Y' Company surrendered.[16]

Meanwhile, Colonel Taylor had been instructed to wait until darkness before finally giving orders for the battalion to make a break, telling them to withdraw to the beach near St Valery in small parties and wishing them Godspeed. One by one, sections began to pull back. Arnold Straw recalls being briefed by the padre before being handed over to the care of Lance Corporals Bill Gamble and Draper, both Sheffield men with previous military experience in India. Having had a chance to get his bearings, Gamble time and again acted as guide through the shattered streets and scattered rose petals of the burning Veules and towards the harbour where the men could see a destroyer standing off shore. With fires all around, the men ran the gauntlet across brightly lit streets where they made perfect targets for any German marksmen but fortunately few enemy patrols had yet penetrated this far. Even as Battalion HQ gathered its equipment, tanks were closing in on the sunken road. Only the lightly wounded stood a chance of escape; those too badly hurt to walk were left in the care of the padre to await capture.

Straw and his party reached the beach and scraped a shallow trench but despite their exhaustion were too tense to sleep. To the west, the men could see the flames of St Valery and hear the firing still going on there. Behind them the battle continued late into the night. Late in the evening, Regimental Quartermaster Sergeant Oakes was approached by the commander of a French artillery unit behind the Dukes' lines. He explained that enemy machine gunners were working their way around the seaward side and asked for help to dislodge them. Despite being under treatment for varicose ulcers contracted in the retreat from Abbeville, Oakes gathered a mixed force of 28 batmen, cooks and store men and led them in a counterattack lasting over an hour, securing the left flank and covering the retreat.

On the cliff tops above the beach, other Dukes were still trying to get away from the relentless onslaught. Cut off from the town and access to the beach, Company Quartermaster John Smith of the 4th Seaforths was also attempting to escape through the Dukes' positions that night. Like many others, he was unable to reach the town and desperately sought a way to climb down the cliffs instead. He unloaded a stock of army blankets from a truck and began knotting them together, strengthened them using rifle slings and secured one end to a three-ton truck.

> We had no idea if the first rope had hit the bottom, and the first few who volunteered to go down didn't know where they were in the dark. Of the first twelve, I think seven were killed. One shouted up 'we need more length at the bottom.' So we passed more rifle slings to the boys who were going down, and they tied them until they eventually made the ground. Quite a number got down that way along with me.[17]

The route was still in use seven hours later in broad daylight.[18] Private Jukes of the DWR would later report that he had climbed down 'a rope made of Frenchmens' belts.'[19]

All night the gathering groups of survivors were joined by men walking along the beach from St Valery. Captain Derek Lang of the 4th Camerons recalled walking along the foot of the cliffs.

> Evidently some of the troops had tried to descend the three hundred foot high cliffs on ropes. Few could have succeeded judging by the smashed bodies lying on the beach, while a hundred and fifty feet above we could see the frayed ends of their broken ropes.[20]

In the early morning mist, ships could be seen off shore but whether they were Allied or German was unclear. Unable to bear the wait, Arnold Straw's friend Doug Dart decided to

Troops retreat past a crater caused by the demolition of a roadway.

find out. Stripping to his underwear, he set out to swim to the nearest ship, over half a mile away, returning some time later with the good news. The evacuation was on.

As dawn broke, the men on the beach faced a new menace. German infantry had reached the cliff tops and were firing down on them. Men sheltered in sea caves at the foot of the cliffs but had to race across the beach under fire to reach the small boats coming to collect them. For the crews of some of these ships, the St Valery operation was considered to be far worse than Dunkirk had been. Already that morning, the ship they had sailed to France aboard – SS *Bruges* – had been sunk by bombers off Le Havre as it waited for the division to reach that port. A queue formed on the nearby jetty and on the beach as naval gunfire rained in to suppress the German positions. As fire came in, the lines scattered, only to reform as soon as the attack passed. Some decided to stay put rather than risk losing their place and stood patiently in the water as bullets whistled around them.

At sea, Arnold Straw was unceremoniously dragged aboard a boat by a Canadian sailor and taken to the steamship *Princess Maud*. He had just got below deck when the ship was hit by a shell just above the waterline. With the hole plugged with mattresses and sealed

St Valery after the battle.

British POWs in St Valery.

with a tarpaulin, the ship headed home. He was, he found out later, lucky. Many ships had sailed direct to Cherbourg and unloaded men there to wait for days to be taken home.

Lying on the beach, already wounded in the arm and chest, Lance Corporal Dickinson suddenly felt a powerful 'kick in the pants'. A few coins in his hip pocket had just stopped a German bullet which hit with enough force to imprint the design of one coin on the face of another. Dickinson would not make his escape. Nor would Bandmaster Doyle. His horse turned loose, Doyle volunteered to stay with the wounded as the Germans closed in. Colonel Taylor had not been seen since he left his HQ and was later reported captured. Captain Gerrard, who had led the rescue of the instruments, was dead. The battalion's war was already over.

Notes

1 Barclay p252
2 War Diary 2/7th Duke of Wellington's Regiment WO167/737
3 Beauman p128
4 Barclay p253
5 Glover p168
6 Ellis p283
7 Ibid p283–5
8 Ibid p285
9 See Glover p173 and Blaxland p367
10 Jackson, J. *The Fall of France* 2003 p103
11 Ellis p285
12 Barclay p254
13 Ibid p254
14 Accounts taken from After Action Report signed by Major Hirst 26 June 1940. Gawthorpe Papers IWM 78/44/1
15 Ibid
16 Peter Walker account accessed at www.dwr.org.uk
17 Saul, D. *Churchill's Sacrifice* p219
18 Williams, D. *The New Contemptibles* London 1940 p77
19 Private Jukes' statement. WO361/45
20 Lang, D. *Return to St Valery* London 1989 p33

Chapter Thirteen

'Non-swimmers stay back!'

Like their counterparts in the 2/7th, the men of the 2/6th Dukes began their long march back down the railway lines on the morning of 21 May. Lieutenant-Colonel Llewellyn had told his officers that 'if the men were to be … moved at all, they would have to do it on their feet, and soon.'[1] A foraging party had been sent out by truck to try to establish contact with any higher formation and to find food supplies but Llewellyn and Taylor had agreed that they could not stay put. Laden with everything they could carry, with no maps or even an idea of the distances to be covered, the lead company set out to navigate by the sun, keeping the railway line on their right as far as possible.

It was an impossible task. With German aircraft overhead constantly, the battalion moved into the cover of nearby woods. The countryside was described as 'so complicated' that contact between companies and platoons was lost, re-established, lost again until it seemed a hopeless task to try to keep the men together. Two platoons of the rearguard company went out to reconnoitre a village and could not find their way back to the main body. As they continued, Llewellyn's men found the commanding officer and 'ten very weary men' of the 2/7th Queen's Regiment who reported having spoken to Colonel Taylor's battalion and that they had just evaded tanks nearby. Llewellyn invited them to join him but the Queen's CO declined, saying he 'wished to take a straight line'.[2] Oddly, Llewellyn doesn't appear to have enquired what was meant by this and instead set out again on his by now chaotic cross country march.

At one point, with his band reduced to just 20 men, Llewellyn stopped to collect stragglers and after a while had increased his force to around 100. Behind him, 'D' Company had taken up position to guard the flanks from the threat of attack from the Abbeville–Rouen road. As they pressed on, the numbers fluctuated as Dukes were lost but stragglers from other units joined until, tired and thirsty, they reached Gamaches. There, two dispatch riders from the Grenadier Guards were waiting with orders for any units arriving to head for a line between Dieppe–Neufchatel. Congratulating himself on 'anticipating these orders to the letter',[3] Llewellyn was disappointed to read that no transport would be available. At his current speed, it would take two days to cover the 25 miles to Dieppe.

By early afternoon, the party had reached Guerville but by now the heat was beginning to affect several men. No food was available and the water supply was found to be contaminated. Two miles further on a special halt had to be called to treat several men who had collapsed. In the distance, troops could be seen and these proved to be a French machine gun section with horse-drawn guns heading in the direction of the nearby village of Melleville. A reconnaissance party made contact and heard from them that Gamaches was now in German hands. The Dukes' rearguard moved into Melleville at around 2030hrs and was fed by the inhabitants with eggs and milk but there was no bread to be had. An hour later, they pushed on towards Ville de Bas and found an excellent defensive position across the Fleuve L'Yeres stream at Val du Roi late that night. Around midnight, the three officers and 62 men still in contact with the CO settled down in barns as torrential rain began outside.

The scattered companies had made varying degrees of progress that afternoon. 'A' Company had reached a wood near Lemesnil and would be on their way again by 0300hrs the next morning. 'B' Company had strayed from the line of withdrawal and were sheltering in the Haute Forêt d'Eu. 'C' Company pushed on through the night, marching from the vicinity of Eu to Criel in six hours – a distance of less than ten miles – and resting for just five hours before setting out again. HQ Company were at Grandcourt, estimated to be about two hours ahead of the rearguard.

In fact, setting out at 0600hrs, it took the rearguard three hours to reach Grandcourt, finding the place cleared of any food supplies after refugees had passed through 'like a plague of locusts'. By 1400hrs progress had dropped to around one mile per hour. Any food supplies left were pooled to provide a hot meal which restored spirits, as did the arrival of Lieutenants Lawson and Smith with a truck filled with beef, biscuits, canned fruit and cigarettes after a successful foraging operation. They also brought news of the other companies and that the Germans were at Eu. That night, at Bethencourt, still more stragglers arrived and guards that night were drawn from the 2/6th, the 2/7th Queens and Engineers.

As the companies reached the British line, they immediately found themselves co-opted for other tasks. 'A' and 'B' Companies arrived at Neufchatel and were put to work loading heavy weapon ammunition supplies from the St Martin dump and digging positions to defend the stores not yet moved, constantly subject to air alerts and grabbing whatever sleep they could. When HQ Company arrived, 33 specialists were taken to join Vickforce and the remainder sent on to Rouen.

'D' Company, still acting as rearguard, was yet to reach the relative safety of Neufchatel. They had woken at 0400hrs to hear machine gun and rifle fire from the direction of Les Vieuxifs. Setting out an hour later, they were met at Envermeu by dispatch riders with the welcome news that transport was on its way from Dieppe to meet them. Llewellyn perched on the back of one of the motorcycles and went into Dieppe for orders. On 24 May, a week after setting out on their journey and three days after being stranded, the last of the Dukes were finally back under British command.

That night, reports began to filter in of German patrols just north of the Neufchatel line but no attack developed. The next day saw air raids over Dieppe but again, no ground attack came. On the 25th, Llewellyn was told to take the 2/6th and the attached men of the Queens to St Etienne du Rouvray, setting out from Rouxmesnil junction after dark. In pouring rain and with an air raid in progress behind them, the troops began the five-mile march past the aerodrome where damaged planes lay on the grass and through a wood where two young civilians on bicycles were seen acting suspiciously at a crossroads and narrowly escaped capture. A low flying plane failed to spot the battalion but rifle fire erupted around them as other units opened up on it.

The force reached St Etienne at around 0200hrs the next morning and was accommodated in an infantry base depot where the men were put to work in the local ammunition dump and preparing defences. They were joined the next day by the last of the rearguard

A Bren gun team in action.

company and news reached them that the battalion transport had been located. For the next few days the battalion worked at various sites around Rouen, a routine only broken when Captain Stell and eleven men in two trucks, equipped with three days rations, drove up to Dieppe to collect the battalion's drums from the 2/7th after their rescue of the band instruments. Hearing that the train was still at Chepy, they borrowed a Bren gun and anti-tank rifle and set out to see what could be recovered.

Arriving at Chepy, Captain Stell found that M. Pruvot had continued his work and the train was now at Le Treport. Masses of paper showed where it had been and shattered boxes lay around, smashed with 'pickaxes and choppers'. Moving to Le Treport, the train was located in a goods yard and as much equipment as possible was recovered. Pausing for a meal with the 2/7th and to return the weapons, Stell's group then set out after the rest of the battalion.

Whilst they had been away, the battalion had been moved yet again, this time to Bruz, just south of Rennes, to re-equip and to undertake intensive training at the Boozer Infantry Base Depot. One of their first tasks on arrival was to improvise a footbath in the bed of a 15cwt truck so the men could soak their blistered feet. Proper washing facilities were not available and water supplies to the camp barely existent, causing problems for arriving stragglers who reached the camp filthy and sometimes infested with fleas and ticks picked up while sheltering in woods and barns. 'Physically', the War Diary notes, 'this battalion was in a poor way.'

The first week of June saw them slowly recovering and able to make arrangements to carry out weapons training with the Bren and the anti-tank rifle – which, as the diarist dryly notes, was 'the first time that the men of this unit had been given this opportunity'. On the 6th, Llewellyn was told that the battalion would soon be required in an operational role and that he should be prepared to move at short notice. Beauman, now promoted to acting Major-General, had given his 'A' Brigade to the 51st Highland Division and the Dukes, together with the 2/4th KOYLI and the improvised 4th

Provisional Battalion (better known to all as 'Symes Battalion') were now their replacements in the Beauman Division.

At 1010hrs on the morning of 7 June, Llewellyn was told to have his men at Bruz station by 1030hrs and, remarkably, managed to get them together and to the station by 1050hrs, only to then wait until 1410hrs for the train to depart. The battalion transport had been sent to Rennes for loading but it was discovered that the loaded wagons were too high to pass under local bridges. They were again unloaded and sent on by road. For the Dukes and the KOYLI following behind, it was an eerie echo of the same journey just over two weeks before as they passed along the same line, finally reaching their destination at Louviers 24 hours after leaving Bruz.

Once again, chaos reigned. The battalion were now back to within a few miles of the camp at St Etienne but seemingly no better organised than when they left at the end of May. Transport arrived with some stores but not the additional Bren guns and anti-tank rifles they had been promised and which were included in the paperwork that came with the vehicles. The Dukes detrained as instructed at Louviers and began to prepare a meal. A few small scale maps were issued that were of little tactical use but at least gave the men an idea of where they were. Where they were, they soon found out, was in the wrong place. When the train carrying the 2/4th KOYLI arrived, it was discovered that the Dukes should, in fact, have been sent further along the line to Pont de l'Arche, a few miles further downstream on the river Seine towards Rouen itself. The KOYLI had been assigned the defence of bridges around nearby Les Andelys but by a fortunate coincidence, Llewellyn knew the area around there anyway – he had spent his honeymoon there and had walked the hills nearby. That helped to clinch the deal. The 2/4th agreed to push on and leave Les Andelys to the Dukes.

The German advance was in full swing and the panzer divisions were bearing down on Rouen. Weygand, in a highly charged meeting with Altmayer and Marshall-Cornwall, had dramatically claimed that if the Germans crossed the Seine he would advise the French government to surrender, declaring the coming fight to be

> … the decisive battle of the war! Every man must fight in his place! Every tank must be a fortress! Everyone must be in the attack! We must tear them apart with our teeth like a dog![4]

Altmayer is said to have given Marshall-Cornwall a sympathetic look. Both men knew that the temperamental and aging Weygand was barely holding on to his command and had already lost control of the battle.

Earlier that day, reports had reached HQ Beauman Division of an incident at Forges-les-Eaux when, at 1000hrs, a column of tanks with French markings approached a British checkpoint. The troops had been warned that French tanks were operating in front of them and cheered as they passed through the roadblock, which had been left partially open to allow infantry the withdraw through it.

> These tanks were captured French tanks manned by Germans. As soon as they had passed through they closed their turrets, turned around and annihilated the posts with MG fire. This enabled further large enemy AFV formations and mechanised infantry to pour through.[5]

The incident highlighted how thin Beauman's defensive screen actually was. By 1500hrs Beauman ordered 'B' Brigade to make for ferries across the Seine downstream from Rouen

German cyclists. Using bicycles, German infantry were able to advance rapidly to support their tanks.

German troops operate a makeshift ferry to cross the Seine.

Riders of a reconnaissance squadron crossing a river.

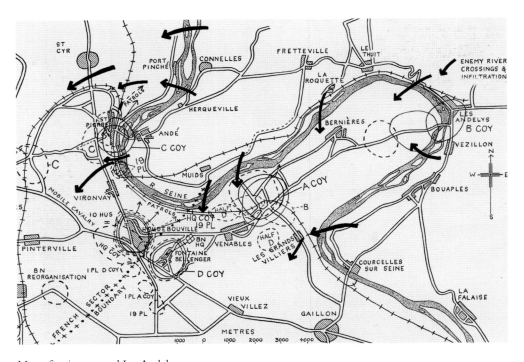

Map of action around Les Andelys.

at Duclair and Caudebec and for 'C' Brigade to head for Pont de l'Arche. The newly arrived Dukes, KOYLI and Symes Battalions would hold the river line as the others withdrew.

The Dukes were asked to take up positions around two bridges, one at St Pierre du Vouvray and another at Les Andelys, where the river curves in a long bend through hilly, rolling country. To the Dukes' left would be the KOYLI, to their right a mixed French force. The twelve-mile front assigned to them was a pre-war tourist destination where people came to enjoy the river. As such it was filled with potential crossing points and 'it was very soon realised that the enormous area of country to guard against infiltrations by portable bridge or boats from all company flanks was impossibly large.'[6] All along the front were riverside villages linked to islands in the river, heavily wooded banks and boats and punts 'abounded everywhere'.

The first bombs had fallen on Les Andelys at around 1100hrs on that Saturday morning and an exodus of the population had begun. As Colonel Llewellyn began his reconnaissance at around 1830hrs, another heavy bombing raid struck the area and a four-horse wagon filled with refugees and their belongings took a direct hit just yards from his car. Pressing on, he established contact with the KOYLI and with the strong French garrison at Gaillon. The iron and concrete suspension bridge at St Pierre was covered by a French 75mm gun as well as 'C' Company of the Dukes, and a mass of refugees had begun to accumulate in the area, hoping for protection. At Les Andelys, 'B' Company had established its positions on both sides of the town bridge, itself already prepared for demolition. At Heudebouville, HQ Company stood in reserve and were patrolling the riverbanks. Alongside them, No19 Platoon, formerly designated as the anti-tank platoon, were dug in near a railway bridge in support of a detachment of French engineers with a small calibre gun. The platoon had just two LMGs and one anti-tank rifle available to cover its objective.

That evening, the enemy were still 45 miles away but their commander, General von Manstein, was determined to strike before the defence line could be completed and ordered the spearhead units of his divisions to push on as fast as possible, 6th Division to Les Andelys, 46th Division towards Vernon and the Pont de L'Arche. 'This was an extraordinary feat to expect,' he later wrote,

> … from troops who had been engaged in a running fight with the enemy for four days past, but there happen to be moments in war when a senior commander must impose the most severe demands if he is to avoid flinging away an opportunity for which his troops may have to fight all the harder later on.[7]

By the following morning, his men were approaching the river. The air raids that had set Les Andelys ablaze had, to von Manstein's annoyance, simply served to announce the approach of his men and put the defenders on their guard so the crossing was likely to be harder than he had hoped.

On the morning of the 9th, the battalion intelligence officer, Lieutenant Cooper, had gone to HQ to request maps, only to be told there were none to be had. He was also told that the KOYLI had been attacked by tanks and were even now holding their ground. With this news, it was decided to withdraw across the bridges and make ready to blow them. Out of the blue, a British armoured detachment of one tank and two machine guns arrived at St Pierre, adding significantly to the firepower available; but Colonel Llewellyn was concerned to find instructions to withdraw to Bernay via Neuberg after dark under the codename 'Nora'. Despite No19 Platoon reporting the presence of growing numbers of Germans on the opposite bank, no attack had yet been made and Llewellyn saw no good reason to suddenly pull back twelve miles. As the Adjutant attempted to contact HQ using the telephone at Fontaine Bellenger, he found his call answered in German and 'several suspicious looking individuals in the village were arrested.'[8] Concerned about fifth columnists, Llewellyn decided to ignore the order. He then managed, with difficulty, to track down the local French commander and explained his decision. 'He thanked me with great cordiality' and told Llewellyn that French infantry and artillery support were on their

German troops take shelter during an artillery barrage.

way to relieve pressure of the Dukes' flanks at Venables. A relieved Llewellyn returned to find orders from British HQ to stay put.

Approaching from the north was the German 6th Infantry Division, its advance led by the mounted cavalry of 1st Reconnaissance Squadron led by the aristocratic Oberleutnant Georg Freiherr von Boeselager.[9] Early on the morning of 9 June, he received surprise orders: 'Division has reached the Seine ahead of schedule – Reconnaissance Section will form a bridgehead against Les Andelys for the division to follow across.' By 0715hrs he had formed a forward troop in vehicles with orders for the mounted squadron to follow behind.[10]

Even in the early hours, the weather was oppressively close and humid as his saddlesore men mounted their horses and followed the heavily laden personnel and supply lorries. By midday, the unit was in the village of Saussay, where his men went in search of a watering trough but found instead 40 French soldiers hiding in a barn. Taking their surrender, the Germans simply pointed the prisoners in the direction of the infantry follow up and left them to make their own way into captivity. Then, maintaining an advance of over five miles per hour, the unit rode via Clery towards Les Andelys. The bridge there was already blown but a small force was sent ahead to try to seize another eight kilometres upstream of the river at Courcelles before it could be blown. As they approached, it too exploded. 'All of a sudden, a violent explosion. Broken masonry rains down and the air pressure shatters windows all around. We are too late.'

The rest of Boeselager's men now assembled on the Bouaffles–Vezillon road, just off the Dukes' right flank. 'B' Company and the French troops had been under mortar and machine gun fire for some time from tanks and infantry on the north bank where the fire was so accurate that all but one of 'B' Company's LMGs were knocked out in the barrage

German troops advance as French POWs are marched to the rear.

and the ensuing air attack, leaving speculation that enemy troops were already directing it from riverside cottages. There was no choice now but to pull back to a line across the main road at Bernieres. Across the river, refugee traffic stacked up as the crossing points were destroyed and the German advance slowed as they tried to force their way through the crowds. Then, according to German reports, the French opened up with machine gun and artillery fire indiscriminately. In terror, civilians ran towards the Germans, crying 'heil Hitler' and taking shelter alongside the troops.

Oberleutenant von Boeselager then seized the initiative when, after scouting 500 metres below Courcelles, he found a crossing point: 'Everybody in my command listen! Non-swimmers stay back!' then, with Leutnant Meier and twelve men, all loaded down with rifles, ammunition, flare pistols and their personal equipment, he began to swim the river. Three men were lost in the crossing as the current swept them away but the rest quickly established themselves on the muddy bank as the non-swimmers provided covering fire.

As the group took control of the far bank, an engineer truck arrived with inflatable rafts and 60 men were sent across along with an anti-tank gun. By the time von Manstein arrived, the crossing was well under way at three points. Satisfied, the general set off to check on the progress of the battle at Pont de l'Arche where, unknowingly, the entire German 46th Division were pitted against just one battalion of their British counter-parts. 'One or two difficulties did crop up in the case of 46 Division, however', noted von Manstein later.

First of all, it had moved off three hours later than was expected. By the time I returned to it after visiting 6 Division it had lost all contact with its reconnaissance battalion, and the latter, wherever else it might be, was certainly not at the Seine, like that of 6 Division.

There was nothing for it but to suggest to the commander of 46 Division that he meet me early that evening at Vernon, his crossing place. He might, I added, at least bring his missing reconnaissance battalion along with him.[11]

Across the river, von Boeselager had taken a small group forward towards Villiers and ambushed a French motor column with grenades and machine guns, sending the French racing for the cover of ditches. Although a small force, the infiltration served to highlight how vulnerable the Les Andelys salient had become. Throughout the night, three French counterattacks failed to dislodge von Boeselager's men.

The Dukes had been bemused by the arrival during the night of French cavalrymen armed with sabres and were not surprised when, at 1400hrs, they rode away. Just one French officer and six of his men seemed determined to make a fight of it and stayed. By now, they knew that German troops were across the river behind them and that it was only a matter of time. Second Lieutenant Reynolds and six men fought with an LMG until their position was finally overrun and by then, Llewellyn had decided that it was time to pull back to a position around Venables to prevent 'B' Company being surrounded from both north and south. Between them, 'B' and 'C' Companies had a front of just two miles but their move had been observed and no sooner had they taken up position than a heavy mortar attack began.

Llewellyn had been summoned to attend a conference at the French HQ at Chateau du Hazy at 1630hrs and left Captain Stell with clear instructions about how to employ the reserve if necessary. Reports from along the battalion front indicated that they were holding but under pressure, especially at the outposts at Andé, to the west of the sector. Llewellyn duly reported at 1630hrs and found Colonel Diggle, commander of Beauman's 'C' Brigade already there, his AMPC battalions being deployed to the left of the KOYLI in the same sector. It was not until 1700hrs, however, that General Malliard arrived and then, after listening to Llewellyn's assessment and request for support, 'carefully explained' that he was in command of the 5e Brigade de Cavalerie and responsible for Sub Sector East. This

Beauman Division mobile column in Normandy.

line ended at Fontaine Bellenger. 'C' Company and No19 Platoon were therefore not his problem but that of Sub Sector Centre. With implacable Gallic logic, Malliard insisted that if Llewellyn wanted help for his beleaguered company, he should apply to Lieutenant-Colonel Watteau at his HQ in the school of St Cyr-du-Vaudreuil, around ten miles to the north. As Beauman's after action report explained,

> … the practice of putting small packets of British troops under Allies is disastrous … the [2/6th DWR] was placed astride a French intercorps boundary. As a result the bn commander received conflicting orders throughout the day from various French commanders. This bn was also moved so far from the rest of the division that supply became impossible, and the bn ran out of food and ammunition.[12]

Llewellyn left the meeting with 'grave misgivings'. He had been asked to use his reserve 'D' Company to extend the line at Les Grands Villiers with the promise that a French detachment would reinforce 'B' and 'D' Companies but also with the news that the local commander did not consider HQ and 'C' Company to be his problem. 'This appeared a strange piece of tactics' noted the war diary, 'as the French, like ourselves, were being outflanked'[13] – and Llewellyn was unwilling to run the risk of having his battalion literally cut in half. His reluctance was later criticised by Malliard, who complained of 'worrying apathy' on the part of the British who, he claimed, 'could only be kept in the battle with difficulty'.[14] By the time he got back, though, the orders were no longer valid. 'A' and 'B' Companies were pinned down by mortar fire and holding off determined infantry attacks. Gradually, they disengaged and pulled back along the line of the railway at the base of the peninsula. 'D' Company's commander, Captain Stell, had been badly wounded during a reconnaissance for the move to Les Grands Villiers when he found the village already occupied. His companion was killed as they came under heavy fire. It was only that evening as the battalion truck was driving the Colonel to visit a position that they saw a body lying at the side of the road and found Stell trying to crawl back to his men.

Fighting in fields of standing corn, the Dukes were by now firing at movements in the crops, 'the method of shooting rabbits in happier times', as the Germans approached within 30 yards of their positions, only to be beaten back. As dusk fell, the fighting slowed. Casualties were evacuated two at a time on stretchers aboard the single small truck the Dukes had with them. Overnight, patrols were mounted to try to prevent more enemy machine gun teams getting across the river. 'C' Company, outflanked on both sides, pulled back three-quarters of a mile to the Heudebouville–St Cyr road but any attempt to get a runner to Battalion HQ was met with a hail of gunfire.

By 0300hrs, the position of No19 Platoon was becoming precarious and in desperation, Llewellyn decided that he had to attempt to contact Watteau, setting out by truck along the road running parallel to the river. After a few miles, near Louviers, he met with a British brigadier with a small force of light tanks who promised to do what he could. Pressing on, he finally found Colonel Watteau who blithely told him that whilst Llewellyn might think his battalion was there, as commander of that sector he could assure him that there were no Allied troops in the Heudebouville area and, furthermore, that the road Llewellyn had just used was impassable because the Germans had already cut it. Realising just how out of touch Watteau had become, Llewellyn went back to his battalion.

As the morning wore on, 'C' Company began its withdrawal in contact so close that its rearguard and the advancing Germans were firing at each other from opposite sides of a crossroads. Suddenly, the British tanks Llewellyn had met earlier 'like a Buffalo Bill story

Abandoned vehicles litter the road to Cherbourg.

Exhausted troops reach Cherbourg on a commandeered lorry.

of Wild West rescue, appeared near the positions occupied by HQ Company and immediately went into action.'[15] They were followed at around 1400hrs by the arrival of nine tanks of the 10th Hussars which meant that apart from the endangered 'C' Company positions, the Dukes' line would now hold. But not so the French.

At 1450hrs, Llewellyn contacted General Maillard, who informed him that the French troops were moving south and that the British should rejoin their lines along the river Eure via Acquigny. By luck and good management, contact was broken off by 1700hrs and with HQ Company as rearguard, the battalion marched through the night. Bypassing the bombed Evreux, they found the once beautiful town of Neuberg in a shambles. There were no civilians but the town was crammed with worn-out French troops and a strange, langorous atmosphere hung over it. Leapfrogging using the battalion transport they reached

Bernay in the early hours of the 11th. From a packed railway station, trains crammed with refugees were constantly leaving, interspersed with hospital trains full of wounded.

Behind them, the battle continued. Arriving in Les Andelys from Paris at the end of the month to check on friends in the area, Andre Montier found the town devastated. His friend Hauchard told him how, on the Sunday morning, he and his family had been amongst the last to leave. Packing everything they owned onto their horse-drawn wagon, he, his son-in-law and his eight sons, along with their dogs, had set out only to find the battle already raging around them.

The bridges were blown and the refugee traffic stacked up as an artillery duel began. The horses, terrified by the noise, bolted and Hauchard was thrown off but managed to find them a short time later, caught in the trees nearby. Others had not been so lucky and at least three people had been killed. Deciding that the risk of being caught on the road was too great, he then found himself looking after around 125 cows and 50 horses in neighbouring farms, ensuring that they were fed and watered over the coming days.

The battle had been followed by the arrival of the Germans, taking over cottages as billets, sleeping up to six in a room. Pontoon bridges had been thrown across the river and the walls of several gardens had been knocked down to widen the tracks from the riverbank. Then came the bombers. British and French aircraft had tried to hit the bridges and to delay the repairs to the Le Manoir rail bridge. Obsolete Fairey Battles of 88 and 103 Squadrons of the RAF had repeatedly attacked with varying degrees of success. One family had spent twelve days sheltering in their cellar before feeling able to venture out.

All that was now in the past. As Montier wandered around, he saw German soldiers sunbathing by the water as if on holiday but the peaceful scene jarred with the ruins surrounding him. In the centre of town, he reported that '95% of the buildings are destroyed entirely and I could recognise only the shells of the Town Hall and Courts. Nothing at all was left of three solicitors' offices.' The cathedral seemed intact but he was told that the vaults had been badly damaged by incendiaries and hand grenades. Every day, they said, bodies were being found in the rubble. Near the station, a Panhard armoured car stood immobile, a huge swastika flag draped over it as a signal to the Luftwaffe. A fire engine stood burned out. On the roads around, he saw signs of battle everywhere.

> At the crossroads on the roads to Villers and Louviers stood a tank, beside it a grave … cases of ammunition stood by a silent gun, military effects lying around as German cars passed by…at the side of the road, evidence of the intense passage, the grass no longer existed and broken branches lay all around. Jars of jam, cigarette packets and boxes of matches lay around and papers were strewn around in the sunshine … Those houses not destroyed had tiles missing and windows shattered by the blasts … On the approaches to the bridge, a burnt out machine gun and another grave, this time that of a young girl … It was very sad, it was total desolation.[16]

Glad to be away and settling in a wood in the grounds of the Chateau Bernay, the Dukes rested as Colonel Llewellyn went forward to reconnoitre Beauman Division's new positions between the Pont d'Ateau and Brionne on the river Risle, staying away until late in the night whilst the men slept out in the open in torrential rain. The next morning, they were visited by the division's Assistant Director of Medical Services, Colonel Austen Eagger..

> Inspected 2/6 DWR. CO evacuated suffering exhaustion neurosis. 50 cases same, morale very low. Reported and suggested Div taken out before more affected.[17]

British trucks aboard an evacuation ship, Cherbourg.

Outbreaks of scabies and lice were also reported, further adding to the misery of the exhausted men. They were, it was decided, 'totally unfit for battle for at least three days.'[18] Despite this, as they settled down to sleep in barns around the neighbourhood, orders were received to supply five officers and 100 other ranks for a volunteer force under the command of Captain Rostron. Volunteers quickly came forward but no further orders reached them until the afternoon of the 14th when they joined with a similar band of

This page and overleaf: British evacuation, Cherbourg.

KOYLI volunteers and were sent to Beaumont Le Roger under Major Archdale. Orders to withdraw arrived at 0100hrs on the 15th and the move was scheduled to begin at 0330hrs via Broglie to Lisieux. Fortunately, by this time the German main thrust had turned south towards the Loire and it was relatively easy to pull back, although there were still disquieting moments.

The rest of the men, only around 300-strong by now, were moved to a rest camp at Sees. Lieutenant Cooper took a truck with 22 wounded men to Le Mans, only to find the hub of the L of C deserted but strangely tidy. Sapper Bill Harvey, one of those evacuating Rennes on the 15th recalled how he and his colleagues opened a NAAFI store and took what they needed but when they pulled out, the stores buildings were neatly locked behind them. Personal items left behind were likewise locked securely away to await the inevitable German plundering. Throwing blankets and food to passing refugees, the base area troops were ordered to head for the ports of Brest, St Malo and Cherbourg, creating huge traffic jams as military police ordered all vehicles to be disabled.[19]

The Dukes, uncertain of what was happening, sent a dispatch rider to Divisional HQ only to find it gone 'without any notification of their whereabouts'. Fortunately, on the 16th, Lieutenant Griffiths arrived with the order to head for either Brest or St Malo. The battalion's single three-ton truck and its water cart now operated a shuttle, again leapfrogging groups of men forward in a race against time. Information became even harder to find. The battalion were told to go to Redon, only to have the order cancelled immediately and instructions from General Marshall-Cornwall who was now, at last and too late, nominated as commander of 'Norman Force', to head directly for the coast. Newly arrived Canadian troops were attempting to hold a defence line across the Cherbourg peninsula but were already pulling back by the hour. The 'second BEF' was no sooner in France than

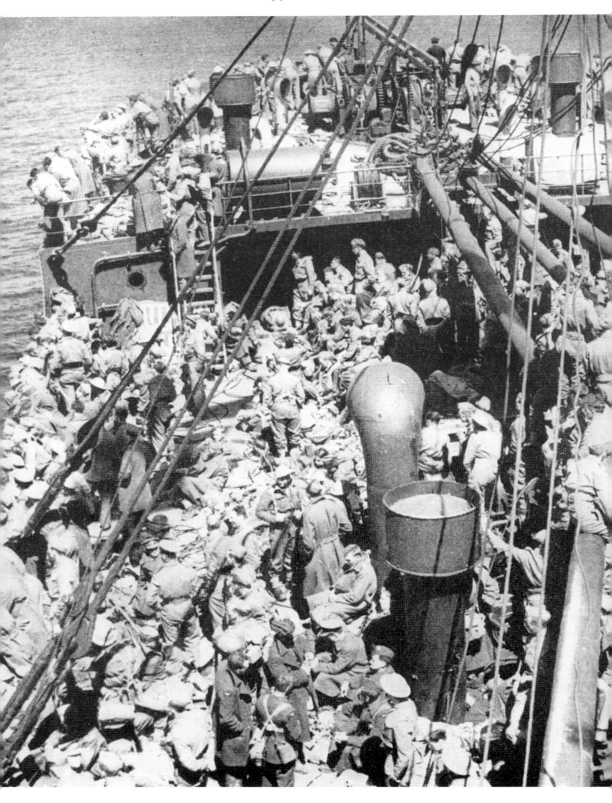

it was being forced out again. The 1st Canadian and 52nd Lowland Divisions, together with the Beauman Division, the remnants of the 1st Armoured Division and their French colleagues – an estimated force of around 30,000 evacuated through Cherbourg alone, with over 20,000 through St Malo – were being pushed out of France by a single German division under General Rommel.

The surrender came on 17 June when the Dukes were three kilometres from the town of Vitre and searching for fuel for their vehicles. On the way they had managed to acquire a few more and were making reasonable progress but Vitre was 'devoid of all British troops and GHQ had evacuated the day before.'[20] As they were gathering what they could, the news came over the French wireless. They then encountered an officer who advised them to get to St Malo, 80 miles away, as quickly as possible. Siphoning fuel from the tanks of three of their vehicles every man crammed aboard the remainder and the trucks raced for the coast. That night, 1,800 men sailed aboard a ship licensed to carry 800. Captain Rostron and his men had reached Cherbourg and the similarly crowded *Duke of Argylle*. Both reached home the next day.

The next day, 18 June, and in keeping with the unit's experiences, rail transport officers directed the battalion's train to Rotherham, where no-one knew they were coming and so redirected them to Leeds. The 46th Division was supposed to regroup in Manchester.

Notes

1 War Diary 2/6th Duke of Wellington's regiment. WO167/736

2 Ibid

3 Barclay p204

4 Marshall-Cornwall p144–5. See also Blaxland p364

5 Report dated 8 June. Beauman Papers

6 War Diary 2/6th Duke of Wellington's regiment. WO167/736

7 Erich Von Manstein in Powell, AG. *Lost Victories*. Chicago 1958 p140

8 Barclay p209

9 Boeselager was killed on the Eastern Front on 27 August 1944. Two days later, he was posthumously promoted to full colonel and awarded the Knight's Cross with Oak Leaves and Swords — one of only 159 German soldiers so decorated in the history of the award. Later it was revealed that he and his brother had been involved in the July plot to assassinate Hitler and had been marching his troops to Berlin when news of its failure reached him. He was able to disguise the troop movement as a move towards the front and initially avoided suspicion. When investigators later contacted his old unit in France to demand that 'First Lieutenant von Boeselager' be detained for questioning, his former comrades recognised the threat and, since he had long been promoted beyond lieutenant rank, replied that they knew no such officer. It seems likely that he chose to die in battle to deny the Nazis the chance to discredit his family.

10 Account of the river crossing and subsequent action is translated from *Oberkommando des Heeres. Tag und Nacht am Feind* Gutersloh 1942 p127–132.

11 Von Manstein, op cit p141

12 Conclusions. After Action Report by Major-General Beauman, June 1940. Beauman papers.

13 War Diary 2/6th DWR

14 *Résumé succinct des opérations de la 5e. Brigade de Cavalerie. Service Historique de l'Armée de Terre*

15 Barclay p213

16 Account translated from http://hvmontier.free.fr/andelys_1940.html

17 Report of Assistant Director of Medical Services, Beauman Division. WO177/436

18 Barclay p214

19 Account accessed at BBC People's War site www.bbc.co.uk/ww2peopleswar/stories/17/a4195217.shtml

20 War Diary 2/6th DWR

Chapter Fourteen

'I was never a boy any more'

When the KOYLI train stopped outside Abbeville on the afternoon of 20 May, Lieutenant-Colonel Hodgkinson had hoped that he could press on around to the west of the city and still reach St Pol as ordered. Pushing ahead of the main party, Lieutenant Lee and the four men of his recently formed Intelligence Section reconnoitred the route ahead. Don Clark, one of the four, would only retain vague memories of the immediate aftermath of the attack on the train but remembered around 40 KOYLIs spending the night in a field wrapped in their groundsheets and that he and Lieutenant Lee found a French 75mm gun position abandoned 'like the *Marie Celeste*'. He would also remember the shock of seeing the endless stream of refugees and his first sight of the enemy approaching in a 'non-stop stream of tanks, guns and motorised infantry' he estimated to include well over 2,000 vehicles. Most of all, however, he would remember the feeling of being left behind.

Soon after crossing the Somme, it became clear to Hodgkinson that trying to advance against the flow of refugees into an uncertain situation was too much of a risk.

Men of the Second BEF embark from the UK aboard a French warship.

Thousands of men left behind are rounded up.

The battalion was ordered to turn back and he was told that a train would be waiting for them. For some reason, though, Clark's party had not received the order. Finding themselves alone, Lieutenant Lee paraded the men and told them to make their way towards Dieppe and to keep going until they met anyone collecting stragglers. In the chaos all around them there would be little hope of staying together so each man should keep the sun on his left in the morning and walk towards it in the evening. That way they should at least reach the coast. The remaining food was shared out – some raisins and a few tins of pilchards – and then the men started out.

Those who had received the order to turn around had made their way back in the darkness across the bridge and turned right onto the tracks, joining the mass of people trudging silently down the line 'like spectators coming away from a football match'[1] carrying whatever they could from their homes. There was no sign of the driver of their engine and no way to contact anyone for help so Colonel Hodgkinson ordered all secret papers to be destroyed and for the men to salvage what they could. The best he could do for now was to tell them to follow the tracks and make for Dieppe. With no maps available, it was the only town they knew the route to that would contain British troops. As they turned away from the train, the huge numbers of refugees made any attempt to maintain contact between groups impossible and Hodgkinson just had to hope that come daylight some sort of order could be restored.

'Walking on the ballast soon made soft feet sore and the alternative of doing a sort of dot and carry step on the sleepers was very exhausting'[2] and after about three miles of this Company Quartermaster Sergeant John Brown was already feeling the strain. At a small bridge, he met a group of British officers and Belgian soldiers who asked who was in charge of his party. Brown replied that he was the senior man. They had a suspected spy they wanted to hand over but Brown was too busy to even consider accepting him and said so. Without trying to force the issue, the officers then told him that they were planning to dump their kit and head for Dieppe as fast as possible and advised him to do the same.

Brown thanked them for the advice and asked about the train standing alongside. That, he was told, was a refugee train and wouldn't be moving for at least two days. Then he noticed the lights of another train up ahead on the track. It was moving at walking pace and he could see one or two men jumping aboard. Taking his leave of the group at the bridge he and his small party caught up and threw themselves into the open door of a cattle truck to find a mixed group of KOYLI and Belgian troops inside. Panting could be heard outside the slow moving train as the suspected spy and his escort caught up with Brown and asked him what to do. Brown told them to shoot him but then, his training as a solicitor's clerk coming back to him, asked if the man had been tried. Hearing that he hadn't, Brown urged the men not to kill him. He was thrown into the next wagon.[3]

The journey was a short one and after covering perhaps four kilometres in half an hour, the train lurched to a halt. The line ahead was blocked – probably by the broken down train the Dukes had cobbled together – and the Belgians were ordered off. As they assembled on the trackside, Brown noticed that the guard appeared but without the prisoner. He decided not to ask questions. Nearby, he spotted a group of around 25 KOYLIs under the command of Lieutenant O'Connor and ran to catch up. Together they set off once again on their trek. The exhausted Brown had to abandon his pack after a short distance just to keep up. Unknowingly, in the darkness they passed through the area held by the Dukes and soon encountered the wrecked train at Fressenville, Brown noticing the decapitated driver and the mourning dog that would still be there the next day when the Dukes arrived. The KOYLI party was too small to do anything. They pushed on.

Just after 0700hrs, they reached a small village. His water bottle empty since the day before, Brown was parched but the locals refused to allow the men to refill their bottles. Instead, in desperation, he agreed to pay 50 francs for a siphon of soda water from the owner of the cafe. There was no food available for them at any price. Moving off two hours later, he reached a footpath just off the main road before he 'laid down and fell into a coma'.[4] The Regimental Quartermaster woke him and gave him a sip of whisky from his flask, encouraging him with the news that transport would be with them soon. Sure enough, a short while later Captain Taylor arrived with one of the battalion trucks and ferried Brown and two other men to nearby Eu.

Behind them, Clark and his party had only just reached the Pont Laviers and crossed the Somme back to the southern bank. Pausing for a rest, they suddenly noticed the refugees scattering as a German motorcycle group appeared less than 70 yards away. Reacting quickly, Clark's Bren killed them before they could open fire. Then they joined the exodus down the line. Oddly, Clark felt safe in the crowd, almost invisible, 'like a tiny fish in a gigantic shoal when predators circle around.'[5]

Collecting points had been set up at Eu and as members of the battalion reached it they were directed to an abandoned hospital at Floques, two miles out of town. As the tired men arrived they found clean clothes being issued from the stores and a large Michelin map pinned to the wall – their first indication of where they actually were. All day men limped in, but by nightfall around a quarter were still unaccounted for. Many seem to have been found by the Dukes and rejoined later but it was a long and anxious wait for news of mates. Lacking any information or orders, Lieutenant Appleyard volunteered to go into Dieppe to make contact with HQ. A 40-mile round trip through dark and unlit roads crammed with carts, people and vehicles, Appleyard had chosen a difficult challenge for his first motorbike ride. He got back around midnight with orders to head at once for the station at Rouxmesnil Junction. Once again, the exhausted men dragged themselves to their feet for a seventeen-mile hike to the station, not arriving until almost midday. There, they were redirected to a camp about a mile away at Arques-la-Bataille to join the Buffs and to extend the defence line along the river Bethune and support the right of the 2/7th Dukes.

As the battalion left for Arques, CQMS Brown was still lost. Captain Taylor had delivered him to Dieppe but had then been told to go to Rouen. Expecting the battalion to arrive soon, Brown and his companions were dropped off by the harbour and were still there when bombers appeared overhead. Brown's first indication that they were enemies was the huge explosion that rocked the hospital ship *Maid of Kent* and the piece of flying masonry that struck his knee. For over an hour the men sheltered as bombs rained down. When it was over, they emerged to find Captain Taylor had returned and had found them a place on a convoy leaving for Rouen in just a few minutes. Grateful to be leaving, they climbed aboard.

A short distance outside Dieppe, the convoy passed Colonel Hodgkinson and Lieutenant O'Connor, and Brown's party jumped off the truck to find approximately 100 men of the KOYLI standing around the station. Anxiously, Brown asked for news of 'B' Company but apart from a few men, the company was still mostly unaccounted for. After about two hours with no news or orders, some began to drift away and to climb aboard trucks leaving Dieppe, regardless of the destination. There was, he noticed, ample transport but no apparent effort to do anything with it. At 2100hrs, after the CO had gone into town, Captain Taylor again arrived and told them to make their way to Rouen as best they could. In sections, they moved off on the start of another agonising march without food or water. At one point, a couple of young refugees even carried Brown's rifle for him. Attempts to force civilian drivers at gunpoint to carry them on the mudguards of their cars failed until, at last, the driver of a lorry crammed with Belgian refugees agreed to make room. At about 2000hrs on the 22nd, after two full days and nights, they reached Rouen and the luxury of a clean bed.

The next day, shuffling around on stiff and sore legs, Brown found some of the KOYLI at an infantry base depot. To his surprise, he found he had been reported killed but was gratified to find he had been regarded as having done well. He was also pleased to find his company commander, Captain Phythian, had made it, although he was clearly tired and shaken and the two men sat talking until late into the night. In the morning, Brown found himself back in the army bureaucracy and tasked with arranging a pay parade for what could be found of the battalion. As he bent to the work, a request came down for two volunteer CQMSs to go to a forward area to act as brigade quartermasters. Brown, feeling it was his duty to go, raised his hand. He had just become the QM of 'B' Brigade, Beauman Division.

After arriving at Brigade HQ at Bosc Bordel, about five miles west of Forges-les-Eaux, Brown was introduced to the aptly named Major Harrowing, acting temporarily as brigadier, who explained that his motley collection of odds and ends were 'a last barrier against the Hun' and that he should expect 'a fight to the finish'.[6] Despite the ominous words, Brown woke the next morning to find all was quiet and, on the following Sunday, he was able to wander down to the local church to admire its ancient wood carvings; the only reminder that this was the front line was the distant sounds of bombing mixed with the thunder of a summer storm.

For the next few days, his existence was a peaceful one interspersed with patrols to chase reports of parachutists or to retrieve shot-down German aircrew in the muddy fields around HQ. On Friday 31st, Major Harrowing told him that the division was being reformed. At that moment, he grinned, their unit consisted of just the two of them. It would soon transform into 2nd Provisional Battalion (Davies Rifles) under the command of the newly promoted Lieutenant Colonel Harrowing.

It was that afternoon that the war returned. Brown was feeling depressed after a week without mail from home and a nagging presentiment of his own doom. The mood was not helped by the court martial of a sentry who had dozed off on duty and the night before, an officer had been shot in the stomach by a suspected parachutist, although no-one had seen it happen. Then, in the middle of the afternoon, a German bombing attack began and planes swooped down to strafe the area. A man was hit nearby and two civilians were killed. The wounded officer died the next day and was found to have been hit by a small calibre bullet but what weapon and where it came from nobody knew.

Over the next few days, the battalion began to move north past Rouen, reaching Bray on 4 June. On the 6th, orders came for Brown to return to the KOYLIs at Rouen. He was terribly torn. Although he wanted to get back to his unit, he also felt it his duty to stay at the front. Harrowing needed him and said so, joking that he would be keeping a close eye on him. There was another reason to stay – on orders that night was his promotion to WO2 and he knew that if he stayed in the post for the next few weeks, he stood a good chance of having it made permanent. The order to return was cancelled by Harrowing.

As the news of his promotion sank in on the 7th, Brown encountered a downed German pilot who would raise his spirits. As the man was brought in, trembling and shaken, Brown found himself moved by pity. 'My heart which I had thought was cold and pitiless turned to water at the sight of him.' Getting him a chair and a tot of rum, Brown talked to him. Finding that he had no cigarettes, he gave him some and, in return, Hauptmann Bernhard Mielks presented Brown with his knife. The souvenir 'which I shall not part with willingly', was, to Brown, a reminder not of the war, but of his feelings at that moment. Although the knife was 'a splendid affair', he wrote that the incident proved 'more marvellous still, a startling change of heart I am glad to note, which proves conclusively that war has not deprived me of human kindness.'[7] That night, 30 men deserted their posts and melted away into the night. On the 8th, Brown crossed the Seine heading north to Neaufles-Saint-Martin.

Far behind him, the KOYLI had spent five days on the Bethune line before being withdrawn. Clark, meanwhile, had become hopelessly lost and had instead used his civilian work skills to attach himself to a mobile workshop of the Royal Army Service Corps at Rouen. After a routine trip to a petrol dump, he suddenly found himself acting as armed escort to a party of nuns and 50 schoolgirls on a bus to Argentan, arriving there in time to see the first of the 'Second BEF' begin to move forward. He would eventually be evacuated via St Nazaire late on the 17th, having repeatedly crossed paths with his unit without ever being able to make contact.

Unsure what to do with them, HQ Rouen had sent the 2/4th back to Rennes on 27 May along with the 2/6th DWR. By 1 June they were back at work on the same railway siding they had left a fortnight before. 'It was a labour that was to prove utterly useless,' the regimental history records, 'and the time could have been so much better spent employed in marching and training, but this was not allowed.' Copies of the *Continental Daily Mail* were available a day late and there they learned about Dunkirk, reading 'Four fifths of BEF now evacuated'. The men wryly remarked that they were now in the last fifth. Colonel Hodgkinson and the battalion quartermaster, Lieutenant 'Tommy' Knott, spent their days trying and failing to obtain the Bren guns their men so badly needed. Instead, the battalion took delivery of 22 butcher's knives and nine small trucks.[8]

The loss of Beauman Division's 'A' Brigade to the 51st Division left them without a third of their men at a time when Weygand was demanding an all-out defence of the Seine. So, on 7 June, orders arrived for the 2/4th to join the 2/6th and to head back to

Rouen. They were once again part of the Beauman Division. Rex Flowers had made it back to Rennes with the battalion.

> It was in the afternoon that the order came. The battalion formed up and we marched in companies and platoons to the railway station, a small one that was nearby. We marched with a light step – we thought we were going home. I mean, everything pointed to it! What difference could we make (we had no illusions) to the situation? Most had gone via Dunkirk, now it was our turn – we thought. It had got to be Blighty! We knew that the battle was lost. We had convinced ourselves, what else could we do? As we waited for the train we could see the QM's staff coming round giving things away (that was unusual in itself). They were carrying large boxes containing these mystery gifts … As they approached we saw what it was; an emergency ration for each of us. Each was in a gold coloured box, which fitted into a special pocket in our battle-dress trousers. When I received mine, I thought Ugh! and a cold suspicion formed in my mind. Why did we need this for going home? It can't be! It can't be![9]

Within hours, the terrible truth dawned as the men began to recognise villages they had passed through before. They were headed for Rouen and the front line. Extra weapons had finally been found and brought aboard at the last minute but they were useless, still encased in the thick grease in which they had been packed and which the KOYLIs had no way of removing now they were on the train.

The battalion had been ordered to move to Les Andelys and arrived at the nearby station of Andé, near Louviers at around 1500hrs on 8 June to find the 2/6th DWR already there. For over two hours the KOYLIs sat on the train whilst the two battalion commanders tried to sort out the mess. The Dukes 'were already in possession and wisely refused to move', so at 1730hrs, they moved off again, this time to take up positions near Pont de l'Arche.

The orders were that the KOYLI were to hold the far bank of the river from the Pont de l'Arche road bridge and to cover the railway bridge at Le Manoir. 'A' Company under Captain G.H. Wilford was on the right covering Le Manoir. Farther north was Captain William Haughton's 'D' Company under the command of a composite battalion of military policemen. 'C' Company at Alizay held the centre of the line under the command of Second Lieutenant Jones and Rex Flowers and his mates of 'B' Company were on the left of the line at Igoville under 25-year-old Captain Jenico Preston, the 16th Viscount Gormanston and usually referred to as simply Captain Gormanston. The battalion was covering about four miles of front and had 'no supporting weapons whatsoever; no artillery, tanks, mortars, – nothing but rifles, bayonets and a few light machine guns.'[10] The men had just 50 rounds of ammunition each.

By the time 'B' Company reached Igoville on the north bank of the river, they found it full of French troops 'so thick on the ground that to put any more would have caused confusion' so Gormanston kept his men concentrated in the village. To add to the confusion, a company of pioneers were also in the area. Whilst they knew about the KOYLIs, the KOYLIs knew nothing about them.

The approaches to the bridge were covered by anti-tank guns and it seemed a strong defence was planned; they were to be cruelly disappointed. At midnight, French guards refused to allow an officer from Battalion HQ across the bridges to the far bank and all contact with 'B' and 'D' Companies was lost. The men were told to get some sleep but it lasted only about an hour before they were woken and told to take up positions outside the village. Throughout the night, Flowers watched as 'for hours troops and guns poured through

Pont de l'Arche area map.

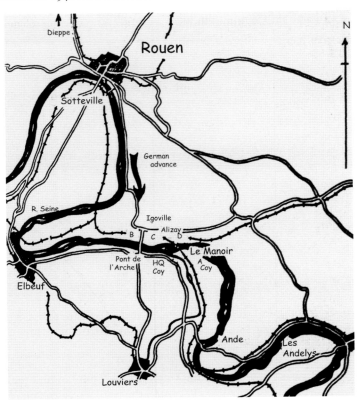

the village and over the bridge. I thought at the time, why don't they stop and have a go at the enemy in the morning?' All that remained as dawn approached were two anti-tank guns and a small group of French engineers but he could see no-one else.

At about 0300hrs, reports began to arrive of German armour approaching and when, 90 minutes later, a column of vehicles appeared, the anti-tank gunners wasted no time in putting a round through the lead vehicle only to discover that it was a refugee group. They were turned away and no sooner had they left the scene than German tanks arrived. The second anti-tank gun fired and scored a direct hit on one light tank. Its two companions withdrew and the three lorry-loads of infantry with them debussed and went to ground in positions overlooking the village to begin reconnoitring by fire, probing the British defences. In a slit trench, Flowers sat by, not reacting to the German fire yet. He needed to conserve ammunition. Their Bren gun had just one magazine.

Across the battalion front, similar scenarios were being played out but no serious attack developed. Later, the British press would make much of how 'twenty Yorkshiremen, with one French anti-tank gun in position, held up a German tank column for nearly three hours.'[11] The officer, 25-year-old John Clemons from Leeds, described how just after 0300hrs a German light tank was stopped by the anti-tank gun but was soon followed by

> … a light reconnaissance tank and two medium tanks of about thirty-five tons − [which] came well into view, just broadside on from our positions only a short distance away. The turrets of the tanks were open and standing in them were men with German steel helmets on … The French lieutenant opened fire and knocked out the first medium tank. Then he opened fire on the second medium tank and knocked it out in turn. This blocked the road for this long column of vehicles, at least fifty in number, coming down the road closely packed together.

He goes on to describe how the Germans 'seemed rather demoralised by the sudden unexpected attack from our hidden positions.' The dramatic account made excellent

An artist's impression of the attack on the German column during the battle at Igoville.

newspaper fodder but the official history tells a slightly different story. It says that after the first tank was hit, 'desultory small arms fire' had broken out.

After an hour or so Flowers heard a voice from behind him. A subaltern warned him to 'Retire to the bridge now, the French will be blowing it up in a few minutes at 6 o'clock' and crawled off to pass the message along. After putting the Bren out of action Flowers crawled off to his right, 'down the road into the village towards the main road, about seventy yards away, with a few well-chosen words on the subject of Anglo-French co-operation'. It was not going to be easy. Between the company positions and the river was about three-quarters of a mile of flat, open ground.

The German positions on the high ground now began to tell as the company made their way through the village streets. To get to the bridge they would have to go to the main road and turn right, through part of the village then under a railway embankment and on a further 100 yards to reach the bridge, much of the way exposed to German fire. They had almost reached the road when the first German tank entered the village and began pouring machine gun fire along it in the direction of the bridge. Retracing their steps, Flowers and his section made their way through a line of back gardens, joined now by a couple of French Senegalese soldiers from a colonial regiment that had also been left behind when the withdrawal took place. Together, the men reached a spot where around 40 KOYLI were crouching at the base of the railway embankment.

Captain Gormanston gathered the men together and explained that they would have to move to the right out of the direct view of the enemy and make a dash for it. If they all moved together, they stood a better chance of getting into cover before the Germans could react.

'We have got to get over this embankment, we will all go over together when I give the word.' We spread out along the base of the embankment. The captain said again, 'When I give the word, all dash over at once and deploy.' He was a brave man; I can see him now in my mind's eye. His revolver in his hand, stood up in full view of the enemy on the ridge under heavy fire marshalling his men.

… away we went a bit sharpish. The rails seemed never ending and we had to jump over wires and so on (I was getting a bit sick of railways). I had a prickly feeling in my back but we all got over to the other side without incident. Stretching away in front of us

French POWs including men of a North African division. Colonial troops from Indo–China, North and West Africa were widely deployed by the French and fought well, but were frequently ill-treated and murdered after surrender. British forces included Indian Service Corps troops, but they did not see action.

was about a hundred and fifty yards of cornfield that was about knee high, and then there was the riverbank.

About half way across, machine guns opened up and the men dropped into the scant cover of the corn. There was no choice but to keep moving forward in a series of dashes and crawls to within a few yards of the sloping riverbank.

I jumped up and ran towards the river, and I noticed that someone else had done the same and we were running almost side-by-side. We had given the enemy too much time to get his sights on us, I think he had noticed my tactics and was awaiting my next move. All at once tracers were all around me, plucking at my clothing on my arms and legs; I think one or two passed between my legs as I was running. I got to the bank and jumped down, rolling on the floor. It was a twelve-foot drop. I looked up to see how my unknown companion had fared. He was dead; his feet caught in some undergrowth or brambles and hung upside down, an ugly sight. God, I had been lucky. It was a French soldier, probably one of the anti-tank crew.

At the riverbank, he found Captain Gormanston and Private Murdoch preparing to swim.

> I came up to them and halted, I wasn't sure what to say or do at first. The Captain said to me, 'Where are you going Flowers?' I replied 'I am going to try and get over the bridge sir.' He then said 'No time, it's going up any time now,' looking at his watch. Nevertheless, I decided to have a go, and made my way to that tantalising bridge. It looked safe and solid; I started to run towards it, there were people running over. I could see their heads over the parapet. That's why I was running. When I was about seventy yards away it just blew up: I can see it now; There were a series of small explosions along the length of the bridge. I was never a boy any more after that.

A non-swimmer, Flowers asked if Gormanston could take him across but the captain shook his head, explaining that the fast flowing river would be enough of a problem even for him as a strong swimmer. Flowers began to scramble along the bank to find some way across. After a few yards, he turned to see Gormanston and Murdoch in midstream. A few steps later he turned again. Murdoch was clambering out. Gormanston was gone. His body was never recovered.

Remembering a western movie, Flowers searched for a log to act as a float and managed to get across the river under fire, to find two soldiers of the Pioneer Corps battalion waiting for him. Soon the group grew to nine, including a Frenchman and two Senegalese infantrymen. They did not know it, but the Senegalese had had a lucky escape. Behind them, six of their comrades had been captured and made to sit at tables outside the village cafe. Each one was shot in the back of the head and as his head fell forwards, it was snatched back and his throat slit.[12]

A bit further downriver, Lieutenant Aykroyd and Lance Corporal Armitage were busy setting up a defence line to cover the river crossing. Last to arrive was Lieutenant Clemons, dragging one of his wounded men. He dived into the water and swam across to a rowing

A bridge being demolished. The sight would remain with Rex Flowers for the rest of his life.

Forgotten men. Privates Jack Speight (top left) and Harry Polson (top right), formerly of the Essex Regiment, arrived in France in 1939 as part of a Pioneer Company. Private Val Thomas (bottom left) was separated from the KOYLI and Private Sékou Diaf (bottom right) from his Senegalese unit after the destruction of the Pont de l'Arche bridges. All four died in battle at the nearby village of Criquebeuf.

boat. Since it had no oars, he then towed it back across and set up a ferry service to shuttle them to safety. Luckily, the Germans were not following too closely.

Downstream, Flowers was attempting to discourage a young Frenchman from trying to recover a boat. The man ignored them and went over to get it. As he stood in the boat, a burst of fire cut him down in full view of the two women he was travelling with. Flowers plodded on.

Meanwhile, Le Manoir bridge had blown five minutes later, taking a number of Germans with it but 'A' and 'D' Companies had escaped without incident, again their young officers swimming the river to bring back boats for their men. 'C' Company was in close contact but managed to get most of its men back. Second Lieutenant Jones then extricated the remaining two platoons and 40 men made their way back to a footbridge across a weir.

By the time the men regrouped, Colonel Hodgkinson had received orders to pull back to Bernay. 10 men had been killed, 23 wounded and 22 known to have been captured. The toll could have been worse. But many men were now lost.

Flowers trudged on. More Senegalese had joined them and he found himself fascinated by the Africans and wishing he could speak French. Gradually, as the day wore on, the group split up. One, with a mixture of Franglais and gestures, indicated for the Britons to follow him and led them through the fields to a small village. This was Elbeuf. He was home and from here the British soldiers would be able to get back to Rouen – if the Germans didn't get there first.

Val Thomas, the reservist Flowers had admired back in training, had had a similar experience. Together with two former Essex Regiment reservists, Harry Speight and Jack Poulson and a Senegalese soldier, Sekou Diouf, Thomas had begun the long march back along the banks of the Seine towards Rouen. They never made it. Their bodies were discovered weeks later at the scene of a small, forgotten battle in the tiny hamlet of Criquebeuf among those of a French detachment who had stood their ground. All across France allies fought and died together as their superiors bickered amongst themselves.

The survivors of the 2/4th began their tiring journey back to Bernay but WO2 Brown, with 'B' Brigade, was still headed the other way. On the 10th, Brigade HQ moved farther north to Roncherolles-sur-le-Vivier, only to be told to turn around and head back. The Brigade had been moved into enemy-held territory and were completely surrounded but somehow, like the 2/4th, made it back towards Bernay, although, he noted, 'the brigadier had said he did not expect us to get through.' Despite his own plight, Brown could still find it in himself to pity the refugees, especially the 'two little girls carrying their dollies' and the young mother bathing her son's blistered feet in a stream. '[They] should not be exposed to such horrors and hardships.'

Gradually, 'B' Brigade made their way to Le Mans only to be turned around yet again and sent back up the line to Authou. 'Lots of men have got the wind up about going back,' Brown wrote. Spirits were lifted by the cheering of the French civilians as they pushed forward but the men knew there would be no sympathy for them in retreat. In passing, Brown heard that only 128 men of his battalion now remained accounted for as he went forward into Authou to check local cottages for use as billets – 'a job I despise' since it involved breaking in. Like many of the sentimental British, he could never get used to the French attitude towards their animals. Dogs were left chained up, cats and cage birds locked inside houses. In Britain, the RSPCA had been inundated with animals brought back by the BEF, 120 dogs being destroyed in one port alone by 5 June.[13] One man was even reported to have been found swimming out to a rescue boat clutching a rabbit intended as a pet for his children. This village was no exception; his men toured the area, releasing any animal they could find. Even as they let loose the abandoned pets, the Germans were closing in on them. Very soon, these humane men would be trying to kill other humans simply to survive.

On the 14th, he pessimistically noted that 'the job we are on here is a suicide one, if we get out we shall be lucky.' But there was good news, too. 'Apparently the vanguard of the second BEF are here.' It was true. The 1st Canadian Division and the 152nd Lowland Division had arrived and taken up positions in the Cotentin Peninsula. Whatever the suicide job was, it was now cancelled. For the next few days, they would be constantly on the move. On the 15th, he travelled by truck to Pont l'Eveque and recorded his food for the day – two slices of bread, one rasher of bacon and a slice of bully beef. Brown realised at one point that he had not removed his boots for a week (he would later be hospitalised when the blisters turned septic) but it no longer mattered as they kept moving, through Lisieux, Caen, Bayeux, Carentan and finally to Cherbourg and a boat home. Collapsing on the deck, he woke to find he 'couldn't understand where [he] was' and had to walk around the boat convincing himself that he was finally going home.

The rest of the battalion had followed much the same route. On the 12th, Beauman Division's medical officer reported that 'morale of men improving, blistered feet etc' and on the 13th, Colonel Hodgkinson had been ordered to Le Mans and had not returned. Step by step and line by line they had retreated in good order and sailed aboard the SS *Duke of Atholl* at 1830hrs on 17 June.

As they disembarked at Southampton the next morning, they were greeted by a cheering man. When the rest of 'B' Brigade had been dispersed to various infantry depots, one man had been left behind to fend for himself. As he stood alone on the quayside, someone had told him that the 2/4th had just arrived. John Brown was home.

NOTES
1 Wylly p118
2 Ibid, p118
3 CQMS Brown's Diary. Imperial War Museum Documents P118
4 Brown quoted in Moynihan, M. *People at War 1939–1945* 1989 p44
5 Don Clark. Personal account. Imperial War Museum documents 99/16/1 p34
6 Brown, op cit p33. See also Moynihan p50
7 Brown p42–43.
8 Wylly p120
9 Rex Flowers. Unpublished personal account
10 Wylly p121
11 'How we held up a German tank column' by 'Eyewitness' in *War Illustrated* 28 June 1940 p700–701
12 James, K. *The Greater Share of Honour* 2007 p252. A memorial was erected in 2005 to the victims, just some of the estimated 3,000 West African soldiers fighting in the French Army murdered between May and June 1940. In light of the extremely high casualty numbers of *Tirailleurs Sénégalais* (out of 40,000 African soldiers engaged in combat with German forces, 17,000 were killed or reported as missing in action), this may be an underestimate. See Raffael Scheck's *Hitler's African Victims: The German Army Massacres of Black French Soldiers in 1940* Cambridge University Press, 2006.
13 *Bradford Telegraph & Argus* 5 June 1940

Chapter Fifteen

Epilogue

Amid the hustle and bustle of the Southampton docks on the morning of 18 June, a tall, drawn figure sat slightly apart, pausing now and again to break off some bully beef from his sandwich and feed it to the small grey kitten perched on his lap. He'd found it in the garden of a house in Rouen and it had stayed with him throughout the retreat – a small reminder of life outside the war. Occasionally men would come up to him and offer their thanks but most felt reluctant to intrude on Beauman's well earned moment of peace.

Behind them, Operation Ariel was still in full swing. Starting on 14 June, Admiral William James C-in-C, Portsmouth Command had been overseeing the evacuation of British troops from the Normandy ports. At the same time, other evacuations were also being carried out from St Nazaire, Brest and Nantes in the Bay of Biscay led by Admiral Sir Martin Nasmith C-in-C, Western Approaches Command. The operation had been going well until 1548hrs the previous day when Junkers Ju88 bombers of Kampfgeschwader 30 had found the *Lancastria*, Cunard's 16,243-ton luxury liner, as it lay off St Nazaire. Aboard, the *Lancastria's* acting adjutant was still desperately trying to compile a list of those boarding from the small fleet of vessels ferrying men and refugees out to the ship but it was an uphill task. He estimated that almost 9,000 soldiers and refugees had crowded onto the ship.

Chief Officer Harry Grattidge, the *Lancastria's* second in command, recalled what happened next.

> The smoke drifted and parted and we saw the most terrible sight the *Lancastria* could offer; the mess of blood and oil and splintered woodwork that littered the deck and the furious white core of water that came roaring from the bottom of the ship in Number 4 hold. I took the megaphone, hearing my voice booming out strangely over the dying ship 'Clear away the boats now … Your attention please … Clear away the boats now.' The *Lancastria* quaked under my feet, a last gesture of farewell.

The ship lurched onto her starboard side, righted again and then listed onto the port side, sending men skidding across the decks.[1]

Walter Hirst of the Royal Engineers was one of those aboard:

> There was panic and chaos. Two soldiers at either end of the ship began to open up with Bren guns on the attacking enemy aircraft. After entering the water a seemingly crazed

LOSS OF THE 'LANCASTRIA'

The Cunard liner 'Lancastria' (16,243 tons) was sunk by a formation of Junkers 87 dive-bombers off St.Nazaire on June 17, 1940. There were about 5,000 British troops on board, and more than 2,000 of them were lost. Our photographs show : above, the 'Lancastria' in her cruise-liner days ; left, settling down after the enemy attack ; below, heeling over, her propellers above water ; bottom, troops clustered on the hull and in the water. Many were rescued by the Royal Navy.

Photos, Associated Press

Report on the sinking of the *Lancastria*.

man tried to remove my lifejacket, but I managed to fight him off. I was in the water for around two hours before being picked up. At one point a large Labrador dog swam past which I later discovered belonged to some Belgian refugee children who did not survive the sinking.

In blind panic, men struggled to survive as German planes returned to mercilessly strafe the sinking ship with machine gun fire. There had been no time for safety announcements. Sapper Cyril Cumbes saw four men whose necks had been broken by the lifebelts they wore riding up as they hit the water. For Ken Belsham of the Royal Army Pay Corps, the abiding memory would be the guilt he carried after having to dive under the water to avoid the clutches of drowning men.

The *Lancastria* was not the only loss that day. Churchill had made a last-ditch effort to keep the French in the war by flying to Paris to meet with the French Cabinet but he had failed. On that Monday afternoon, he and his staff flew back from Paris. Aboard the plane, General Sir Edward Spears was looking out of the window at a coast he had sailed two years before

> … when suddenly I beheld a terrible sight. A great ship was lying on her side, sinking. Hundreds of tiny figures could be seen in the water. It was the *Champlain*, with two thousand British troops on board. We cut across Brittany. We were flying low and the entire countryside seemed to be on fire, for there was smoke everywhere. I thought it was the Germans burning villages, but was told later they were British Army dumps being destroyed. There must have been many of them.[2]

Churchill arrived home to news of the *Lancastria*. 'I forbade its publication' he later wrote.

> The newspapers have got quite enough disaster for to-day at least. I had intended to release the news a few days later, but events crowded upon us so black and so quickly that I forgot to lift the ban, and it was some years before the knowledge of this horror became public.[3]

Survivors still remain bitter about this cover up, claiming, as does Churchill, that it was 'years' before news was released. However, the story was known. As details became available, the weekly *War Illustrated* devoted a centre spread and two more pages to the story in its 9 August issue and more photographs of the sinking itself in later editions. It even hinted at the scale of the disaster with the story of Lieutenant R. Haynes of 50th Company AMPC who boarded the ship with 250 men, of whom just 40 survived. The fact was, stories of ships carrying men from France was old news by now and amid the fear of imminent invasion, the tale of the *Lancastria* was quietly put to one side. Even today, though, the true story remains unclear. Estimates of casualties range from as low as 2,500 to over 6,000 lives lost in a matter of minutes.

Don Clark had, quite literally, missed the boat. He had arrived in St Nazaire but during a bombing raid he had been hit in the knee and the last stages of his journey had been painfully slow. He arrived to find the ship had sailed. Along with the few men left there, he debated the pros and cons of returning to camp. There were no boats nearby and at least they would be able to find transport to take them south towards the Spanish border. Later that afternoon, a small convoy drove away. Clark could never remember the name of the port or the ship but somewhere around Nantes, they found a way home. Pushing their trucks off the end of the quay, they passed through a Military Police checkpoint and onto the gangplank. As they boarded, a Rabbi and a group of Jewish refugees asked for spaces aboard ship but was told that the ship could take only British citizens. The Rabbi pleaded for 'sanctuary' but was refused. Finally, in desperation, the families offered £1,000 for any British soldier who would marry one of the young girls. Again the Major refused. The group gave up. Clark saw them turn towards the south.[4]

The ship left harbour on the 19th and sailed due west for two days, raising Clark's hopes of a trip to America but on the third day it turned north. News had reached them of the *Lancastria* and the captain had wanted to be well out to sea and away from the German bombers before the run for home. The ship eventually reached Plymouth on Tuesday 25 June – the last day of Operation Ariel. As the men marched from the docks, 'there were thousands of women waiting for us. The women lined the two sides of the narrow corridor which had been formed through which we would have to march.' As the men formed up a car backfired, sending them diving for cover. Embarrassed by this display of nerves, they regrouped and set off through the crowds.

> Many wanted to know if we had seen their husbands, sons and boyfriends while on our way to the coast in France. They held out photographs of their missing loved ones and pleaded with us for news.

Clark, not knowing the fate of even his closest friends, could only shake his head and keep walking. 'It was a harrowing, unbelievably sad and grief-stricken struggle for us to get through them and up to the station.'[5]

By then, over 30,600 men of the 52nd Division and Norman Force had been evacuated from Cherbourg alone during Operation Ariel. Nearly 20,500 men, mainly Canadians, had escaped via St Malo and thousands more through St Nazaire, Brest and dozens of smaller ports along the west coast. A further 11,000 men had been evacuated before Ariel began from Le Havre in Operation Cycle. The British garrison at Marseilles would make its own arrangements to evacuate via Gibraltar and these withdrawals would continue into mid-August. In all, official figures record that 191,870 British, French, Canadian, Czech, Polish and Belgian soldiers left France in the weeks after Dunkirk.[6] The last men offering the Germans any resistance at Cherbourg were Major Nightingale and 50 AMPC reservists of 1 Company, No 10 Docks Labour Company. Armed with rifles and a single Bren 'which nobody knew anything about', the company manned the last perimeter until the fighting troops had left. They had arrived on 10 September 1939 'without stores or cooking utensils' and finally left for home on the morning of 18 June – claiming with some justification that they had been 'first in and last out'. 'It wasn't a glorious affair,' Nightingale later observed, 'but the Pioneers could at least be proud of their part in it.'[7]

When the BEF arrived home from Dunkirk, Police Inspector Richard Butcher had seen sparks flying along the London–Dover line as broken men pitched their weapons out of the window.[8] The recently created Local Defence Volunteers scoured the tracks collecting what they could for their own use when the Germans came, as it seemed they inevitably would. Some soldiers contacted their families, changed into civilian clothes and simply walked away. Many more, though, found themselves treated not as a defeated army, but as returning heroes. They chalked the letters 'BEF' on their helmets and some even had unofficial shoulder badges made up as they enjoyed a warm welcome home. 'Enjoy it while you can lads,' one Sergeant Major advised them, 'it won't last.'

By the time the ships began returning from Cherbourg two weeks later, the novelty of the 'miracle of Dunkirk' had already worn off. For most of the returning men,

German tanks and infantry advancing.

homecoming was an anti-climax. They travelled alone or in groups to stations where no-one knew or cared what they had been through. Dunkirk was already a memory and these men were, after all, not the heroic fighting regiments of the BEF that people had read so much about in the papers, they were just the 'useless mouths' of the Lines of Communication. When Beauman went to Whitehall to submit his recommendations for awards to men under his command he was greeted by the Assistant Military Secretary of the BEF with a surprised 'Oh, did you have any fighting?'[9] Later, he was interviewed by the Military Secretary.

> In view of the fact that I had just returned from an operation which had proved, to say the least of it, both exacting and difficult, and that he had been sitting in a comfortable armchair at the War Office since the early days of the war I felt that I was entitled to a courteous reception, even if I could not be given any encouragement regarding my future. The Military Secretary was both exceedingly abrupt and discouraging. He finally said that he could see little hope for further employment for me unless there was an invasion and heavy casualties amongst senior officers.[10]

A year later Colonel Vickery, the former commander of Vickforce, wrote to Beauman expressing sympathy and telling him that he had gained the support of 'a higher Chief' who would fight his case. It was clear, Vickery, said 'that M-C [Marshall-Cornwall] was obviously making you a scapegoat for his deeds.' A command was being formed and Beauman was, apparently, in the running. A dispirited Beauman noted that the news 'sounds hopeful but probably too good to be true.'[11] Eventually, Beauman got his promotion and command of the North Riding District at Catterick. He was retired again in 1944.

General de Fonblanque, who might have been able to fight Beauman's corner, had been exhausted by his efforts and died soon after his return. In the aftermath of the evacuation, Dill's staff complained bitterly that not enough had been done to save precious supplies, ignoring the fact that they themselves had continued dispatching fuel and ammunition through ports in the Bay of Biscay for the second BEF even as de Fonblanque was evacuating the same materials through Cherbourg. In some cases, there were tales of stores being unloaded from one ship only to be placed aboard the ship tied alongside for return to the UK. Around St Nazaire, the 6th Royal Sussex had continued railway building right up until the French surrender before they had downed tools and marched to a waiting ship, their efforts serving only to complete the groundwork for the Germans to finish for their own needs.

Almost immediately, a committee was set up to consider the lessons of the campaign and by early July were ready to present their results. Their recommendations were confusing. The army, they said, should be decentralised and allow its junior officers more scope to use personal initiative, as the Germans did. This, though, was far too radical a change for many senior officers to contemplate so it was tempered with instructions that having achieved a breakthrough, they should immediately be taken back under the control of the divisional commander who would, as one training manual later put it, control his troops much as a conductor controls his orchestra – there should be no improvisation. Vague orders were blamed for the disaster so troops should be given clear written instructions that gave no room for interpretation. The returning men, at Churchill's insistence, were put through intensive drill to instil instant obedience to orders. Recruits at all levels were told that they were 'not paid to think' and the whole resulted in an army that, in theory, valued personal initiative but did everything it could to eradicate it. It was a policy that would handicap operations for the rest of the war, bringing bitter criticisms from Britain's American, Canadian and Australian allies in all theatres.

The aftermath was also a time when senior officers looked to their careers. Gort, feted as a hero, was never given another operational command and quietly slipped away. Marshall-Cornwall's memoirs show that his actions in France had been governed by his concerns that he might be court-martialled for a wrong decision and so chose to cover himself carefully. His report published in the *London Gazette* in 1946 made it clear that he blamed, chief amongst others, Beauman for not being aggressive enough and allowing his men to make their own decisions about withdrawal on the battlefield rather than simply fighting to the end in their trenches as the out-of-touch Weygand had demanded. He seemed to see no contradiction in saying that the division was not a 'fighting formation' but then complaining that it failed to act as one. Nor in saying that his job had been to prevent unnecessary casualties but that the Beauman Division was not his responsibility and that more British troops should have been ordered to fight 'last man, last round' battles to shore up French lines that had already vanished. In all, he said, too many British soldiers outside of his control were 'looking over their shoulders for a good abri [shelter]'.[12] On his return from France, Marshall-Cornwall was sent to the Middle East to take up another liaison mission and later was given a command of forces in north-west England. He was sacked in 1942 for deciding that he, as local commander in Liverpool, was better able to judge what was needed than his superiors in London.

All that summer, news filtered back about the fates of some of those left behind. Each week, local newspapers carried reports of letters bringing news of men now confirmed killed or prisoners. In many cases it was an agonising wait. On 12 October, the *Halifax Weekly Courier and Guardian* reported that the family of 46-year-old Arthur Stead of the AMPC were 'considerably relieved' by news that he was alive. A week later, it noted that there had been a mistake. He had drowned aboard the *Lancastria*. So had 26-year-old William Galloway of the 2/6th Dukes and so had Corporal Arthur Fenwick of the Royal Engineers – three weeks after his brother had become the 2/5th West Yorkshire Regiment's first casualty. Others of 137 Brigade were almost certainly among the casualties but no-one knows for certain. The official search for missing men continued into 1942 as statements were taken from survivors of Pont de l'Arche, Veules-les-Roses and the retreat about who they had seen alive when they pulled out. In 1944, some of the more seriously ill prisoners came home, bringing stories of the missing, the dead. They also talked of the irrepressible Bandmaster Doyle's prison camp concerts and his unstinting efforts to keep his lads going.

Throughout that summer and autumn of 1940, other men continued to make their way home. Lance Corporal John Warner of the Queen's Regiment was amongst them. He had surrendered at Abbeville: 'I felt I was the biggest fool in the army, until next morning we were joined by 10,000 French and 1,200 British prisoners.' As the prisoners were being marched towards Arras, he managed to obtain some civilian clothes from a Frenchman and made his break. Stopped by a soldier, his poor French was not noticed because the German spoke it even more badly and he was able to slip away, claiming to be going to his wife in Arras. He was given a bicycle by a Frenchman and cycled south to the Spanish frontier. The gendarme on duty refused to let him pass without an exit visa but the police commander pointed out that there was a perfectly safe route into Spain across the nearby hills. Warner reached London in time for his 21st birthday.[13]

Lance Corporal Downing and Private Ash of the KOYLI made it into the unoccupied zone of France but were detained by the French and handed over to the Germans when the Vichy government was taken over in 1942. Their comrade Private Winslade was more successful. Without a map, money or any ability to speak either language, he travelled through France and into Spain, making it to Gibraltar and home.[14]

In the West Yorkshire mess, Richard Camrass walked in after reading his own obituary. Captain Wilkins, last seen outside Robecq in May 1940, was treated to a hero's welcome when he reached home on 14 August 1941 after over a year on the run.

The escapers were aided by a network of civilians willing to risk their lives to help the British. One such was Maurice Marland. On 10 June, Marland, an employee of the Suez Canal Company, left the British Embassy in Paris for the port of Granville on the west coast of the Cotentin to set up a branch office and liaise with the British Foreign Office. After the ceasefire, Marland discovered that there were 52 British soldiers in the area, mainly survivors of the 51st Division. Local fishermen could not leave the harbour without drawing fire from the German garrison in the barracks overlooking the port but Marland managed to persuade a few to start making the run to the Channel Islands at night. All 52 were evacuated by the 27th. By July, though, the route was no longer viable. When three Scots led by Robert Craig were brought in on 7 July, Marland had no choice but to hide them for almost four years. 'Bob was not a senior officer, nor one who it had taken much time or effort to train – he was not worth the risk of a speedboat' was how one member of the group explained it later.[15] Marland then continued to act as a guide and resistance leader until his arrest and execution on 22 July 1944, one of many who never accepted France's surrender.

As its battered units reached home, 46th Division regrouped in the grounds of the Belle Vue Park and Zoo in Manchester. The gaps in their ranks were filled with new recruits – the next registration of men aged up to 28 for military service had begun on 15 June – and, when it reached full strength again, the division was shipped to Iceland to act as a garrison.

In 1942, the division was reorganised. On 20 July, 137 Brigade was taken out and converted to an armoured brigade of the Royal Armoured Corps. 2/5th Battalion The West Yorkshire Regiment was overnight transformed into 113th Regiment, Royal Armoured Corps. The 2/6th Dukes were now 114th Regiment and the 2/7th became 115th. The brigade was not called upon for overseas duties and was disbanded on 26 September 1943. Gradually, the men were whittled away to other RAC units, the Dukes holding on to a few vestiges of their identity in 'Dukes Squadrons' but they would never again be the battalions that had left for France in 1940. The rest of the division carried on, taking part in the invasions of Sicily and Italy.

Clark went on leave and came back sporting the unofficial 'BEF' badges that had become popular only to be told in no uncertain terms that 'there's no bloody BEF here' and be forced to get rid of them. Weeks later, as a skilled tool maker, he was discharged. Travelling home, by chance he met with his old RSM and records that the man had been found guilty of weak leadership and 'a lack of moral fibre'. He was on his way home to Southern Ireland. As ever with the army, some men stayed with their regiments for the rest of the war. Some moved on. Major Haughton, who had commanded 'D' Company of the KOYLI at Pont de l'Arche, was killed serving with 2nd KOYLI in Burma in February 1942 and Major Clemons, MC, the young lieutenant whose story had aroused so much interest, died at Salerno. WO2 Brown received a commission in 1941 and spent the rest of his war in Burma with the Royal Armoured Corps attached to 33rd Indian Division.

General Alan Brooke later wrote of Weygand that

> like Hitler in a similar position four years later, the seventy-four year old Generalissimo met the onslaught of superior and better-equipped force by the fatalistic expedient

of ordering outnumbered units to fight to the death where they stood. The inevitable result was that those who obeyed their orders were either surrounded or killed while the weaker fled, carrying panic and disorder along every highway.[16]

Writing later of the destruction of the Pont de l'Arche bridges and the stranding of the KOYLI, Beauman said

> I should hesitate to blame the French for blowing the bridge behind our troops on this occasion … Stringent orders had been issued by the French High Comand that regardless of the local situation bridges were to be blown as soon as the enemy approached them … the French officer in charge had justification for his action.[17]

Rex Flowers, though, took a different view: 'It looks pretty certain to me that the French sacrificed us.'

In the immediate aftermath, King George spoke for his generals when he said; 'Personally, I feel happier now that we have no allies to be polite to and to pamper.'[18] In the years since then, British and French historians and politicians have argued and criticised each other. Britain, it is said, was let down by the cowardice and incompetence of 'cheese eating surrender monkeys'. There is an element of truth to this. An aging, unimaginative French High Command in which commanders refused to see the need to have radio communications connecting their Vincennes HQ to forces spread far and wide lost command and control capability within the first few days of the battle. Within five days of the German attack, a France riven by political factions – who sometimes saw German occupation as preferable to life under a left wing government – and where senior commanders viewed their allies with greater contempt and suspicion than their enemies, had lost the will to fight. All that was at the root of the French collapse, along with the almost contemptuous attitude French officers had towards their own conscript army. Yet there were many thousands of brave men who fought well and hard. The North African troops of 1st DINA, for example, having fought from Sedan to Dunkirk, escaped to safety only to return immediately to carry on the battle in Normandy. Their courage should not be forgotten.

For the French, the events of those weeks more than confirmed their belief that 'perfidious Albion' had deserted them in their time of need and, as expected, had run for home at the first opportunity. Yet for the villagers of La Herliere that never seemed true. The speed of the German advance had caught many civilians before they could flee so the people of the area knew about Private John Lungley, a 34-year-old Bren gunner of the 5th Buffs. On 20 May he was left alone in a slit trench as the Germans closed in. They broke off their attack and called on him to surrender. He refused. They attacked again. Again he held them back. A tank was called up and he died at his post. That night, and every night, flowers appeared on his temporary grave. When it was decided to take his body to the local cemetery, so many locals turned out to honour him that the angry Germans cancelled the ceremony and buried him at night. No-one at La Herliere believed the British had deserted them.[19]

A German account of the battle for France records the comments of a sergeant in 'the Yorkshire Regiment' taken prisoner at Dunkirk.

> My regiment has suffered great losses, every tenth man has been killed. The German artillery is very good, the German infantrist [sic] fights very courageously. Yes, we have great respect for you … We knew that your Division had fought in Poland, and has been called since 'the bloody dogs.' That is true. But we will beat you next time all the same.[20]

Left: The strain of captivity etched on his face, Private James Laidler of the Tyneside Scottish on his release from Stalag XXa in 1945. (courtesy Else Laidler)

Below: A field burial.

A report produced by the German IV Corps described the British troops they encountered as men who 'did not complain of hardships. In battle he was tough and dogged … In defence the Englishman took any punishment that came his way.'[21]

Like the rest of the digging divisions, 137 Brigade had arrived in France 'untrained and virtually unarmed'. They were asked to stand against the combined might of the German air and ground blitzkrieg. With little more than a rifle and bayonet against tanks and artillery, they were told that the fate of their country depended on them standing their ground. So they stood. Knowing that their leaders had let them down, that they had not been given the tools for the job, that their allies were running away around them, that the men who should have been in their place were even now escaping, they stood. Because they had been asked to.

Outgunned, outnumbered, defiant and doomed, Lungley's lonely last stand epitomises the spirit of the forgotten men of the digging divisions.

NOTES

1 This and subsequent accounts are to be found at the website of the *Lancastria* Association of Scotland at www.lancastria.org.uk

2 Spears. *Assignment to Catastrophe*, n.d. p619–620
When the SS *Champlain* was built in 1932 for the French Line she was the largest, fastest, and most luxurious cabin class liner afloat. From the start of the war she had been engaged in transporting thousands of refugees to America. On 17 June 1940, she struck a German mine whilst at anchor in the waters off La Pallice and quickly heeled over. Despite claims that as many as 300 people lost their lives, in fact only around a dozen fatalities were recorded. A few days later a German U-boat fired a torpedo into the hulk, which remained largely above the water. The wreck was eventually cleared in 1965.

3 Churchill *The Second World War* Vol 2 p169

4 Clark. Imperial War Museum Documents 99/16/1

5 Ibid p91

6 Blaxland p387

7 *History of 1 Company*. RPC Museum Archives

8 Collier. Sands of Dunkirk p233

9 Beauman p175

10 Ibid p175–6

11 Colonel Vickery letter to Beauman 14 May 1941. Beauman Papers

12 Marshall-Cornwall Report dated June 1940. WO216/116. See also Marshall-Cornwal. *Wars and Rumours of Wars* p155

13 *War Illustrated* 23 August 1940 p193

14 Wylly p125

15 For more on M. Marland, see www.etab.ac-caen.fr/lycee-hotelier-granville/resist.htm. See also www. christopherlong.co.uk for information about other networks set up to aid BEF soldiers escape France.

16 Bryant. *Turn of the Tide* p164

17 Beauman p164

18 Caddick-Adams, P. 'Anglo-French Co-operation during the battle for France' in Bond, B & Taylor M. *The Battle for France and Flanders Sixty Years On* Pen & Sword 2001: p49

19 Blaxland p131

20 Von Altenstadt, HG. *Unser Weg zum Meer* Berlin 1940 p182

21 Quoted in Thompson p301

Bibliography

Adamthwaite, A., *France and the coming of the Second World War, 1936–39* London: Frank Cass (1977)

Anonymous, *The Diary of a Staff Officer* London: Methuen & Co (1941) *Infantry Officer* London: Batsford (1943) *Harder than Hammers: the 1st Battalion of the Black Watch* Tyneside Scottish Association 1947)

Baggs, C.S.M., (IWM 94/49/1) Personal account

Barclay, C.N., *The History of the Duke of Wellington's Regiment 1919–1952* London: Wm Clownes & Son (1953)

Barnett, C., *The Collapse of British Power* London: Eyre Methuen, (1972)

Bartlett, Captain Sir B., *My First War* London: Chatto & Windus (1940)

Beauman, A.B., *Then a Soldier* London: Macmillan (1960)

Beauman, A.B., personal papers

Benoist-Méchin, J., *Sixty Days That Shook the West: The Fall of France, 1940* Translated by Peter Wiles and edited by Cyril Falls New York: G. P. Putnam (1963)

Bet-El, I.R., *Conscripts* Stroud: Sutton Publishing (2003)

Blaxland, G., *Destination Dunkirk: The Story of Gort's Army* London: Wm Kimber (1973)

Bond, B., (Ed) *Chief of Staff: The Diaries of Lieutenant General Sir Henry Pownall* London: Leo Cooper (1972) *British Military Policy Between the Two World Wars* Oxford: OUP (1980)

Bond, B. & Taylor, M., (Eds) *The Battle for France and Flanders Sixty Years On* Barnsley: Leo Cooper (2001)

Bonnaud, S., 'Le 9e Bataillon de Chars de Combat. Pt II.' In *Histoire de Guerre Blindés & Matériel* No75 Fevrier/Mars 2007

Bradford Telegraph & Argus May–Oct 1940

Brown, J.S., (IWM P118) Diary

Bryant, A., *The Turn of the Tide* London: Collins (1957)

Burdock, C. & Jacobsen, H-A., *Halder War Diary 1939–42* California: Presidio Press (1988)

'Ça Ira' Journal of the West Yorkshire Regiment Vol IX No 3 Dec 1939

'Ça Ira' Journal of the West Yorkshire Regiment Vol IX. No 4 March 1940

Chapman, G., *Why France Collapsed* (1968)

Chatelle, A., *Dunkerque Ville Ardente* Caen: Ozanne et Companie (1949)

Churchill, W.S., *The Second World War: Vol 1 The Gathering Storm* London: The Reprint Society (1952) *The Second World War: Vol 2 Their Finest Hour* London: The Reprint Society (1952)

Clark, D., (IWM 99/16/1) A Personal History of the 1940 Normandy Campaign

Collier, R., *The Sands of Dunkirk* London: Fontana (1974) *1940: The World in Flames* London: Penguin (1980)

Coilliot, A., *Mai 1940: Un Mois Pas Comme Les Autres* Arras (1980)

Corrigan, G., *Mud, Blood and Poppycock* London: Cassell (2003)

Coster, D.Q., 'Behind German Lines' *Readers' Digest*, November 1940

Cox, S., 'British Military Planning and the Origins of the Second World War' in B.J.C. Coercer & Roch Legault *Military Planning and the Origins of the Second World War in Europe* Westport CT: Praeger (2001)

Daily Telegraph 30–31 March 1939

Derry, T.K., *The Campaign in Norway* London: HMSO (1952)

Edgar, D., *The Day of Reckoning* London: John Clare Books

Ellis, L.F., *The War in France and Flanders, 1939–1940* London: HMSO (1954)

Flowers, R., unpublished personal account provided by Kim James

Freiser, K-H., *The Blitzkrieg Legend* Anapolis, Maryland: Naval Institute Press (2005)

Friesen, B.H., 'German Flank Guard Actions During the 1940 French Campaign' *Armor Magazine* Jan–Feb 1994

Führungshauptamt SS, *Damals: Erinnerungen an Grosse Tage der SS - Totenkopf - Division im Französischen Feldzug 1940* Stuttgart (1942)

Gates, E M., *The end of the affair: The collapse of the Anglo-French alliance, 1939–40* London: George Allen and Unwin (1981)

Gaultier, P., & Montier, A., personal account, accessed at http://hvmontier.free.fr/ande-lys_1940.html

Gawthorpe, J.B., '137 Brigade: A Formation of the TA in the First Year of War 1939–40' *'Ça Ira' Journal of the West Yorkshire Regiment* Vol XII June 1948

Gawthorpe, J.B., (IWM 78/44/1) After Action Report signed by Major Hirst 26 Jun 40. After Action Report signed by Colonel Taylor 2 Jun 40

Glover, M., *The Fight for the Channel Ports* London: Leo Cooper (1985)

Halifax Courier May–Oct 1940

Hamilton, N., *Monty: The Making of a General 1887–1942* London: Hamish Hamilton (1981)

Hammerton, Sir J., The Second Great War Vol 1 London: Waverley (1941)

Hatherill, G., *A Detective's Story: George Hatherill of Scotland Yard* New York: McGraw-Hill (1972)

Hawes, L.A., 'The Story of the "W Plan": The Move of Our Forces to France in 1939' *Army Quarterly* 101 (1970–71): 445–56

Hayward, J., *Myths and Legends of the Second World War* Sutton Publishing (2004)

Higgs, H., 'The Geddes Reports and the Budget' *Economic Journal*, Vol. 32, No. 126. (Jun., 1922)

Hingston, W., *History of the KOYLI Vol 5 Never Give Up 1919–42* London: Lund HMSO *The NCOs Musketry Small Book* London (1915)

Humphries (1950)

Holmes, R., *Tommy* London: HaperCollins (2004)

Howard, M., *The Continental Commitment: The Dilemma of British Defense Policy in the Era of Two World Wars* London: Temple Smith. (1972)

The Iron Duke: The Magazine of the Duke of Wellington's Regiment (West Riding) Vol XVI No 45 Feb 1940

Jackson, J., *The Fall of France* Oxford: OUP (2003)

Jackson, R., *Dunkirk* London: Cassell (2002)

James, K., *The Greater Share of Honour* Leicester: Troubadour Books (2007)

Karlsake, B., *1940: The Last Act* London: Leo Cooper (1979)

Kelly, D., (Ed) *Time Unguarded: The Ironside Diaries, 1937–1940* New York: D. McKay (1963)

Kennedy, P., *The Realities behind Diplomacy* London: Fontana (1981) The Rise and Fall of British Naval Mastery London: Penguin, (2004)

Laidler, J.C., *A Slice of My Life: The War Diary, Letters and Photographs of Private James C Laidler* privately printed, Wakefield Library

Lannoy, F. de *Dunkerque 1940* Bayeux: Heimdal (2004)

Liddel-Hart, B., *The Rommel Papers* London: Collins (1953)

Lord, W., *The Miracle of Dunkirk* London: Penguin (1984)

MacLeod, R. & Kelly, D., (Eds) *Time Unguarded: The Ironside Diaries, 1937–1940* New York: D. McKay (1963)

McKersher, B.J.C., 'The Limitations of the Politician-Strategist: Winston Churchill and the German Threat 1933–1939' in Michael I. Handel, John H. Maurer (eds) *Churchill and Strategic Dilemmas Before the World Wars: Essays in Honor* of Michael I. Handel. London: Routledge, (2003)

Marshall-Cornwall, J., *Wars and Rumours of Wars* London: Leo Cooper (1984)

Martineau, G.D., *A History of the Royal Sussex Regiment* Chichester (1953)

Messenger, C., *Call to Arms: The British Army 1914–18* London: Cassell (2005)

Montgomery, B.L., (1958) *The Memoirs of Field Marshal the Viscount Montgomery of Alamein KG* London: Companion Books

Moor, R., diary provided by his son, Mr Jeremy Moor

Moynihan, M., *People at War 1939–1945* London: David & Charles (1989) *Forgotten Soldiers* London: Quercus (2007)

Mulcahy, R., 'Blitzkreig's Beginnings' *World War II* magazine March 2006

National Army Museum *Against All Odds* London: National Army Museum (1990)

Nicholson, W.N., *Behind the Lines: an Account of Administrative Staff Work in the British Army* Cape Publishing (1939)

Nobecourt, R.G., *Les Soldats de 40: dans la premiere Bataille de Normandie* Luneray: Editions Bertout (1986)

Noble, W., personal account, details provided by his son, Mr Adrian Noble

Oberkommando des Heeres *Sieg über Frankreich* Berlin (1940) *Über Schlachtfelder Vorwärts!* Berlin (1940) *Tag und Nacht am Feind* Gutersloh (1942)

Pile, Gen. Sir F., *Ack-Ack* London: Harrap (1949)

Post, G. Jr. *Dilemmas of Appeasement: British Deterrence and Defense, 1934–1937* Ithaca, NY: Cornell University Press (1993)

Rhodes, A., *Sword of Bone* London: Buchan & Enright (1986)

Rissik, D., *The DLI at War 1939–45* Durham: Depot DLI (1952)

Sandes, E.W.C., *From Pyramid to Pagoda, The Story of the West Yorkshire Regiment (The Prince of Wales Own) in the War 1939–45 and Afterwards* London: FJ Parsons (1951)

Scheck, R., *Hitler's African Victims: The German Army Massacres of Black French Soldiers in 1940* Cambridge University Press (2006)

Sebag-Montefiore, H., *Dunkirk: Fight to the Last Man* London: Penguin (2007)

Shaw, F. & J., *We Remember Dunkirk* Oxford (1997)

Straw, A., personal account, accessed at: www.bbc.co.uk/ww2peopleswar/stories

Sydnor, C., *Soldiers of Destruction* London: Guild Publishing (1989)

Terraine, J., *To Win a War: 1918 The Year of Victory* London: Macmillan (1978)

The Times, 11 November 1932

Thompson, J., *Dunkirk: Retreat to Victory* London: Sedgwick & Jackson (2008)

Tschimpke, A., *Die Gespenster Division* Munich (1940)
Von Imhoff, C., *Sturn Durch Frankreich* Berlin (1941)
Walker, P., personal account, accessed at: www.dwr.org.uk/dwr.php?id=119&pa=121
Whiting, C. & Taylor, E., *The Fighting Tykes* London: Leo Cooper (1993)
Wilkinson, R., 'Hore-Belisha – Britain's Dreyfus?' *History Today* Vol 47 Issue 12. December 1997
Williams, D., *The New Contemptibles* London (1940)
Yorkshire Post May–Oct 1940
War Illustrated 28 June 1940

Other Files

WO 177/436 Report by Assistant Director Medical Services, Beauman Division
WO197/118 Polforce/Macforce/Petreforce Reports
WO361/113 Beauman Division
WO 208/92 Correspondence between Lord Hankey and General Ironside March 1940
WO 216/116 Report by Marshall-Cornwall. June 1940
WO106/1775 Bartholomew Committee
WO 361/ 45 Duke of Wellington's Regiment
WO 361/46 West Yorkshire Regiment
Inskip, Defence Expenditure in Future Years, Interim Report By The Minister For Co-
    Ordination of Defence, C.P. 316(37), Cab. 24/273
Service Historique de l'Armée de Terre: Résumé succinct des opérations de la 5e. Brigade de Cavalerie

Parliamentary Debates

Hansard House of Commons Debate 03 March 1919 vol 113 cc69–184
HC Deb 07 July 1919 vol 117 cc1567–70
HC Deb 11 December 1919 vol 122 cc1743–58
HC Deb 15 December 1919 vol 123 cc87–147
HC Deb 06 July 1932 vol 268 cc515–9
HC Deb 10 March 1932 vol 262 cc2007–73
HC Deb 15 March 1932 vol 263 cc241–2
HC Deb 08 March 1939 vol 344 cc2161–302
HC Deb Debates 27 April 1939 vol 346 cc1343–464
HC Deb 26 May 1939 vol 347 c2703

War Diaries

WO 166/4375 2/4th Bn King's Own Light Infantry Oct 1939–Mar 1940
WO166/4730 2/5th Bn West Yorkshire Regiment Sep 1939–Mar 1940
WO 167/709 1st Bn Tyneside Scottish
WO 167/736 2/6th Bn Duke of Wellington's Regiment
WO 167/737 2/7th Bn Duke of Wellington's Regiment
WO 167/765 7th Bn Royal West Kents
WO 167/777 2/4th Bn King's Own Light Infantry April - June 1940
WO 167/829 2/6th Bn East Surreys
WO167/837 7th Bn Royal Sussex Regiment
WO 167/853 2/5th Bn West Yorkshire Regiment May-June 1940

German officers relax after reaching the coast.

Index

A Lewis gun crew provide what air cover they can.

Exhausted surviving members of the digging divisions sleep on deck at Cherbourg prior to evacuation. Some were so drained they slept through air raids.